passion *to* PROFITS

Business Success for New Entrepreneurs

First Edition

Rhonda Abrams

with Alice LaPlante

the**Planning**shop

The Planning Shop
Palo Alto, California

Praise for Books from The Planning Shop

"User-friendly and exhaustive … highly recommended. Abrams' book works because she tirelessly researched the subject. Most how-to books on entrepreneurship aren't worth a dime; among the thousands of small-business titles, Abrams' [is an] exception."

—*Forbes Magazine*

"You have done a great service in establishing your publishing company and in helping so many people to learn all the ins and outs of what can be a daunting experience. You've also saved people like me lots of money in the interim, as we learn and do what we can to realize our dreams."

—*S.M. Lourenco, VP, Imaginas, LLC, New York*

"If you'd like something that goes beyond the mere construction of your plan and is more fun to use … this book can take the pain out of the process."

—*"Small Business School" (PBS television show)*

"This book stands head and shoulders above all others … and is the perfect choice for the beginner and the experienced business professional."

—*BizCountry*

"Your book has been both an inspirational read as well as a comprehensive guide. … Being relatively inexperienced with entrepreneurship, your book has not only given me the ability to create a solid roadmap for planning, but has also provided an encouraging and easy way to cope with the enormous amount of information and organization needed."

—*Simon Lee, Entrepreneur*

"I'm growing my business by purchasing a commercial building, and I needed a real estate loan to make the purchase. *Business Plan In A Day* was THE source I used for writing my plan, and the bankers and brokers I spoke with all commended my plan as being very strong and well written. Thanks to you, I've secured my loan and the transaction is going through. I feel so fortunate to have found this book."

—*Lisa Stillman, GardenWalk Massage Therapy, St. Louis*

"Rhonda Abrams knows her target market. She did not try to be all things to all readers. This book is for people who want to be serious entrepreneurs … It comes down to the numbers … Rhonda Abrams makes sure you'll take care of the Bottom Line numbers."

—*Sean Murphy, Ernst & Young, LLP, New York*

"I have to say—I reviewed several options on the Internet, and after much searching, ordered four different books that I thought would be the best to consider using in the course. The other three didn't even come close. This is a great book, especially for non-native speakers of English. Good work over there!"

—*Julie Carbajal, Fonty University of Applied Sciences, The Netherlands*

It is my No. 1 recommendation to SBDC clients … I have always liked the layout, order of presentation, sidebar notes, and real-world perspective on the planning process, components of the plan, etc."

—*David Gay, Small Business Development Center, College of DuPage*

"There are plenty of decent business plan guides out there, but Abrams' was a cut above the others I saw. *The Successful Business Plan* won points with me because it was thorough and well organized, with handy worksheets and good quotes. Also, Abrams does a better job than most at explaining the business plan as a planning tool rather than a formulaic exercise. Well done."

—*Inc. Magazine*

"At last, a straightforward book that demystifies the process behind conducting effective business research … gives business practitioners and students an incredibly useful tool to enable them to find accurate and timely information for business plans, academic papers, and other business uses."

—*Molly Lavik, Practitioner Faculty of Marketing, Graziadio School of Business and Management, Pepperdine University*

"As a small business advisor, I use the Electronic Financial Worksheet (EFW) tool extensively in analyzing my clients' financials. I recommend the Planning Shop's EFW for any small business. It's the best cash flow financial planning tool on the market today."

—*Joe Lam, Certified Business Advisor, Texas State University Small Business Development Center*

I just finished reading Rhonda's *Trade Show in a Day* and thought it was an excellent book and one that will stay close by my side during my next dozen shows. I highly recommend the book to anyone who wants to increase their productivity and profitability at their next trade event.

—*Gene Muchanski, President, Dive Industry Association*

Passion to Profits: Business Success for New Entrepreneurs
©2008 by Rhonda Abrams. Published by The Planning Shop™

ISBN: 978-0-9740801-9-2

Managing Editor: Maggie Canon
Project Editors: Mireille Majoor, Jill Simonsen
Cover and Interior Design: Diana Van Winkle

Services for our readers

Colleges, business schools, corporate purchasing:
The Planning Shop offers special discounts and supplemental teaching materials for universities, business schools, and corporate training. Contact:

> info@PlanningShop.com
> or call 650-289-9120

Free business tips and information:
To receive The Planning Shop's free email newsletter on starting and growing a successful business, sign up at: *www.PlanningShop.com.*

> The Planning Shop™
> 555 Bryant Street, #180
> Palo Alto, CA 94301 USA
> 650-289-9120
>
> Fax: 650-289-9125
> Email: info@PlanningShop.com
> www.PlanningShop.com

The Planning Shop™ is a division of Rhonda, Inc., a California corporation.

Cover Photo © istockphoto.com/Juan Monino
Back Cover and Inside Photos © istockphoto.com, dreamstime.com, and gettyimages.com
Inside Illustrations © clipart.com

"This publication is designed to provide accurate and authoritative information in regard to the subject matter covered. It is sold with the understanding that the publisher and author are not engaged in rendering legal, accounting, or other professional services. If legal advice or other expert assistance is required, seek the services of a competent professional."

— from a Declaration of Principles, jointly adopted by a committee
of the American Bar Association and a committee of publishers

Printed in Canada

10 9 8 7 6 5 4 3 2 1

Who This Book Is for

You have a passion—perhaps for a hobby, a profession, something you want to invent, or a social goal you want to achieve. You have talent. You have training, skills, and insights. You're ready to strike out on your own and launch your business. But what do you do first? How do you find clients or customers? How do you know what to charge and how to make sure you get paid? What about taxes, financing, and hiring and firing employees? Your head is spinning with questions.

Perhaps you're in school learning a profession in the engineering, health care, arts, law, or culinary fields. You know that one day you'll want to be your own boss or that you want to be self-employed or start your own business. How do you prepare yourself for that day? What do you need to know to make sure you can succeed?

Perhaps you're a consultant or self-employed independent contractor. How do you find more clients or customers? How do you stay motivated? Get organized? Manage your time and workplace?

Passion to Profits: Business Success for New Entrepreneurs answers all of these questions and more, providing the business advice and basics new entrepreneurs need to successfully start running their own businesses. If you want to start your own business, are running a business already, or are a student who one day is likely to find yourself starting a company of your own, this book is for you!

Passion to Profits: Business Success for New Entrepreneurs is for you if you want to:

■ Turn a personal passion or goal into a sustaining source of income

■ Use your education, skills or training to go into business yourself

■ Turn your talent and insight into a business that gives you the flexibility and autonomy you want and need

■ Acquire the skills you need to take the business you've already started to the next level

■ Create the type of workplace you've always dreamed of working in

■ Live your dreams

In particular, this book is designed for:

■ Anyone who wants to transform their interests, talents, or training into a financially rewarding enterprise or who wants to live the life they've always imagined—making money doing what they love

■ Students—engineering, technology, the arts, culinary, health care, law, and more—who one day want (or need) to turn their education into a business that can support and sustain them

■ College professors and instructors who want to make sure their students are well equipped to face an entrepreneurial future

■ Mid-career professionals ready for a career change or looking to leverage their years of experience to strike out on their own

■ Retirees wanting to turn their golden years into profitable ones by entering the world of entrepreneurship

■ Independent consultants and solo practitioners who want to treat their business like a business—learning how to market themselves, differentiate their offerings, provide legal protection for their businesses, and more.

■ Anybody who wants to learn more about business, get a solid business foundation, and make more money.

About The Planning Shop

The Planning Shop specializes in creating business resources for entrepreneurs. The Planning Shop's books and other products are based on years of real-world experience, and they share secrets and strategies from entrepreneurs, CEOs, investors, lenders, and seasoned business experts. Products from The Planning Shop are known for their practical, honest advice and information, their easy-to-use format and worksheets, and their understanding of the real needs of businesspeople today.

Millions of entrepreneurs have used The Planning Shop's products to launch, run, and expand businesses in every industry. Since chief entrepreneur and CEO Rhonda Abrams founded The Planning Shop in 1999, more than 600 business schools, colleges, and universities have adopted The Planning Shop's books as required texts.

The Planning Shop's expanding line of business books includes:

- The *Successful Business* series, assisting entrepreneurs and business students in planning and growing businesses. Titles include *Successful Business Plan: Secrets & Strategies, Successful Marketing: Secrets & Strategies, Six-Week Start-Up, Successful Business Research, The Owner's Manual for Small Business,* and *What Business Should I Start?*

- The *In A Day* series, enabling entrepreneurs to tackle a critical business task and "Get it done right, get it done fast.™" Titles include *Business Plan In A Day, Winning Presentation In A Day, Trade Show In A Day, Finding an Angel Investor In A Day.*

- The *Better Business Bureau* series, helping entrepreneurs and consumers successfully make serious financial decisions. Titles include *Buying a Franchise, Buying a Home,* and *Starting an eBay Business.*

At The Planning Shop, now and in the future, you'll find the business information, books, and tools you need to make your business dreams a reality and your business plans a success. Learn more and register for our free business tips newsletter at *www. PlanningShop.com.*

About the Authors

RHONDA ABRAMS

Entrepreneur, author, and nationally syndicated columnist Rhonda Abrams is widely recognized as one of the leading experts on entrepreneurship and small business. Rhonda's column for *USAToday*, "Successful Strategies," is the most widely distributed column on small business and entrepreneurship in the United States, reaching tens of millions of readers each week.

Rhonda's books have been used by millions of entrepreneurs. Her first book, *The Successful Business Plan: Secrets & Strategies,* is the best-selling business plan guide in America. It was named one of the Top Ten business books for entrepreneurs by both *Forbes* and *Inc.* magazines. She is also the author of more than a dozen other books on entrepreneurship and has sold more than a million copies of her books. Rhonda's other books are perennial best-sellers, with three of them having reached the nationally recognized "Top 50 Business Bestseller" list.

Rhonda not only writes about business—she lives it! As the founder of three successful companies, Rhonda has accumulated an extraordinary depth of experience and a real-life understanding of the challenges facing entrepreneurs. Rhonda first founded a management consulting practice working with clients ranging from one-person startups to Fortune 500 companies. Rhonda was an early Web pioneer, founding a website for small business that she later sold. In 1999, Rhonda started a publishing company—now called The Planning Shop—focusing exclusively on topics of business planning, entrepreneurship, and new business development. The Planning Shop is America's leading academic publisher focusing exclusively on entrepreneurship.

A popular public speaker, Rhonda is regularly invited to address leading industry and trade associations, business schools, and corporate conventions and events. Educated at Harvard University and UCLA, where she was named Outstanding Senior, Rhonda now lives in Palo Alto, California.

Register to receive Rhonda's free business newsletter at The Planning Shop's website, www.PlanningShop.com.

Other books by Rhonda Abrams include:

- *Successful Marketing: Secrets & Strategies*
- *The Successful Business Plan: Secrets & Strategies*
- *Six-Week Start-Up*
- *Business Plan In A Day*
- *The Owner's Manual for Small Business*
- *Successful Business Research*
- *What Business Should I Start?*
- *Winning Presentation In A Day*
- *Trade Show In A Day*
- *Wear Clean Underwear: Business Wisdom*
- *Finding an Angel Investor In A Day (Editor)*

ALICE LAPLANTE

Alice LaPlante is a business writer based in Palo Alto, California. She has worked with The Planning Shop on numerous books, including *Starting an eBay Business*. Alice also teaches creative writing at Stanford University and San Francisco State University. She received the prestigious Wallace Stegner fellowship from Stanford University. Among her seven books is *The Making of a Story*, published by Norton.

How to Use This Book

Entrepreneurs tend to dream big. They see opportunities in challenges and profits in their passions. But it's not enough to have a great idea, an awe-inspiring talent, or even a boatload of business smarts. *Passion to Profits: Business for New Entrepreneurs* shows first-time entrepreneurs how to combine all of the above—plus lots more—into a business that can sustain them for years to come.

By focusing first on the *passion*—your unique set of skills, talents, and training and how those can inform a unique business concept—and then on the profits—how you can pull all of these together to run a viable business—this volume provides a blueprint for entrepreneurial success.

If you're long on ideas but short on real-world business experience, not to worry: *Passion to Profits* shows you how to leverage those ideas to meet a market need and then how to get your business up, running, and profitable. And if you're an expert at managing people, a whiz with numbers, but sick of punching someone else's time clock, you've come to the right place as well: *Passion to Profits* will get you thinking like an entrepreneur, helping you to identify opportunities and design a business around them.

Organization

Divided into four main sections plus a special section on independent consultants and solo practitioners, *Passion to Profits: Business Success for New Entrepreneurs* leads you step-by-step through the process of transforming your entrepreneurial dreams into a viable business:

- Part One: Choosing a Business

- Part Two: Starting a Business

- Part Three: Marketing, Pricing, and Sales

- Part Four: Running a Business,

- Special Section: Independent Consultants/Solo Practitioners,

Choosing a Business

Sure, you have an idea, a talent, a passion—but what's the best way to turn those into a money-making enterprise? Part One: Choosing a Business shows you how to turn your *avocation* (your hobby, interests, talents, training) into a *vocation*. It helps you find the ways to make your *dreams* (of autonomy, flexibility, riches) into *reality*. In this section, you'll learn how to think like an entrepreneur and how to translate your personal vision into a business vision. You'll then get help identifying just the right kind of business for you. In this section, you'll also learn how to identify opportunities, figure out exactly who the best customers are for your product or service, get a better grip on your competition, and get your bearings on how to do business in a socially responsible way.

Starting a Business

Once you know what you're going to do, who your best customers are, and what's up with the competition, it's time to get down to the details of getting your business underway. Part Two: Starting a Business takes you through all the steps of doing just that. It starts with creating an identity, figuring out the best way to get your product or service to market, and finding the ideal location. Then, it takes you through the not-so-fun parts, too: legal aspects, taxes, licenses, and insurance. Then comes money: financing and financial projections. Finally, you'll get to creating your business plan—always a crucial step. Along the way, you'll find a wealth of tables and worksheets to help get your creative juices flowing and to compare your options.

Marketing, Pricing, and Sales

The key to business success, of course, is having customers and charging them enough to make a profit. Part Three: Marketing, Pricing, and Sales illuminates the range of marketing options available to you—from the tried-and-true traditional methods (such as advertising) to the most affordable (such as networking and word-of-mouth) and the most up-to-date online marketing tools. You'll also brainstorm creative options to help devise your first marketing plan. This section helps you tackle the thorny issues of setting prices and getting customers to buy from you, offering practical, real-world advice. It will even help you create a knock-'em-dead sales pitch.

Running a Business

You've hung out your shingle, opened your doors, and let the world know you're in business. And—surprise, surprise—customers are flocking in. Now, you just have to figure out how to keep it all going—and going efficiently and profitably. If you're like most entrepreneurs, you got into the game—at least in part—because you wanted to run things yourself. And that means *managing*—operations, people, and finances. Part 4: Running a Business shows you how. As you work your way through the chapters in this section, you'll learn how to provide the infrastructure, equipment, processes, and procedures that enable you to deliver your product or service in a profitable way; what you need to do to hire and retain the best employees; and the steps you need to take to ensure that your cash continues flowing and flowing.

Independent Consultants/ Solo Practitioners

You may be in business by yourself, but that doesn't mean you have to go it alone. Recognizing that one-person shops represent by far the largest business category today, *Passion to Profits: Business Success for New Entrepreneurs* includes a special section devoted exclusively to solo entrepreneurs. Whether you're a business consultant, doctor, artist, chef, writer, lawyer, jewelry-maker or are in any of the thousands of industries and professions dominated by self-employed individuals, this section covers the issues unique to striking out on your own—including setting up a home office, legal and tax issues, working with an agent, building a virtual team of your own, and much more!

Special Features

Passion to Profits: Business Success for New Entrepreneurs is packed with worksheets to help you turn your ideas into action. Like all books from The Planning Shop, this volume contains a range of tools to help you quickly grasp the information you need and help you get going fast, including:

■ **Business Buzz Words.** No one can intimidate you by tossing around a bunch of business jargon! *Passion to Profits: Business Success for New Entrepreneurs* makes you an instant insider in the world of business by giving you clear, real-world definitions of the business words you're most likely to encounter. After all, it's much easier to get by—and thrive—if you speak the language.

■ **Case Studies.** While every business is unique in its offerings, operations, and culture, many share common challenges. Seeing how other entrepreneurs have thrived or tackled thorny issues will both inspire and educate you. With this in mind, we've sprinkled a few case studies of real businesses throughout this volume, so that you can learn from others' successes.

Contents

Part Three: Marketing, Pricing, and Sales 129

Part Four: Running Your Business 173

Special Section: Independent Consultants/ Solo Practitioners 207

Index 217

Part One:
Choosing a Business

chapter 1

Profits from Your Passion

You have a dream. And that dream involves more than just following others, punching a time clock, or showing up at a cubicle on a schedule created by someone else. Even if you're doing that now to earn a living, you know that your long-term goals involve satisfying a much more important need: following your passions, talents, skills, and desires. Your dream is to someday—maybe today—start and run your own business.

You have a passion. Perhaps you're a snowboarder and spend all spring, summer, and fall waiting for that glorious moment when you can buckle your board on your boots and really begin living. Or you're a craftsperson devoted to designing and building custom cabinetry from recycled or sustainable sources. Or maybe you're an avid fashion designer with an eye for predicting which styles are going to become the Next Big Thing. You want to make your avocation your vocation. But you're not sure how to begin.

You have training and talent. You're a highly skilled pastry chef. Or you've just graduated from engineering school with top honors. You're good at what you do, but that won't be enough out there in the marketplace. Most professions require you to do more than simply practice your skill or craft well. You need business skills to back up your flair for design, your knack for software programming, or your talent as a musician. But how do you acquire those skills?

You want more than what conventional employment options will provide. You may have—or be planning to start—a family, and a nine-to-five job isn't compatible with your parenting ideals. Or you're a free spirit who would feel hampered by a traditional employer-employee relationship. Or you want to earn the kind of money that just wouldn't be possible on a salary, perhaps even become truly wealthy. Yet when you search the Internet job boards, all you see are ads for the usual. You want to take control of your own destiny. But how do you proceed?

You want to move your business forward, but you're being held back by your lack of business knowledge. Or you may have jumped feet first into a business before realizing you don't quite have all the know-how you need to make a go of it. Whether you're one of the scores of freelance technical writers struggling to differentiate and market themselves to potential clients, or a software engineer with a brilliant idea but no clue how to turn that into an actual business, you need to acquire the business skills to support your vision.

In all these cases, you have a passion—and a talent—for something that would place you beyond the boundaries of most traditional employment situations. And you are either dreaming of being able to turn that passion into a sustainable living, or have already started down that path. Most importantly, you want to take control of your own destiny. This book is designed to help.

Think Like an Entrepreneur

What you are dreaming about is called *entrepreneurship*. The origin of the word is *entreprendre*, French for "to undertake." Notice that this word emphasizes an attempt to act, and not the outcome of that action: you *undertake* something, and the implication is that what matters is that you have started on a journey and accepted that it's an open-ended one. Someone who needs an extremely high level of security might be challenged by an entrepreneurial lifestyle, yet a lot of people who don't think of themselves as embracing risk become entrepreneurs. The key is that although a successful entrepreneur takes risks, those risks are *measured.* Though entrepreneurs frequently go out on limbs, the ones that make it generally test that limb first to make sure it has a good chance of bearing their weight.

Entrepreneurship can be applied to virtually any field or profession. No matter what products and services are currently on the market in your area of expertise, there are always opportunities to improve them and to better serve the customers who buy them. That said, if you're a true entrepreneur, you likely possess the following key characteristics:

- **You are driven to succeed.** You're so motivated to achieve your goals that you are prepared to overcome obstacles that would likely discourage or stop others.

- **You are a self-starter and go-getter.** Rather than waiting for someone to issue instructions, you take initiative. And you can be innovative—you constantly think "out of the box" when attempting to meet challenges.

- **You routinely see opportunities where others see problems.** Rather than feeling defeated when you encounter roadblocks to your goals, you feel energized. Challenges spur rather than deter you.

- **You take control of your own destiny and bear responsibility for your own actions.** The buck truly stops with you when it comes to dealing with the results—both positive and negative—of decisions you make or actions you take.

- **You are willing to give up the security blanket of corporate life.** You don't mind working without the safety net of a regular paycheck or the benefits and social structure that an established employer provides.

- **You thrive on change.** In the entrepreneurial world, change is a given. But rather than fearing it, you welcome it and enjoy the excitement of the ride.

- **You understand the importance of making a profit.** You know that all of your best intentions and actions are for naught if you aren't actually making a profit—that is, bringing in more money by selling a product or service than it costs you to provide it.

The Economic Importance of Entrepreneurship

Entrepreneurs make enormous economic contributions to societies around the globe. In the U.S., for example, according to the Small Business Administration (SBA), small businesses represent 99.7 percent of all employer firms, employ half of all private-sector employees, and are responsible for more than 45 percent of the total private payroll. Moreover, they generate between 60 percent and 80 percent of new jobs annually. In terms of innovation, they also lead the pack: small firms produce 13 times more patents per employee than large businesses, and their patents are twice as likely to be among the top 1 percent cited by other inventors submitting new patents.

Most importantly, entrepreneurship is a road to financial freedom. The U.S. Federal Reserve reports that equity in unincorporated businesses made up the second largest share of total household wealth, second only to home equity.

Passionate and Powerful: Surf Divas Make Waves in Southern California

Twins Isabelle, "Izzy," and Caroline, "Coco," Tihanyi always knew they'd start a business together one day. The only question was, which one?

One thing was certain: the business would have to revolve around something the women absolutely loved. "We believe that you have to be passionate about what you do if you want to succeed," says Coco. Agrees Izzy, "Going into business without that passion is like getting married without being in love. It just won't work in the long run."

In the end, founding Surf Diva, one of the world's most successful surf schools for women—and one of the few women-owned businesses in the male-dominated surf industry—turned out to be the most natural decision in the world.

Having grown up by the ocean in San Diego, both women gravitated toward the outdoors and sports in general and the beach and surfing in particular. Izzy was a championship surfer who put herself through college at the University of California, San Diego (UCSD), teaching others how to surf. Coco, after earning her degree in communications, also at UCSD, was employee No. 4 at Reef Sandals, a local startup that made surfers' shoes which is now a globally recognized entrepreneurial success story. And it was a warm May evening in 1996 when the sisters sat down to have a glass of wine and found themselves talking about their dreams. "Izzy said she wanted more girlfriends to surf with. I said I wanted to design clothes and do business development," recalls Coco. "We thought we saw an unmet need in the local surfing industry. We got all fired up and said, 'Let's give it a try!'"

The fact that Izzy only had $324 to her name to begin with didn't deter her one iota. They were determined from the beginning to be self-sustaining and not take outside money, and today they still plow all excess cash back into the business. "We both worked other jobs for almost three years before we were able to quit and do Surf Diva full time," says Coco. "We felt it was very important not to go into debt."

With their company still privately held, the women don't divulge their annual revenues, but at last count they had between 50 and 70 employees—more in the summer, due to the seasonal nature of the sport. The Surf Diva Costa Rica Surf Adventure, which the sisters founded in 2004, takes women and families on a high-end all-inclusive surfing vacation in Costa Rica, and has become one of the most popular women's adventure destinations in the country. In 2007 they acquired the La Jolla Surf Camp for Kids, in La Jolla, Calif., and the Australian Surf Academy, a co-ed surfing school for teenagers. "We believe in always trying new things," says Coco. "That's part of the fun of having your own business."

Both women urge would-be entrepreneurs to follow their dreams—but also to not be shy about paying their dues in more traditional ways. "We didn't jump into this when we were 19 years old," says Coco. "We did our internships when we were students, got our degrees, worked for other people, and climbed the business ladder before we felt the time was right." Agrees Izzy, "you should never think of a job as just a job. Think of it as an education that comes with a paycheck. There's so much you can learn from others, even when you're just making the coffee."

Sooner or Later, Everyone Is an Entrepreneur

Entrepreneurial endeavors are nothing new. Yet we seem to be entering a golden age of entrepreneurship. Although much attention is paid to technology-based startups—particularly those related to the Internet—you can find entrepreneurial behavior throughout all industries and geographic locations around the world. There are a variety of reasons for this:

■ **No more "company men" (or women).** The days when people assumed they would be working for one company all their lives are long gone. The reasons for this are many. For starters, a large number of businesses today run extraordinarily "lean." Rather than hiring full-time permanent employees, many businesses are opting for part-time personnel or temporary or contract workers. And those that do hire full-time workers find that the average tenure of an employee is much shorter than it used to be. This is likely exacerbated by the fact that lifelong full employment is no longer a given. The average person born in the later years of the Baby Boom has held 10.5 jobs from age 18 to age 40, according to the Bureau of Labor Statistics of the U.S. Department of Labor. Indeed, many people have two or even three "careers" over the course of their lifetimes as their interests change and evolve.

Technology is also dramatically accelerating the rate at which markets—and therefore new businesses—are created or evolve. First of all, businesses that once required a huge upfront investment in infrastructure, equipment, and staff can now do a lot more for less. What can't be automated in house can easily be outsourced to partners who are seamlessly connected electronically so that they become part of the "virtual" team. And then there are the businesses that have sprung up to provide technology solutions to entrepreneurs. Web design firms, search marketing specialists, third-party IT services providers, and all sorts of consultants represent just a few of the new types of business opportunities that have emerged.

■ **Lifestyle drives career choices.** Increasingly, surveys asking about job satisfaction bump up against the same fact: people are willing to forgo larger salaries to meet their ideal lifestyle goals. These generally involve more flexibility in work hours, less time spent commuting, and more time for family, hobbies, exercise, or interests other than those that actually generate income. Indeed, possessing a dream of a lifestyle that couldn't be satisfied by a traditional job is one of the key reasons that people choose the entrepreneurial path.

■ **Financial considerations.** Many people simply don't feel they can meet their financial goals by working for an hourly wage—or even a professional-level salary. The publicity given to young multi-millionaire founders and early employees of high-tech startups has fueled many people's dreams. No surprise that a lot of people feel that they can achieve their financial goals more fully and easily if they're self-employed—or employ others.

business
BUZZ
words

"entrepreneur"

According to the Miriam-Webster Dictionary, an entrepreneur is one who organizes, manages, and assumes the risks of a business or enterprise. In his book *Venture Capital Investor*, David Gladstone says that one of the key characteristics of an entrepreneur is a desire for independence and autonomy. Furthermore, entrepreneurs would rather manage than be managed. Entrepreneurship, therefore, has much to do with a need for personal, as well as professional, control.

Does Failure Mean You've Failed?

One of the key defining factors for successful entrepreneurs is the ability—or rather, determination—to not view failure as failure. Rather than taking setbacks personally or becoming discouraged by them, successful entrepreneurs seize them as an opportunity to learn—and to apply that lesson to their next attempt. Indeed, many venture capitalists and other investors in entrepreneurial ventures won't provide funds to anyone who hasn't had at least one failed business.

There are any number of people who eventually made it big who tried and failed first. More than a decade before releasing its iPhone to huge success, Apple introduced an early personal digital assistant (PDA), the Newton, which died a quick death. The founder of FedEx, Frederick W. Smith, got a "C" on a business paper outlining his idea when he submitted it to a professor at Yale. The now-ubiquitous Post-its failed all the market tests that 3M routinely uses to determine whether to release a product to market. Scratch the surface of most successful entrepreneurs, and you'll find at least one significant "failure" that they've used to gain valuable experience.

The Advantages of Entrepreneurship

As many books and motivational speakers will tell you, there are numerous advantages to the entrepreneurial life. These advantages fall into three general categories: personal, professional, and financial.

- **Personal benefits.** Much of the payback people get from their entrepreneurial ventures is personal. Having the independence and flexibility to make time for family, hobbies, or other activities is a huge draw to the entrepreneurial life. It also provides an opportunity to do something you have a passion for than spend the majority of your waking hours performing tasks you have little real interest in. And, increasingly, location independence is a huge benefit: many people want to live in a particular geographic area—say, close to the mountains or by the ocean—or perhaps in a place where there aren't an abundance of jobs. Avoiding long commutes is a growing priority, as is the ability to work virtually from anyplace to enable a more footloose lifestyle.

- **Professional benefits.** You will also reap extensive professional benefits from your entrepreneurial endeavors. For starters, you can advance more rapidly than you would in a traditional office setting. You won't be limited by what your boss thinks. You won't be held back because you lack experience or seniority. You will succeed or fail on your own merits.

  You'll also be able to fully leverage your creativity and ingenuity. Rather than simply carrying out other people's ideas or implementing their visions, you reap the professional benefits of any exciting insights or "ahas" you get. You can be aggressively proactive at pursuing exciting new ideas for products and/or services, and you can pave a path or create a legacy for those who come after you.

  Finally, you will thrive due to the sheer adrenaline factor. Entrepreneurs are challenged and surprised every day, and because of this they grow at a much faster rate professionally than their counterparts in traditional employment situations. And because you're the boss, you can invest in further education and training as you want or need it.

■ **Financial benefits.** The financial benefits of running your own firm can be substantial. Research performed by Thomas Stanley and William Danko for their best-selling book *The Millionaire Next Door* found that self-employed businesspersons were four times more likely to be millionaires than those in traditional employer-employee roles. Your earning potential is theoretically unlimited—you can go as far as your business idea will take you. You also benefit directly from your success. The fruits of your labors belong to you. You can take as much or as little out of your business as you choose. And you are untethered from the economic ups and downs—and whims—of a traditional employer. You make, and reap, the financial rewards of your own hard work.

The Challenges of Entrepreneurship

Naturally, entrepreneurship isn't without its challenges—and risks. There are a number of things you will inevitably have to confront and surmount on your journey. Among other challenges, you will need to find ways to manage the following realities:

■ **Your income may fluctuate considerably.** You won't have the comfort of that steady paycheck. What you sell to customers or bill clients is what you get. You will inevitably experience dry spells or have times when your resources are stretched. And you may need to look beyond your own means for the cash to grow your business or even to keep your doors open if times get tough.

■ **You'll need to be self-sufficient.** You must be a disciplined self-starter. And depending on the type of business you start, your goals, or the speed at which you grow, you may be working on your own most of the time. You won't have the traditional "network" of coworkers to turn to for support or assistance. If your computer breaks down, you'll have to figure out how to get it up and running again—either yourself or by hiring outside help. You'll either do your own books or find a good accountant. And you won't have the built-in social structure of the traditional workplace.

■ **You'll work hard.** This is a given of the entrepreneurial life: self-employed individuals tend to work longer hours than the typical employee. You don't get paid for the time you're not working. This means that you will lose revenue for each day you are sick and for vacation days. Moreover, it may take time to get adequately paid for the work you actually *do*; many entrepreneurs have to continue doing their "day" jobs until their entrepreneurial ventures are established.

■ **You must be a fast learner.** Unless you are a very unusual person, you will be largely jumping into the great unknown when you start your business. You may have a deep understanding of your professional field—nursing or engineering or culinary arts—yet it's a given that you will be confronted hourly with unanticipated challenges. Your ability to learn the ropes and pick up on things quickly will be one of the prime determinants of your success.

■ **You'll need benefits.** Even employees of the largest companies are not being provided with the same level of insurance and retirement benefits as in the past. When you're starting your own business, you have the same kind of decisions to make as the largest Fortune 100 companies: What kind of health benefits will you be able to afford—both for yourself and for any others you employ? Which insurance company (or companies) will provide them? How will you fund these benefits? Likewise for retirement savings—both your own and for any employees. Will you contribute to a 401K? What you decide will depend upon your personal as well as business priorities and resources.

■ **You must cope with constant change.** The one constant you face is change. And just when you think you have everything under control, something new will come along—count on it. You will need to develop your capacity for dealing with the unexpected.

Traditional to Entrepreneurial

Just about any skill that has historically been harnessed to fulfill a traditional job can be turned into an entrepreneurial venture. Likewise, people are increasingly leveraging their hobbies to build successful businesses. Here are some examples of how traditional jobs and skills can be applied to entrepreneurial goals.

TRADITIONAL JOB/HOBBY	ENTREPRENEURIAL APPLICATION
Skilled cook/baker	Open a restaurant, bakery, catering company; start a line of specialty food products
Associate in law firm	Open your own legal practice; contract your services to other law firms
Clotheshorse	Open a retail clothing store; design clothes; start a fashion company
Engineer in large manufacturing company	Found a startup based on a new idea in your field; become a consultant to manufacturing companies
Sports enthusiast	Develop new equipment; open sporting goods store; offer personal training services; start a sports camp
Animal lover	Open a grooming business; offer pet training services; open a doggie daycare facility; start a dog walking service

chapter 2

Your Vision

To begin building a business, you have to start at a very high level, first identifying your overarching vision and then drilling down deeper into the opportunities until you come up with an actual concept for a real business.

■ **The vision.** You have a vision. There are two aspects of this vision: personal and professional. Your vision encompasses your passions and talents; your business, personal, and financial goals; your lifestyle; and everything else that will determine the quality of your life as you start and run your business.

■ **The opportunities.** Next, identify the opportunities that exist in your chosen field. How will you apply your vision to the real world? What are the new or improved products or services you can offer?

Finally, you get down to the specifics. How do you exploit the opportunities you've identified to create an actual business? Your business concept must include all the details about making the product/service, financing it, and getting it to market.

The Four C's

When you start out, it's important to understand your personal goals. Some entrepreneurial ventures fail and others flounder precisely because their founders or executives are uncertain of what they really want to achieve. They don't structure the company and their responsibilities in ways that satisfy their personal needs and ambitions.

Most entrepreneurs' personal goals can be summed up by the Four C's: *creativity, control, challenge,* and *cash.* Of course, everyone wants all four of these to some degree, but knowing which ones you most want or need can help you structure your company to best achieve your goals.

Which of the Four C's motivates you most?

■ **Creativity.** Entrepreneurs want to leave their mark. Their companies provide not only a means of making a living but a way for them to create something that bears their stamp. Creativity comes in many forms, from designing a new "thing" to devising a new business process or even coming up with a new way to make sales, handle customers, or reward employees.

If you have a high need for creativity, make certain you remain involved in the creative process as your company develops. You'll want to shape your business so it's not just an instrument for earning an income, but also a way for maintaining your creative stimulation and making a larger contribution to society. But don't over-personalize your company, especially if it's large. Allow room for others, particularly partners and key personnel, to share in the creative process.

CASE STUDY

Mona Lisa Sound:
Rocking the Classical World

What happens when classically trained musicians take on Pink Floyd? An entrepreneurial success story emerges that all music majors should hear.

The Grammy-nominated Hampton String Quartet was created in 1985 by RCA, which wanted to record an album of Christmas music played by a classical ensemble. The debut album of the group, "What if Mozart Wrote 'Have Yourself a Merry Little Christmas,'" was a smash hit, selling more than a million copies. The quartet is made up of Regis Iandiorio, first violin; Abe Appleman, second violin; Richard Maximoff, viola; and John Reed, cello.

After releasing another best-selling album that featured the Rolling Stones' "Sympathy for the Devil," the group received so many requests for its classical arrangements of popular rock songs that the group's cellist, Reed, along with his partner, Janna Glasser, created Mona Lisa Sound, a sheet music publishing company and record label, in 2000. The Hampton String Quartet later released three albums through Mona Lisa Sound.

"When we started publishing our sheet music, we expected to sell the arrangements primarily to professional musicians—quartets like ours," says Reed. "But, surprisingly, we've really found our niche in the education market." What apparently happened, says Reed, is that high school string teachers discovered Mona Lisa Sound's arrangements and eagerly snapped them up for students bored with the usual classical repertoire. Once he realized what was happening, Reed placed advertisements in the American String Teachers' Association (ASTA) magazine, *String Teacher*, and in *String* magazine, and participates each year in ASTA's annual convention. So popular are Mona Lisa Sound's arrangements that Reed has to operate two booths there.

One of Reed's biggest challenges is managing the intellectual property issues that arise from arranging the work of other composers. For each new work he arranges and publishes, he has to track down the copyright holder—which is not necessarily the composer of the work—and negotiate a licensing deal. "When we started, no one would pay attention to us when we asked to license the music," he recalls. "It took us two years to break through. Finally, we actually went to England and asked Led Zeppelin's manager personally if we could license 'Stairway to Heaven.'" The members of that band got so excited about Reed's arrangement that they convinced Warner Bros. to license the rights to their music.

But there was a major gotcha in all the licensing arrangements. Try as Reed might, he could not get a copyright on his arrangements—the copyright for all the music, no matter how much he changed his versions from the original, belonged to the people or businesses that held the print rights to the music. "There was no way to protect our intellectual property," he says. "It was a hard pill to swallow."

Despite that, Mona Lisa Sound is thriving. It has plans to release two more Hampton String Quartet CDs, and its list of sheet music arrangements keeps growing. It makes the majority of sales via its website, although it also has a catalogue that it sends out every other year to 35,000 music educators and schools.

Reed credits the firm's ability to turn a profit on its low overhead. "We financed it all ourselves and never borrowed any money," he says. They also chose to self-publish the sheet music on demand rather than use an offset press, which would have been considerably more expensive. "To make offset printing cost-effective, you'd have to print thousands of copies," he says. "But we're always tweaking our music—fixing typos or changing a note, and so we bought our own printer and only print music when we get an order in."

Reed believes that every classically trained musician should be thinking entrepreneurially. "The odds of making a living as a classical musician are horrendously low," he says. Yet by being creative, musicians can come up with very viable businesses, he says. "I would absolutely encourage young musicians to try."

■ **Control.** Many people start businesses because they want more control over their lives. Perhaps you want more control over the way your good ideas are implemented. Perhaps you want, or need, more control over your work hours or conditions so that you can be more involved in family, community, or hobbies. Control is a major motivation for most entrepreneurs—usually more important than money. But how much control you need—especially on a day-to-day basis—directly influences how large your company can be.

If you need or want a great deal of control over your time, you'll most likely need to keep your company smaller. In a large company, you have less immediate control over many decisions. If you're a person who needs control, you can still grow your business larger. You'll simply need to structure communication and reporting systems to ensure that you have sufficient information about and direction over developments to give you personal satisfaction. If you seek outside funding in the form of investors, understand the nature of control your funders will exert and be certain you're comfortable with these arrangements.

■ **Challenge.** If you're starting or expanding a business, it's clear you like challenge—at least to some degree. You're likely to be a problem-solver and risk-taker, enjoying the tasks of figuring out solutions to problems or devising new undertakings. Challenge-hungry entrepreneurs can be some of the most successful businesspeople, but they can also be their own worst enemies—flitting from one thing to another, never focusing long enough to succeed.

If you have a high need for challenge in your business life, it's important to develop positive means to meet this need, especially once your company is established and the initial challenge of starting a company is met. Otherwise, you may find yourself continually starting new projects that divert attention from your company's main goals. As you plan your company, establish goals that not only provide you with sufficient stimulation but also advance—rather than distract from—the growth of your business.

■ **Cash.** Every entrepreneur wants to make money. Perhaps it's just enough money to provide a decent income; perhaps it's so much money you can buy a jet. How much you want or need affects how you'll develop your business. Will you need investors and when? Will you sacrifice control to grow the business quickly?

Keep in mind there are sometimes trade-offs between personal goals. For example, wanting more cash often means having less control, while staying at the center of the creative process can necessitate having a partner or growing slowly—once again trading off control or cash.

business
BUZZ
words

"monetize"

Monetizing is the process of transforming something—an idea, invention, or creation; a website or software programming; or an action—into a product or service that someone else deems valuable enough to pay for. For example, writing and selling a book can be seen as monetizing one's thoughts into a product that people will have to purchase. Accepting ads on a "free" website monetizes that website for its creators. Likewise, building a company to sell your new invention can turn an abstract idea into something that actually brings in money.

The Four Aspirations

Once you have considered the Four C's, you must continue to define other aspects of your vision. A good way to proceed is to choose which one of the following Four Aspirations fits your personal, professional, and financial goals:

- Actualizing Activity

- Solo Sustainer

- Balance Business

- Visionary Venture

Actualizing activity

Everyone likes to make money, but for some entrepreneurs, making money is not the primary reason to start a business. Actualizing Activity businesses are those launched by entrepreneurs who are primarily interested in meeting personal interests or fulfilling personal goals. The key factor is that money made in the business is not critical for financially supporting the business owner's lifestyle. The fortunate individuals who launch Actualizing Activity businesses already have other sources of income—for example, pensions, spouses or partners who are already bringing in sufficient revenues, or investment income. These people can choose which business to start based on how it meets their personal goals rather than their financial needs. Thus, a previously successful engineer might open a gallery to fulfill a need to be involved in the arts or a model railroad enthusiast might establish a retail hobby shop to satisfy a desire to build a local community of like-minded individuals—even if those businesses don't make them much money.

Solo sustainer

The largest number of all businesses fit into this classification. These are one-person ventures that provide critical income for the entrepreneur—and often the *only* source of income for the entrepreneur's family.

Solo Sustainer businesses represent the classic self-employment business model—frequently called "sole proprietorships" (see the Independent Consultants/Solo Practitioners Special Section at the end of the book). These businesses are owned by one person, are typically non-incorporated, and it's not unusual (although never

recommended!) for the entrepreneur to mix business and personal expenses. Self-employed accountants, physicians, and others who provide professional services fall into this category.

Businesses in this group share these characteristics:

- Income from the business is critical to maintaining the lifestyle of the entrepreneurs and their families.

- The entrepreneur generally works alone (or perhaps with the aid of part-time administrative assistants or independent service providers, such as attorneys and accountants).

- The business generates current income for the entrepreneur rather than creating ongoing income streams that could continue even if the entrepreneur were to leave the business.

In other words, in Solo Sustainer businesses, the business sustains the entrepreneur, and the entrepreneur sustains the business. Once the entrepreneur stops working, the business stops—period. In essence, the entrepreneur is the "product" that the company sells, and is the sole income generator for the business. There is no "business" independent of the entrepreneur.

Balanced business

When someone uses the term *small business,* they usually mean this type of business. "Balanced" doesn't mean that the books are balanced. Nor does it refer to any other specific aspect of the business' management or financial well-being. Rather, it means that the goals of the venture's founders are fairly well balanced in that:

The business is designed to be a career for the owner.

And

The business provides jobs for others.

The business is designed to provide income for the entrepreneur.

And

The business may be capable of building value independent of, and lasting longer than, the entrepreneur's personal involvement.

The business is small enough for the owner to be able to control it.

Yet

The business is big enough to be able to support growth.

Ideally, a Balanced Business will develop value in addition to the annual income it produces for the owner and the paychecks it generates for employees. With good planning and development, many of these businesses can be sold to others when it comes time for the entrepreneur to retire. They can also be passed down to family members or employees. Restaurants fall into this category, as do construction companies, automotive repair shops, and just about any kind of Mom and Pop retail stores.

Visionary venture

The entrepreneur who starts a Visionary Venture has a different kind of ambition than those who start other types of businesses. Yes, they may be starting small, but their vision doesn't stop there. These entrepreneurs have plans to grow big. Their goal is to develop a company that will grow into a major enterprise—one worth many millions of dollars. They envision a company so substantial that it will become a household name, with publicly traded stock. Or they may hope that an even larger corporation might acquire the business in the future. Don't be surprised, these entrepreneurs think, if one day you see them on the cover of *Fortune* magazine. Google founders Larry Page and Sergey Brin right from the beginning hoped to make it really big by creating search technology that would harness the chaos that was the early Internet. Ray Kroc saw the possibilities in a small hamburger franchise and grew the McDonald's empire based on his vision of applying mass production concepts to a service industry (food preparation). And every day venture capitalists are presented with business plans from would-be entrepreneurs whose definitions of success go well beyond simply earning a decent living.

Visionary Ventures are the types of new companies that get a lot of press. They are exciting, innovative businesses that aspire to new heights and to break new ground. They are also risky. Since an entrepreneur creating a Visionary Venture wants to create a company with huge potential, the entrepreneur often has to put personal considerations—such as the business' ability to generate current income or provide financial stability—second to the need to find a concept that can support the growth of a large enterprise.

Because Visionary Ventures inevitably involve finding and securing big markets—or developing new products or technologies—they typically require a great deal of money to get started. This means that the entrepreneur not only has to spend a lot of time seeking financing, but they also will probably have to give up a significant portion of the ownership of the company to investors.

business
BUZZ
words   ## "corporate culture"

At its most basic level, a corporate culture is made up of the aggregate attitudes, experiences, beliefs, and values of all employees at a business. According to Charles W.L. Hill and Gareth R. Jones in their book *Strategic Management* (Houghton Mifflin, 2001), corporate culture can be defined as "the specific collection of values and norms that are shared by people and groups in an organization and that control the way they interact with each other and with stakeholders outside the organization." A corporate culture can be one in which employees work very hard but also play hard. Or it could be one in which individual workers possess a great deal of autonomy – to the point where they don't need to come into the office except for meetings or other special occasions. Some businesses attempt to formalize their corporate cultures by writing down their corporate "values"; in other cases, the culture is simply the spirit that infuses the organization more spontaneously.

Your Personal Vision

Visions differ from goals in that they tend to be large, grand, and encompass a broad range of factors. Goals tend to be the tangible, nuts-and-bolts accomplishments we set to fulfill our visions. When creating a business, you start at the very top with the personal vision, and gradually work your way down through business vision to opportunities to actual goals and milestones that you can check off a list. To better define your vision, you'll need to:

■ **Identify your passion.** First, what are you passionate about? What truly interests you? What will keep you up at night, thinking and working, long after you should be asleep? This is your passion, and you should always pay attention to what you are passionate about. Aligning your vocation (how you earn your living) with your avocation (how you prefer to spend your time) is one of the most satisfying things you can do. In many cases, it's the reason entrepreneurs have become entrepreneurs.

■ **Identify your skill sets in this field.** Once you know what your avocation is, you need to decide how personally qualified you are to pursue it. You may have a passion for helping people in emotional difficulty and think you want to be a psychologist, counselor, or even a psychiatrist operating your own practice. But what are your inherent skills that make this an appropriate choice of profession for you? Are you naturally intuitive and insightful when it comes to understanding other people's emotional states? Likewise, if you would like to head your own business consulting firm, what specific skills do you possess that would make this a good match? Do you have an analytical mind that can spot problems and come up with solutions? Do you have the people skills to convince people you have the answers to their questions? Taking a long, hard look at yourself is an essential first step in starting a business.

■ **Assess your training/education.** Once you've identified your inherent skills and talents, it's time to investigate how well you're prepared to go into this field based on your formal training and education. It may turn out that your native skills are enough to qualify you to jump into a profession with both feet—for example, dog grooming does not require a degree or certificate—but in many cases you will need to have a credential, academic or trade, or some sort of formal proof that you are qualified to do what you want to do.

■ **Evaluate your experience.** Likewise, experience often matters—sometimes even more than a formal education. In the software field, for example, someone's innate programming abilities coupled with hands-on experience writing computer programs are often worth more than a degree from even the most prestigious university. As has been often noted, Bill Gates never graduated from Harvard. Instead, he took his talent for programming and his experience experimenting with computer languages to found his own software company, Microsoft. The rest is history.

■ **Assess your lifestyle goals.** How you want to live your life is a big part of your vision. Are you willing—or even eager—to devote 60 hours a week to your business? Or is your ultimate goal to leave the running of your day-to-day operations to someone else while you relax on your sailboat? Do you want to grow a business that employs hundreds of people, or do you want to remain an independent sole proprietor? Do you want to work out of your home, or do you wish to establish boundaries between your personal and professional lives by getting an outside office? The more you can articulate this aspect of your vision, the more prepared you will be later to identify the actual goals and milestones for judging whether you're meeting them.

■ **Identify your geographic preferences.** Where would you like to live? Do you want to be able to travel extensively, and to run your business from wherever you happen to be? Or do you want to reside in a particular location? Technology is enabling people to run "virtual" companies that can be operated from anywhere, so depending on the specific type of business you hope to start, you may have a whole gamut of choices that were previously unavailable to entrepreneurs.

■ **Articulate your financial dreams.** Finally, there is the very important question of money: you may simply be hoping to get enough to support yourself (and your family) and save sufficiently for retirement. Or you may be more ambitious, and have visions of accumulating real wealth. Whatever your goals, it's best to articulate them upfront as part of your vision so you can plan your business accordingly.

Your Business Vision

Once you've articulated your personal vision, it's time to consider your business vision. This includes thinking about the type of company you want to build and run at a fairly high level. Some questions to consider:

- **How big a company do you want to build?** As you begin to think about your business, keep in mind that the business itself may dictate the size. Some people deliberately keep their business vision small: they want to be sole proprietors and have no interest in employing others or growing a business that requires more than their particular input. Those with professional skills like accounting or business consulting often fall into this category. Big ideas often require big companies to make them come to fruition. It would be difficult to run a furniture manufacturer with mass-market reach with just three employees. A lot of this comes back to control. It's hard to maintain a high degree of control over a larger company—although some people certainly try.

  The Four Aspirations outlined on pages 14–15 provide a good yardstick for determining the size business you will run. If, for instance, you come to realize that your aspiration is to start a Visionary Venture, you'll be able to eliminate ideas that can only sustain one or two people. If, on the other hand, your aspiration is a company that is a Solo Sustainer, you'll want to avoid businesses that require you to invest a great deal of money up front.

- **Do you want to work by yourself or with other people?** This is a critical question. You may be a self-sufficient type who prefers being in control of every aspect of your business to delegating responsibility or partnering with others. Or you may be gregarious and socially inclined and need others to support you, to bounce ideas off, and to socialize with. Or your business may absolutely require others with complementary skills to make it a success.

Your preferences in this regard will determine the type of business you will start.

- **What business values/corporate culture do you want to create?** What's important to you about the nature of the business you build? How will you treat your employees? Interact with your community and the world in general? What code of ethical conduct will you adhere to when doing business? Management style plays into this: you may prefer a buttoned-down, traditional workplace. Or you might want to foster a more fun environment that includes scooters, video games, and even nap rooms. Here is where your commitment to socially responsible behavior comes into play, as does your vision of how you want to be viewed by others in your organization. Do you want to create a role for yourself as a traditional authoritarian boss or nurture a more collaborative, "flat" organizational culture? You can be very specific about the rules and mores of your business: for example, Kinkos for many years had a strict organizational mandate against gossiping. Other organizations are committed to family values, allowing four-day workweeks and guaranteeing that employees can leave at 5 p.m. Your business values represent an important aspect of you business vision.

- **What are your business skills?** What are your leadership/management qualities or other personality traits that stand you in good stead pursuing this passion? Do a careful inventory of your business skills at this point, because it will determine whether and how you should bring in other individuals to complement your skills, or what additional education or training you need if you hope to go it alone. Can you motivate others? Can you communicate? Are you willing to learn these skills if you don't currently possess them? Keep in mind that your inventory of business skills should include not just the ones you have now, but also the ones you're willing to work on or develop.

worksheet: Your Personal Vision

To help bring your vision into sharper focus, fill out the following worksheet. Don't be shy about writing down your wilder dreams—that's often how the most innovative and successful businesses begin!

What's your passion?

_____

_____

What are your skills/talents in this field?

_____

_____

What's your education/training?

_____

_____

What's your experience?

_____

_____

What's your optimal lifestyle?

_____

_____

Where would you like to live (geographic location)?

_____

_____

What are your financial goals?

_____

_____

worksheet: **Your Business Vision**

Now it's time to focus on the vision you have for your business. After filling out the following worksheet, you will have a better idea of what your business goals are and what you need to do to achieve them.

How big a company do you want to build?

_____

_____

_____

Do you want to work by yourself or with other people?

_____

_____

_____

What are your business values? What kind of corporate culture do you want to create?

_____

_____

_____

Which of your leadership/management qualities or other personality traits will stand you in good stead pursuing this passion?

_____

_____

_____

What business skills are you willing to develop to make your venture a success?

_____

_____

_____

Your Business Opportunities

What exactly *is* a business? According to the American Heritage Dictionary, the word *business* "pertains broadly to commercial, financial, and industrial activities." Although the definition doesn't mention profit per se, it is generally accepted that making money is one of the key—if not *the* key—goals of business. Yes, there are non-profit businesses whose objectives are to create a different kind of value altogether. However, the discussion in this book is focused on for-profit businesses, where the desire to make money from an activity—whether that involves making and/or selling a product or performing a service—is an essential component for embarking on an entrepreneurial venture.

What Is a Business Opportunity?

A business opportunity occurs when you see a chance to provide a product, service, or even information to other people. What you provide can be something new. Or it can be a better or cheaper version of an existing product or service, or a more convenient way of delivering an existing product or service. In its most basic form, an opportunity means that something is missing from current market choices, and that circumstances are ripe for taking advantage of that lack.

Frequently, business experience itself leads to insight into opportunities for other businesses. If you're intimately familiar with the home theater design business due to working in a big-box retailer, for example, you might realize that a certain important component could be better designed. Or you might see that most competitors aren't doing a very good job of providing service to customers, and you could do better. There are the kinds of "aha" moments from which very successful businesses arise.

What Is a Viable Business Opportunity?

Lots of business opportunities exist, but that doesn't mean they're all viable. To qualify for that, the opportunity must lead to a *sustainable* business. And a business is only sustainable if it's 1) profitable (that is, it brings in more money than it costs to run), and 2) those profits are of sufficient volume to meet your financial goals. There are a lot of business ideas that simply can't be made profitable, or that are profitable but don't generate sufficient income to support a single person, much less a family or group of employees. This is frequently the case for solo inventors, who may create a small and much-needed product or service but find the market for it too small to generate enough revenue to make producing it worthwhile.

Toxair: Necessity as the Mother of Invention

In Spring 2003, Dave Srebro had just been laid off from his job with an environmental contractor that had finished a project cleaning up a waste site outside Chicago when he had his "Aha" moment. As a part-time real estate agent, he was attending a training class required as part of his continuing education for keeping his license up to date when he began hearing about the very serious mold problem that was plaguing a lot of area homes. "I hadn't realized it was such a big problem," he says. "A light bulb went off." Toxair was born.

Srebro went home and began tinkering with a prototype of an inexpensive attachment to a standard vacuum cleaner that could be used to perform air sampling in the home. Says Srebro, "I ended up inventing a scaled-down version of what the professionals use."

The Airhound air sampling system is Srebro's brainchild. It's a long molded plastic tube that attaches to a vacuum cleaner and provides detailed information about the air in a particular room. It not only determines the presence of contaminants such as mold spores, carbon dioxide, dust mites, and carbon monoxide, but it also tells users the *amount* of contamination that exists. Srebro markets the Airhound as an inexpensive way for people to test the air in their homes before buying an expensive high-efficiency particulate air (HEPA) cleaner. He sells solely over the Internet, from his website (www.toxair.com).

As a one-person operation with very limited funds, Srebro needed to leverage his time and energy. Since he was attending graduate business school at the University of Illinois at Chicago when he was building Toxair, he paid a fellow student to draw up the engineering diagrams for his invention. He then asked around and got the name of a Chinese manufacturer that would do plastic injection molding at a price he could afford. "I didn't want to go offshore," says Srebro, "but U.S. manufacturers were just too expensive." As it turned out, his experience outsourcing to China was only positive. "They did a really good job. First they sent samples, which I was able to check over for errors and tweak. Then they delivered the final product right to specifications."

Srebro is in the middle of applying for a patent for Airhound, and he says one of the things he learned that other entrepreneurs should be aware of is that many lawyers will do pro bono work for new cash-strapped businesses. "Sometimes their law firms require it, sometimes they just want to give back to the community, but it's a tremendous resource," he says. "I got pro bono help with my patents, which amounted to thousands of dollars of advice. I couldn't have applied for my patents without it."

His other advice: become friends with your business associates. "Go beyond the business relationship to a personal relationship. Believe in your dream, and surround yourself with people who believe in it, too."

Success Factors

There are a number of factors that can contribute to the viability and success of a business:

- **More innovative.** You deliver something to the market that is either new or improves upon an existing offering. Sometimes this involves finding a new use for an existing product or service (or category of product/service). Sometimes this means deploying new technology. In the case of Tom's of Maine, it meant taking a "mature" product category—toothpaste—and innovating by using all natural ingredients. Voila! A successful entrepreneurial venture is launched—and sometimes later sold. In 2006, Colgate-Palmolive Co. bought a majority stake in Tom's of Maine for $100 million.

- **Higher quality.** Offering a product or service that is of noticeably better quality than what others currently offer can create a very valuable business opportunity. Being dissatisfied with what's out there now is a good sign that an opportunity is waiting to be discovered. Steve Ells, the founder of Chipotle, loved Mexican food but was struck by the fact that so much of it was simply not healthy. He thought others might want to enjoy this cuisine without the guilt and used the techniques he'd learned in cooking school to create great-tasting burritos and tacos using only fresh and natural ingredients. His instinct was correct: Today, there are more than 600 Chipotle restaurants, and the eatery was at the forefront of new trend in the prepared food industry—that is, providing the same high quality of food that's found in full-service restaurants in fast food environments.

- **Lower cost.** Being the low-cost leader is a time-honored strategy. But be aware that if your only key differentiator is that you provide a cheaper product or service, it is fairly easy for someone else to beat you at your own game. Unless you have some sort of strategic advantage, such as a unique source of supply or arrangements with partners that make your own expenses *consistently* less than anyone else's, this can be a strategy that is difficult to sustain in the long term.

- **Better service.** A number of very successful companies recognized and seized business opportunities made possible by the less-than-optimal customer service being offered by competitors. For example, JetBlue has built its reputation around providing flyers with more amenities—not just in first or business class but also in economy. Likewise, clothing retailer Nordstrom is famous for accepting returns of merchandise, no questions asked. Providing customers with personal attention and superior service is generally the way that smaller firms attempt to compete with larger ones that have more resources.

- **More convenient.** Making a product or service available in a more convenient way for customers can create a viable business opportunity. A neighborhood hardware store might have higher prices, but its location means that customers don't have to travel to one of the big box retailers. Likewise, a mobile pet grooming service might provide the same basic services as a storefront, but because it goes directly to customers' homes, will carve out a very profitable niche for itself.

business
BUZZ
words

"key differentiators"

What makes your product or service truly different from competitors? Is it price? Is it quality? Whatever it is that makes customers want to choose you over others—that's your key differentiator.

■ **Easily available.** Frequently the fact that a given market is underserved by a particular kind of business can be the basis for a successful enterprise. For example, a masseuse wanting to open an independent practice could look for a town or city in which the demand currently outstrips supply and build a very lucrative client base that would be difficult to establish in an area already saturated with massage therapy businesses.

Degree of innovation

Innovation can take many forms. There is a whole spectrum of possibilities for how you can innovate to exploit the opportunities you see around you:

■ **Tried and true.** Sometimes you don't need to innovate at all. You can simply recognize that there's room in the market for another doctor in private practice, accountant, graphic designer, or restaurant. Yes, you have to be good at what you do, so providing high quality is generally a prerequisite for succeeding in this area. But ordinary rules of supply and demand can make it possible to be very successful in an existing market that's not oversaturated. These businesses often have the least risk and are easiest to start.

■ **New and improved.** Another possibility is going the "better faster cheaper" route by improving on the quality, effectiveness, or price of existing products or services. You're basically putting a new twist on an existing theme. For example, there are a plenty of Web hosting businesses prepared to act

Better, Faster, Cheaper

In the high-tech industry, "smaller, faster, cheaper" has become the mantra for how to differentiate your product or service from other like products or services. (Sometimes that mantra is modified to "better, faster, cheaper.") The concept applies to all types of business opportunities. The beauty of this mantra is its simplicity: people are indeed always looking for a better, cheaper product. And Faster can apply to either a way of getting a product out there more quickly and easily or the fact that the product is more current or actually performs faster. Either way, this phrase captures what you should be trying to do as you assess the viability of a business opportunity. In other words, ask yourself: Is your product better, faster, or cheaper than the competition?

as an electronic "home" for your website, but by offering a lot of additional services—such as the capability to sell things on your website, track who visits it, or place advertisements on it—a number of Web hosting firms have managed to distinguish themselves in a crowded market.

business
BUZZ
words
"innovate"

Innovation is the act of producing something truly new. According to basic economic theory, to innovate is to produce something significantly different, not just make a minor change in an existing idea, product, or service. And that thing you produce must provide value to someone. In an economic context—which is what business is mostly concerned about—creating something new that no one values does not qualify as true innovation. You might design a cool, new household gadget, but if no one needs it, it's not a true business innovation.

Are You an Industry Insider?

Precisely because they are so immersed in a particular product or service industry, some people see opportunities that others less familiar with the territory would miss. For example, no one would be in a better position to know what types of kitchen utensils are missing from restaurants and high-end cooking shops than a working chef. Likewise, a manager of rock bands might see the need for better software to track bookings and billing and have a better understanding of how to go about building this kind of Web application tool than would a software engineer likely to be recognized only by industry insiders. No matter what your industry or area of expertise, you should be constantly looking to spot these kinds of opportunities.

- **Something completely different.** You can also strive for true innovation—creating a new type or category of product or service. This approach has the most risk: It's difficult to be truly different; research and development costs are high; the market may not be ready; and you may even fail. And even if you succeed, competitors may eventually appear. But this approach also promises huge payoffs. In the early days of the Web, for example, you had to know and type in the exact name of a website. Then online directories came along, and one of them—Yahoo—became a huge company. Others kept continue to innovate with ways of finding information, and many search engines were launched. Google came up with innovative, effective mechanisms based on algorithms—and it became a multi-billion-dollar company.

Identifying Opportunities

The best way to think about opportunities is in terms of people's *needs* and *wants*. If you know what they are—and have a plan to satisfy them—your business will have a much better chance of succeeding. Knowing what *you* want and need is not enough. You'll need to step outside yourself and see what potential customers are looking for.

Here are some questions you can ask to identify opportunities:

- What is missing from the current field you're interested in?

- What sorts of things do *you* (as someone passionate about this area) need or want?

- What sorts of things are people always asking you (as someone in the field) to help with?

Degrees of Innovation

FIELD/INDUSTRY	TRIED AND TRUE	NEW AND IMPROVED	SOMETHING COMPLETELY DIFFERENT
Food service	Sandwich shop	A shop offering sandwiches made with freshly baked bread and special coffee drinks like espressos and café lattes.	A sandwich shop/Internet café where people can bring their laptops and have access to free WiFi.
Pet grooming	Walk-in storefront	Satisfaction guaranteed or money back policy	Mobile pet-grooming unit
Communications device	Telephone	Cell phone	PDA with camera and cell phone capabilities

worksheet: Identifying Opportunities

Filling out this worksheet will help you identify areas of opportunities in the business you'd like to explore.

What industry/market/area are you passionate about serving?

_____

_____

_____

_____

What are some of the biggest trends in this industry/market/ area?

_____

_____

_____

_____

What sorts of products/services do you wish were available?

_____

_____

_____

_____

What are people always asking you about/for?

_____

_____

_____

_____

What products/services could improve your field?

_____

_____

_____

Researching Opportunities

Knowledge is power. With accurate information at your fingertips, you can better judge whether the opportunity you've identified is a viable one. And the only way to get this information is through research. Research can be as simple as interviewing people who are already doing what you hope to do. Or it can involve looking up some basic facts about your particular industry on the Internet. Think of research as a reality check that will align your vision with what's really happening in the world. You will do more, and more in-depth, research after you come up with your specific business concept (see Chapter 4) and begin formulating an actual business plan (see Chapter 16).

At this preliminary stage of research, you may want to view historical trends in your chosen field or industry: for example, how many vegetarian restaurants have opened in your area over the past year few years—and how many are still in business? If only a few such restaurants opened, and they're all thriving, that niche might represent a good opportunity. You can also look for data to help forecast future trends. For example, if you'd like to go into the business of decorating and staging houses for sale, you'd want to both see how many houses had been sold in recent months—and at what prices—and what future house sales projections are. And if the housing market is in a slump, you'll probably want to find another opportunity. Your research can help you learn from mistakes others have made—and avoid them in your own entrepreneurial efforts.

Don't try to be exhaustive in your preliminary research efforts; it's not necessary or possible. You are merely looking for information that will answer key questions about the particular opportunity you have identified. At the same time, your research must be thorough enough to give you insight into whether you should proceed along the path you have chosen or investigate other options.

For example, if you're thinking about manufacturing dolls, one of the questions you might ask yourself is, "How large is the market for my product?" For this, you may only have to consult one source, the U.S. Census Bureau, which can provide free-of-charge information about the size and location of a demographic group (such as young girls) to get a reliable

answer. However, answering other questions, such as "What are the current trends in doll-buying habits," may require consulting three or four industry sources, paying a professional researcher, or conducting your own market research to compile information you trust.

Questions to consider in preliminary research:

- Historical trends
- Future economic projections
- Demographics
- Market size
- Competitors

Research resources

An almost unlimited number of resources exists, which you can consult to find out just about anything you want to know about any topic. With the advent of the Internet and electronic search capabilities, you have a wealth of information at your fingertips.

- **People.** People will provide you with some of your best resources for discovering details about just about any topic under the sun. Interview current and past business owners about their experiences. You might think that such people could be reluctant to share information with a would-be competitor, and in some cases this is true. But in many instances, people are delighted to provide up-and-comers with informational interviews about their experiences and lessons learned. Indeed, there are associations—many of them national, with regional or local chapters—that exist primarily for like-minded business-people to share ideas and experiences, and to provide assistance to one another. The local Small Business Development Center is always a good place to start to find help as well.

- **Libraries.** A business library or large branch of your local library is one logical place to start. You'll find books devoted to your area of interest, years' worth of magazines that you can search through—increasingly via electronic means—and online databases. The reference section will have books or binders of business research that are usually updated annually, if not quarterly. Librarians are trained in research and are enthusiastic about helping you find information on your chosen area. They can be one of your most valuable research resources. If you live near a college or university, chances are good it has a business library with specialized resources for entrepreneurs. If you are not a current student or alumni, such libraries will generally issue you a day or week pass for a nominal fee.

■ **Internet searches.** The breadth of what's available about every industry and field is extensive. Typing in relevant keywords causes relevant websites, articles, book references, speeches, and other resources to pop up on your screen. Frequently you'll get hundreds if not thousands of "hits." The problems are understanding what information is reliable and accurate, and taking the time to truly dig deep.

■ **Business research databases.** Business information is valuable. For this reason, the most reliable and useful information is often collected by business research companies and compiled into databases. These are often available in university and public libraries. In the past, most for-fee business databases were only accessible at libraries or via subscription. Today, an increasing number of them will provide you with a specific article or report on the Internet for a one-time fee. Sometimes this fee is quite reasonable, but it can range up to thousands of dollars for in-depth market research reports by top-tier companies.

You might wonder why you would spend money on research when you can do a Google search for free. The answer lies in the *quality* and *timeliness* of the information you get from professional research and analyst firms, which specialize in doing original primary research based on the kind of custom surveys and complex analyses that are well beyond the means, and expertise, of most entrepreneurs (or even established businesses). With access to the databases and reports of professionals, you hear about emerging trends ahead of people *not* subscribing to these resources. And the opposite holds true: if you don't pay for this market wisdom—that is, you may well find yourself behind the curve. You may have to hand over what seem to be significant dollars to get your hands on industry reports. But it might a smart use of your marketing dollars—especially when you're researching the possible opportunities out there.

There are specialized databases such as Lexis (for performing legal research) and Nexis (for business-related topics) (www.lexisnexis.com). Other leading for-fee market research databases include Factiva (www.factiva.com), Dialog (www.dialog.com), and Alacra (www.alacra.com). Generally, whatever you want is out there in one form or another—and increasingly it's online and accessible from your computer.

■ **Government resources.** Government resources can be some of your best sources of information, and for the most part, they are free. An increasing proportion of them are available online. Occasionally, you'll have to pay for a hard copy of a report, but that's generally a minimal fee designed to cover printing and postage costs. Some reports are still only available by mail, and you have to request them specifically. Among the best resources for entrepreneurs are the website of the Small Business Administration (SBA) (www.sba.gov), the U.S. Census Bureau (www.census.gov), and Statistics Canada (www12.statcan.ca/english/census/index.cfm).

Industry Associations

One of the best sources of information about virtually any type of business or industry is the appropriate industry association. An association exists for every market niche you can imagine: Restaurant owners have the National Restaurant Organization; businesses centered around clothing, sports, or outdoor equipment have the Outdoor Industry Association; exterminators have the National Pest Management Association; and on an on. These groups routinely collect industry news, statistics, and trends and make it all available to members to help them run their businesses better. Most sponsor conferences and training events as well. One of the smartest things you can do is join the trade association for your type of enterprise. For a list of industry associations, go to www.planningshop.com/tradeassociations.asp.

The government collects data on a mind-boggling breadth of topics, ranging from growth projections in a broad range of industries to population demographics—segmented by state, county, even city—to analysis of economic trends. Always do a search to see what the government might have already collected and analyzed for you before doing your own research or paying someone else to do it for you.

■ **Research firms.** There are market research companies that charge for the research they routinely perform into various industries, markets, and subject areas. Some of the largest and most reputable ones include Gartner (www.gartner.com), Yankee Group (www.yankee.com), International Data Corp. (www.idc.com), Frost & Sullivan (www.frost.com), and Yankelovich (www.yankelovich.com). The research from these firms is usually quite pricey—but it can be worth it once you get serious about a particular business area.

These research houses do extensive primary research, generally in the form of surveys, on just about every area of business you can imagine, and produce comprehensive reports in which specialists in a particular field—say, the music business—analyze what the survey results mean. Most established firms in the majority of industries routinely subscribe to the services of these research houses on the premise that everyone else in their industry is reading them, and they don't want to miss an important emerging trend.

Researching an industry

When you're researching opportunities, you'll generally be interested in resources that give you information at the industry, rather than specific company, level. (You'll want to research specific competitors once you have narrowed down your specific business concept.) Here are some resources that provide detailed industry data.

Free resources

These are generally available through government agencies, particularly the U.S. Census Bureau.

■ **American FactFinder Quick Reports.** Your source for population, housing, economic, and geographic data in the U.S. Use it to uncover everything from economic projections for specific industries and geographic locations to population trends and housing statistics by country, state, county, or city. (www.factfinder.census.gov).

■ **Statistics Canada studies and reports.** In addition to carrying out a Canadian census every five years, Canada's central statistical agency conducts surveys on virtually all aspects of Canadian life, the results of which can be viewed at the agency's website (www.statcan.com/menu-en.htm).

■ **Economic Census.** The U.S. Economic Census provides a detailed portrait of the nation's economy once every five years, from the national to the local level. Use it to gauge what is likely to happen in a particular industry or geographic region. (http://factfinder.census.gov/jsp).

■ **Industry Statistics Sampler.** Takes data from the U.S. Economic Census and provides snapshots of particular industries. Use it to discover historical trends as well as the current facts about a particular industry. (www.census.gov/econ/census02/data/industry/index.html).

Fee-based resources

Many research resources for up-to-date business industry information require that you pay—sometimes quite a lot—for their data. (Free access to some of these resources may be available through your public, college, or university library.)

■ **ABI/INFORM Global.** Offers abstracts and full-text articles from leading publications. You can find out anything that's been published about a particular market or industry in a major business or trade magazine by searching through this database (www.proquest.com).

■ **Mintel.** A global supplier of consumer, media, and market research. You can use these custom reports to find out what is going on in a broad range of markets and industries (www.mintel.com).

■ **Plunkett Research Online.** Provides market research, company profiles, analysis, trends, statistics, data, and business information. This is an excellent resource for researching potential competitors (www.plunkettresearchonline.com).

■ **Standard & Poor's NetAdvantage.** Comprehensive gathering of in-depth business and investment information. One of the top business databases, this provides independent research, data, and commentary on stocks, bonds, funds, and industries—all of which helps entrepreneurs get the "big picture" of what's going on in their chosen markets and/or industries. *Note:* available only through libraries (www.netadvantage.standardandpoors.com).

■ **Business & Company Resource Center.** A premier online research site that is of special use to entrepreneurs, Business & Company Resource Center has its own content and search engine that allows users to look up detailed information about potential competitors; often available at public libraries (www.galegroup.com/BusinessRC/).

Successful Business Research

The basics of business research and a wealth of both free and for-fee research services are listed in a companion publication to *Passion to Profits*. *Successful Business Research* walks you through how to get verifiable numbers to support your business plans in a step-by-step manner. Harnessing the often-difficult-to-master power of the nation's leading public and private data sources, this book not only takes you to the information, it shows you how to filter it, interpret it, and use it to your business' advantage. Find it at your bookseller or at www.PlanningShop.com

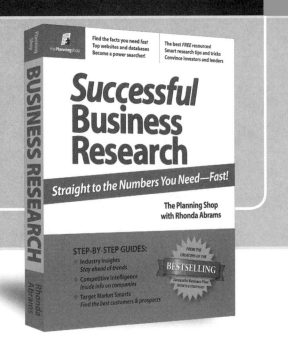

worksheet: Industry Research

This is a good time to test the research waters by using some of the free resources listed on the preceding pages to begin to uncover facts about your chosen industry or market. Use the worksheet below to record some rudimentary facts.

Question	Research Reveals	Opportunities Suggested by Research Results
Describe the economic history and past business trends of this industry or market in terms of the following characteristics: —Demographics —Market size —Competitors —History of industry		
What are the future projections for this industry or market?		
What are the demographics?		
What is the size of this market or industry?		
Who are the main competitors?		

chapter

4

Your Business Concept

You've articulated your personal and business vision and identified opportunities in your area of interest. Now it's time to start honing in on your business concept.

Meeting needs is the basis of all business. You can devise a wonderful new machine, but if it doesn't address some real and important need or desire, people won't buy it, and your business will fail. Even Thomas Edison recognized this fact when he said, "Anything that won't sell, I don't want to invent."

Typically, entrepreneurs get their original business inspiration from one of four sources: 1) previous work experience; 2) education or training; 3) hobbies, talents, or other personal interests; or 4) recognition of an unanswered need or market opportunity. Occasionally, the impetus comes from the business experience of a relative or friend.

As you begin to move from defining a business opportunity to a concept, keep in mind that a successful business incorporates at least one of these elements:

- **Something new or improved.** A new product, service, feature, or technology, or an improvement on an existing product or service encompassing more features, lower price, greater reliability, faster speed, or increased convenience.

- **An underserved or new market.** A market for which there is greater demand than competitors

can currently satisfy, an unserved location, or a small part of an overall market—a niche market—that hasn't yet been dominated by other competitors. Sometimes, markets become underserved when large companies abandon or neglect smaller portions of their current customer base.

- **New delivery system or distribution channel.** New technologies, particularly the Internet, allow companies to reach customers more efficiently. This has opened up many new opportunities for businesses to provide products or services less expensively, to a wider geographic area, or with far greater choice.

- **Increased integration.** The occurs when a product is both manufactured and sold by the same company, or when a company offers more services or products in one location.

Your business should incorporate at least one of these factors—more than one if possible. Ideally, you can bring a new or better product or service to an identifiable but underserved market, perhaps using a more efficient distribution channel. Evaluate the ways your business concept addresses the elements described above. Your concept should be strong in at least one area. If not, you should ask yourself how you plan to make your company truly competitive. To help answer these questions, fill out the following worksheet.

worksheet: **Is Your Business Concept Sound?**

To determine how sound your business concept is, answer the following questions about your proposed product or service:

Is your product or service new or improved? Does it fill a gap in the current market or improve on what's already available? If so, describe how:

_____
_____
_____
_____
_____
_____

Is it serving an underserved or new market? If so, describe that market:

_____
_____
_____
_____
_____
_____

Does it allow companies to reach their customers more efficiently? If so, state how:

_____
_____
_____
_____
_____
_____

Does it build on products or services you already offer, or can you both manufacture and sell it?

_____
_____
_____
_____
_____

Traditional to Entrepreneurial

PRODUCT/SERVICE	WHERE THE IDEA ORIGINATED
No Fear	No Fear is a sports company founded in 1989 by three surfer buddies whose inspiration was to spread positive messages of self-esteem and to encourage all people to perform to their potential. At the same time, the founders eschewed traditional corporate values in favor of socially responsible and ethical business practices that emphasized an approach to commerce that transcended merely chasing profits. Originally selling T-shirts plastered with existential slogans that defied traditional fears of danger or mortality, they promoted wholehearted engagement with life, and expressed contempt for established social mores. No Fear now has an entire line of products, including SoBe No Fear energy drinks under the same brand, in a joint venture with SoBe, and No Fear trucks in partnership with GM and Nissan. The company currently employs about 450 people.
Martha Stewart	Martha Stewart, a former stockbroker and fashion model, built a business empire based on the domestic arts. She founded a catering business in 1976 and became well known in New York society circles for her talent at planning and executing parties. Her first book, *Entertaining,* was a cookbook that featured recipes and photographs from parties Stewart had catered. It became the best-selling cooking book since Julia's Child's classic *Mastering the Art of French Cooking*. From there, Stewart went on to write many more books and rapidly became a media personality through her newspaper and magazine articles and appearances on national television. In 1990 she created her successful homemaking magazine *Martha Stewart Living*. In 1997, Stewart gathered all of her domestic arts ventures under the business Martha Stewart Living Omnimedia (MSLO), Inc. In 2006, MSLO reported revenues of $288.3 million. Although in 2004 she was convicted of lying to investigators about a stock sale and served five months in prison, Stewart has successfully emerged from that scandal and has continued to expand her empire, including creating a 24-hour satellite radio channel and inking deals with department store Macy's and warehousing firm Costco to deliver Martha Stewart–branded frozen foods.
Whole Foods Markets	The Austin, Texas-based natural foods store currently has hundreds of shops throughout North America and the United Kingdom, but its roots are humble. In 1978, a 25-year-old college dropout and his 21-year-old girlfriend wanted to open a small organic grocery store. They borrowed $45,000 and founded Saferway—an ironic twist on the name of supermarket giant Safeway—in Austin. At one point, the couple was so strapped for cash they were actually living in the store, in violation of local zoning laws. They changed the name to Whole Foods after merging with another natural grocery in town in 1980. In 1984, it began expanding to new markets, frequently by acquiring other, local health food stores. In 2007 the firm reaped $6.6 billion in revenues, and it has regularly reported annual growth rates in excess of 20 percent.

Positioning Your Product or Service

A crucial factor in a successful business is a clear strategic position that differentiates you from your competition—and the ability to maintain your focus on that position. All too often businesses fail because management loses sight of the central character of the enterprise.

Defining a clear strategic position enables you to capture a particular place in the market and distinguish yourself from your competitors. Different companies may sell a similar product, but each may have a very different sense of what the business is all about.

Suppose four companies are making jeans. Company A defines itself as selling work clothes; Company B sees itself as a sportswear manufacturer; and Company C identifies itself as being in the business of selling youth and sex appeal. But Company D has never clarified its mission—it just sells jeans.

These different positions affect the way each company markets itself, how it designs its jeans, what subsequent products it produces, and even the employees it hires. The first three companies may all succeed and rarely be in competition with one another. But Company D, which misses the big picture, is almost certain to fail over time as it flounders in its attempt to compete with all of the other, more focused companies.

A second aspect of positioning your company and maintaining focus is the development of a company style or corporate culture. By creating a consistent style that permeates every aspect of your enterprise—from the design of your stationery to personnel policies—you give your customers and employees a sense of trust in your company.

The best way to figure out your key differentiator or differentiators is to make a direct comparison to the other companies—or products or services—that are most like yours. In doing so, you're looking to find a clear, objective differentiator that will truly distinguish you in the marketplace.

- **Similarities.** First decide what will make your company, product, or service like other successful ones. In what way does it resemble the market leader? When pitching to investors to fund a new business, entrepreneurs always have to provide in-depth information about other companies doing similar things. The reason for this is that investors want to determine whether there's interest in the area and judge whether others also see this as an opportunity.

It's important to identify similarities because you want to ascertain that there actually is a potential market for your service. If there is absolutely nothing out there that even remotely resembles what you are trying to offer, it may be because no one wants it. You have to consider that possibility. Investros certainly will. Another reason to come up with comparisons is to give people a reference point as they try and understand why they should buy your offering. Although true innovations do exist—just think of phones, cars, radio, or television—generally even those can be compared to existing products or services to help the market understand their value. Radio, for example, although truly innovative at the time, was originally described to the public as just like listening to a stage play or concert, only in the privacy of their homes. Television, likewise, was advertised as "radio with pictures." People need something they can relate to, or you will have trouble selling your product or service.

Is First Best?

Believe it or not, being the first to bring a product or service to market isn't always the best route to success. Often the maker of a truly innovative new product or the provider of a creative new service has to break down all sorts of barriers: such entrepreneurs frequently have to educate people on how something works or why it offers value. The second or even third business in a market may be the one that profits from the groundbreaking work of others.

■ **Differences.** Think about what will make your business different from others attempting to solve a similar problem/need. Why would anyone care that yet another clothes designer or rapid-copy print shop, or painting contractor has entered the market? This is where your "key differentiators" come in.

Do you pride yourself on your sense of workmanship or customer service? Does your product or service provide unique features that competing products or services don't? Are you serving a different market? Are you simply cheaper than competitors? Anything that sets you apart needs to be identified and emphasized as you establish and grow your business.

What Is Your Business Model?

Now that you've articulated a vision for your business, you need to consider a number of other factors as you begin to ground your vision in reality. These real, practical nuts-and-bolts aspects of running a business will ultimately determine how successful you are. No matter how brilliant the idea, execution in business is everything!

One of the first things you will do is create a business model. This is the business term for describing how you're going to make money. Are you going to sell directly to consumers or use intermediaries? For example, if you're manufacturing a product, will you use distributors or retailers to reach the actual users, or will you open your own brick-and-mortar storefront or e-commerce website? If you're selling a service, will it be for a flat fee, via a subscription, or on a time-and-materials basis? In other words, what structure are you putting in place to make your money?

Your business model is important because even the best concept will have a hard time succeeding if it's not supported by the right business model. For example, AOL—which created an Internet empire based on charging people a fee (based on hourly usage) to provide Internet access and email—found itself floundering in the early 2000s as a plethora of low-cost Internet service providers (ISPs) flooded the market, and industry giants like Microsoft, Yahoo, and Google offered email for free.

worksheet: Similarities and Key Differentiators

Use this worksheet to write down all of the key things you plan to deliver to your customers. For example, if you're an accountant, you would put down "preparing tax returns" and "financial planning services" as key features of your business. Then, you would explain how the products or services mentioned are both similar to and different from your competitors.

Key Feature of Your Business	How Do You Resemble Other Businesses in Your Market?	How Do You Differentiate Yourself from Competitors?

Losing subscribers at a rapid place, AOL changed its business model to a monthly flat fee and began giving away email services to the public. By doing this, it was able to slow the drain of people from its popular portal and thus stabilize the revenue inflow from advertisers—from whom AOL derived the bulk of its profits, since advertising is a major component of its business model.

How Will You Make Your Product or Perform Your Service?

Next, you have to begin to think about how you will make your product or perform your service. If your business is based on a product, will you manufacture it yourself or provide design specs to a contract manufacturer and let them handle that aspect of the business? Where will you get your raw supplies? Where will you store your supplies and your finished products? There's a range of issues you need to start thinking about now—even before you spend the first penny on establishing your business.

If you will be providing people with a service, what supplies will you need? If you are baking organic breads, where will you get your ingredients? Will you need a secondary backup supplier in case your primary supplier can't deliver for any reason on a given day? Will you be performing the service on your own or will you need partners or employees? Will you perform the service at the customer site, at your location, or somewhere else? Will you require a special permit or license? Insurance? These are all important questions you need to consider. It's never too early to start sketching out a plan that addresses all of these, and other, issues. Not having the answers can prevent even the best business concept from ever becoming a thriving operation.

How Will You Get Your Product or Services to Customers?

You will also have to decide how you will be *distributing* your product or service to customers. Will you do this directly, or will you hire intermediaries to do it for you? One term related to distribution is *sales channel,*

or the specifics of how you will sell your product or service to the end user.

It's actually much easier to come up with a new product or service than to change the ways that customers currently buy that product or service. For example, two darlings of the dot-com bubble were Pets.com (a pet supply company) and HomeGrocer (a grocery delivery service). Each spent millions (if not billions) of dollars trying to get customers to purchase products in a new way: over the Internet. Yet both bombed because people had not yet become comfortable buying things online. Today, such businesses might succeed. But it takes time for people to change their buying habits.

How Will You Price Your Products or Services?

Your pricing strategy is critical: in fact, it will determine whether you will have a sustainable business. Price your product or service too low, and you won't generate enough money to pay your bills, much less make a profit. Price it too high, and you may have trouble getting people to buy it. Formulating the right pricing strategy will involve researching prevailing market rates and conditions as well as accurately identifying all of the costs you will incur in making your product or providing your service. (See Chapter 20 for more on pricing.)

Pricing is about more than just covering your costs, however. It's also a competitive tool that shapes how your products and services are perceived by the market. For example, do you want to be considered the "low-price leader?" Or do you want to build a reputation for selling the premier product or service in your market? Low prices aren't necessarily always the best way to go when attempting to build a business and capture customers.

Who Is Your Customer?

Your business concept must also take into account whether you will be selling to other businesses, to consumers, or to both. For example, you may be selling office supplies, but only in the kind of large quantities that businesses would be interested in, and therefore might not even have a storefront, but only a warehouse from which you make deliveries to client locations.

Alternatively, if you wanted to sell into the consumer market, you could open a retail stationery store that catered to individual buyers. B2B is the business term that stands for *business to business*; B2C, in contrast, represents *business to consumer*. Generally B2B and B2C companies sell through different channels and at different price points, and use different marketing strategies to reach their desired customer bases. Until you know exactly whom you'll be selling to, your plans for starting a business will be incomplete. (See Chapter 5 for a more on customers.)

What (or Who) Is Your Competition?

In many cases you'll know exactly who your competitors are: the restaurant down the street, the other big law office in town, the overseas manufacturer who produces the same component as you, or the other Web-based payroll service in your areas. Other times, though, your competitors might not be who you think they are. Sometimes competition comes from indirect sources. If you provide landscaping and lawn maintenance services, your *direct* competitors would be other like services. But your *indirect* competitor would be the local hardware store or superstore, because they sell supplies and equipment that allow people to maintain their own properties. As you price your services, you might have to keep in mind that new products and equipment make lawn do-it-yourself outdoor maintenance easier and are coming down in price significantly.

How Big Is the Market?

You might have the highest quality, most innovative and in-demand product or service in your particular market segment. But if the market for your product or services is too small, you won't be able to earn sufficient income to sustain your business. Inventors frequently run into this problem: they may come up with a device that performs a task extraordinarily well, but if it will only be of interest to a small number of people, the resulting revenues won't sustain a business.

On the other hand, you probably can't be all things to all people. If you view your market as huge, chances are good it's crowded with lots of competitors, and it could be harder to differentiate yourself than if you'd chosen a specific niche within that market.

business
BUZZ
words

"channel"

The sales channel is simply the means by which you get a product or service from you, its originator, to the end user or customer.

Direct, wholesale, and retail refer to different types of channels; typically, the wholesaler is a middleperson between the creator of the product or service and the retailer, which is the business that deals directly with the user. You may actually be a retailer yourself—in which case, you have a "direct" channel, or you may choose to supply others with your product or service and create a "retail channel."

Sales channels can include trade shows where potential distributors or retailers find out about new products and services. Depending on your distribution strategy, you may need to reach these kinds of people rather than the end users themselves. In technology and engineering markets, for example, products are frequently sold through third-party intermediaries who install or otherwise add value to the product. (Indeed, these individuals/companies are commonly referred to as *value-added resellers*.) For example, rather than simply selling the software that operates an electronic cash register for a small retail business, a value-added reseller might also install that software (along with other technology tools) and provide ongoing maintenance.

The way to gauge whether a market is a good size for your business is by seeing how expensive it is to reach and advertise to them. Are there trade shows, magazines, and websites aimed at your target market, and can you afford to be part of them? If you have to use general consumer media—such as TV or the most popular websites—to reach your market, you've probably defined your market too broadly.

How Will You Let People Know About Your Product or Service?

Reaching your target market can take some ingenuity—as well as cash. This is where further research (yes, more!) and marketing and advertising come into play. After all, just because you build it, that doesn't necessarily mean that customers will come. Entrepreneurs must understand how to get the word out—not only to let people know their products and services exist but to make people aware that those products or services are superior in some crucial way to competing products and services. This is called marketing, and there are a variety of ways to do it—indeed, different businesses will require quite different marketing strategies. (For more on marketing, see Chapter 17.)

How Will You Finance Your Business?

Where will the money come from? You may not have enough personal funds to jumpstart your business or keep it going until you're able to turn a profit. Restaurant owners, for example, routinely face this challenge. It takes a lot of capital to set up an operation, buy all of the necessary equipment, pay the staff, and purchase the ingredients for the meals they will serve. Few individuals possess these kinds of resources, and most must look elsewhere—to friends, family, angel investors, venture capitalists, or financial institutions—to bankroll their business visions.

Without a viable plan for funding—even if this just means "bootstrapping" your venture or using only your own money without any outside financing—you won't have a viable business. Spend some time thinking about this upfront and be realistic about your comfort level owing other people money (called "debt") or perhaps sharing ownership with them (called "equity"). (For more on financing, see Chapter 15.)

Location, Location, Location

If you're a retailer or service provider, you'll be concerned about the neighborhood or business district you operate in. What other businesses are nearby? What kind of automobile or foot traffic do you need to be successful? Will you depend on "drop-ins" or expect that people will make a special effort to come see you? The chart below shows how your business needs relate to your choice of location.

TYPE OF BUSINESS	BUSINESS NEEDS	BEST LOCATION
Seafood restaurant	Populated area, vacation crowd	Seaside/tourist town
Women's clothing boutique	Foot traffic, upscale clientele	Retail business area near a financial district
Dentist	Convenience, near neighborhoods	Well-traveled roads where people see your sign
B2B IT services	Close proximity to a business center	Street visibility not required, but close proximity to customer sites is important
Graphic designer	Internet connection	Can be located anywhere with the right technology infrastructure
Caterer	Industrial kitchen for food preparation	The right facilities within short driving distance of most likely customers

worksheet: **Making Your Concept Concrete**

With the worksheet below, you have a chance to finally write down everything you've been thinking about for your business concept. Anything you leave blank because you don't know the answer indicates you need to do more research before you continue.

What is your product/service idea?

_____

What is your business model (how will you make money)?

_____

How will you make your product or perform your service?

_____

How will you get your product/service to customers?

_____

How will you price your product/service?

_____

Who are your customers?

_____

Who are your competitors?

_____

How big is the market?

_____

How will your market your product/service?

_____

How will you finance your business?

_____

chapter 5

Your Customers

Your customers are the individuals or businesses that purchase your goods or services. Keep in mind, however, that your customers may differ from the end users of your product or service. In other words, one person might pay for your product or service, while another person may end up buying or using it. For example, a hardware store might pay you for your line of power tools, but home contractors are the actual end users.

It's critical to clearly define your customers—both primary and secondary—because many of the other decisions you make about your business will follow from knowing who they are. If you don't know who your customers are, you won't know how to tell them about your product or service or how to get it to them. You could waste money placing ads in the wrong magazines or putting up signs in inappropriate parts of town. Or you could misjudge the price your customers are willing to pay. *Know thy customers* should be one of your business mantras from Day One.

Are They Out There?

First and foremost, you need to figure out if potential customers actually exist. Companies have been built—and have failed—on the false premise that customers for a given product or service are in fact out there. There are a number of ways you can attempt to

determine whether your customer base is real. You can start with basic market research, and perhaps progress through customer surveys, sampling, testing, or interviewing potential customers in focus groups. These activities will tell you what actual members of your target customer base think about what you're planning to offer. Or you can start testing in small markets to see the response to your offering. McDonald's does this all the time: offering new specialty sandwiches at a number of selected restaurants to gauge market reaction.

Notice the word *attempt* in the preceding paragraph. It's important to understand that you may not be able to judge whether you have customers based on traditional methods of market research. This is especially true if you're offering a truly innovative product or service. The more innovative it is, the longer it will take for customers to become familiar with it, grow comfortable with it, and begin to buy it. It's much easier to market high-end ballpoint pens to stationery stores at a good price than to convince people to purchase a new device that allows them to input text into a computer without typing.

And there's the fact that customers don't always know what they want until they try it. Once, if you'd tried to sell bottled water to the mass market, they'd have laughed all the way to the kitchen tap. And almost certainly if asked whether they would pay $70-plus a month to have a mobile phone, the vast majority of

If You Build It, Will They Come?

One of the biggest mistakes entrepreneurs make is focusing more on their product or service than on understanding their customers. You could have what you think is the coolest new idea on the planet, but if no one is interested in buying it, you don't have a business. During the Internet boom, Web Van was a media darling—its plan to deliver everything from groceries to prescriptions, dry cleaning, and movie rentals to people's houses seemed like a brilliant concept. The only trouble was, not enough people were willing to pay for the service. The company's demise was one of the most spectacular during the so-called "dot-com bust."

Americans would have answered with a resounding *no.* Even savvy businesspeople make mistakes of this kind. Every market test 3M conducted of Post-its predicted failure. The newer something is, the longer it takes to catch on.

The Costs of Switching

Another point you need to consider is how hard it will be for potential customers to switch from an existing product or service to your offering. Just as there are barriers to entry for businesses (for example, it's difficult to embark on a new semiconductor manufacturing business because of all the specialized staff, equipment, and facilities required), there are also barriers to switching for customers. These barriers can be physical—for example, moving from videocassettes to DVDs took a long time because it involved replacing a pricey machine as well as personal libraries of movies—or they can be emotional. You'll see this in the high-tech world all the time: the time and energy it takes to get files and data from an old computer to a new one causes many people to put off purchasing the latest and greatest machine, no matter how much of an improvement it represents over their existing one.

End User vs. Customer

If you were asked to say *precisely* who your customers—or potential customers—were, how would you answer? You might say that your customers are all of the people who purchase and use your product or service—but you would be wrong. You must be careful to distinguish between your customer and the end user of your product or service. You may be selling directly to your end users. Or you may be selling to an intermediary—or *middleperson*—and that intermediary may well have other intermediaries.

Primary and Secondary Customers

Your primary customers are the ones you spend the most time (and money) targeting. For example, if you're an outdoor apparel manufacturer, your primary customer could be a snowboarding or surfing enthusiast. Yet you might also have "secondary" customers—customers you wouldn't necessarily expect to be interested in your product. Many outdoor product manufacturers have strong secondary markets among people who aren't active in a particular sport but are attracted by the brand image. Surfboard maker O'Neill, for example, has a strong secondary market selling T-shirts displaying the company logo to the general population, who aren't surfers but perhaps wish they were!

Finding Your Niche

Rather than view the world as your oyster, you should focus on a niche within a market or industry. That way, you can hone in on a particular set of customers' wants and needs rather than create a generalized product that's aimed at everyone but, in fact, appeals to no one. Say, for example, you want to turn your knack for design into a fashion business: Telling yourself that everyone needs clothes isn't going to help you design products that stand out in the marketplace. On the other hand, choosing to design and sell clothes for plus-size women or, even more specifically, business attire for plus-size customers will allow you to differentiate yourself in a smaller but still viable marketplace.

Let's say you've created a new breakfast cereal for children: Yummy Tummy Oats. You've packed it with good things: vitamins, minerals, and great nutritional value. You figure you're going to wipe out the competition because all parents want their kids to have a nutritious breakfast.

There's only one problem: Who's your customer? Is it the mom or dad pushing the grocery cart down the cereal aisle comparing the nutrition information on the side of the box? Or is it the end user (the "consumer") of your product—the kid—who couldn't care less about nutrition but wants cereal that tastes sweet, and has cartoon characters on the package and toys inside the box?

Or is your customer the cereal buyer for the grocery store? This person couldn't care less about nutrition or cartoon characters either. The store cereal buyer's concerns are more down to earth: how much money you're going to spend on advertising, how quickly you'll replenish inventory, and whether you'll pay them a "stocking fee" to obtain shelf space. Parents and children aren't going to have a chance to buy or eat Yummy Tummy Oats if you don't meet the supermarket buyers' needs first. On top of that, if you don't have your own sales and distribution force, you may first have to find a cereal distributor and convince them to carry your product.

The parent. The child. The store buyer. The distributor. That's a lot of "customers" you have to satisfy with each box of Yummy Tummy Oats. And you'll give yourself a competitive edge by thinking of each of these "customers" and planning for their needs and motivation.

Being responsive to the details that are important to distributors, retailers, sales representatives, and others helps you plan your marketing materials, operations, packaging, even the nature of the product itself. If yours is an industry where sales reps must purchase their samples, for instance, you can set yourself apart by supplying samples free. If retailers can fit more square packages on a shelf than round packages, you'll be more competitive by choosing a square package.

business
BUZZ
words

"market segmentation"

This is the process of dividing a market into sections that are perceived as having something in common—either they behave in similar ways, or they have similar requirements. The goal of market segmentation is to tailor your product or service to appeal to each segment. This "tailoring" can take the form of adding or deleting specific features or of marketing, pricing, or distributing it differently. For example, Nike segments its shoes into different customer categories depending on the sporting activity they engage in: running, basketball, baseball, and so on. Likewise, automobile manufacturers segment their marketing messages to appeal to different ethnic groups.

Even if you think you'll market "directly to consumers" on the Internet, you'll discover that there are still many entities between you and your "customer" in cyberspace. In the case of Yummy Tummy Oats, your intermediary might be the online grocery store, the health food site, a children's site, or a search engine that will help customers find you. So you'll still have more than just parents and kids to please.

The same thing goes for services. For example, you might run a spa that does a booming business in gift certificates, where the target market is not solely composed of the people who will actually get the massage or facial, but also of the spouses and friends who will be giving the gift. In such a case, your marketing campaign could stress the gift's power to impress the gift certificate recipient.

worksheet: Who Are Your Customers?

Identify your customers in each of the following categories. You'll find that the number of customers in each category grows the closer you get to the end user.

End Users / Consumers

Purchasers / Decision Makers (if different from above)

Retail Sales Personnel

Retailer Decision Makers

Wholesale / Distributor Sales Personnel

Wholesale / Distributor Decision Makers

Others:

Market Size

Ever wonder why there are three or four fast-food joints at the same intersection? Or why, all of a sudden, not one but three big office supply stores open in a community? The answer is they're all relying on similar statistics to analyze a market. They look for certain factors: population density, characteristics of nearby residents (age, gender, income), and the number and type of local businesses (among others).

Big corporations hire consulting firms to compile these statistics. However, you have got an even bigger consulting group doing it for you—free! The U.S. government, particularly the Census Bureau, compiles all sorts of information that's useful for businesses, and it's put much of that information on the Internet.

A few of the most useful websites:

- **Fedstats (www.fedstats.gov).** The main portal for finding government statistics. The government has tried hard to make this accessible, but if you don't know what you're looking for, you may find it difficult to find at this site.

- **U.S. Census Bureau (www.census.gov).** This site gives you access to all Census data, including facts about people, businesses, trade, and much more.

- **County Business Patterns (www.census.gove/eped/cpb/view/cbpview.html).** If you want to know what's going on in your hometown, this is the place to go. This easy-to-use database provides detailed information about businesses in any area, down to Zip code level.

- **Quick Facts (http://quickfacts.census.gov/qfd/index.html).** This is an easy way to access a wide variety of information about population characteristics at the state or county level.

- **American FactFinder (www.factfinder.census.gov).** The gateway site of the Census Bureau to specific information on people, housing, economic, and geographic data.

- **The U.S. Economic Census (www.census.gov/epcd/www/guide.html).** Compiled every five years, the Economic Census gathers very detailed information on business activity, by industry and subsectors of industries, down to Zip code. This site can provide you with very specific information for your target area.

- **The Census Bureau's State Data Centers (www.census.gov/sdc.www/).** The U.S. Census Bureau maintains this site, linking to each state's main statistic site.

Know Your Customers

As you begin to define your customers (both end users and intermediaries), you should have a good idea of their various attributes: age, location, industry, purchasing patterns, buying sensitivities, and "psychographics" (what motivates them). Although you might not have enough research data at this stage to fully understand all aspects of your customer, you should have some idea who you're targeting with your product or service. Of course, not all products and services require that you know *everything* about a customer. If you're a software engineer with a new add-on to an Internet browser, for example, you don't need to know the age and sex of your target customers—merely that they use that browser and are looking for functionality of the kind you can provide. Still, it's good to guesstimate what your "typical" customer might look or act like before you actually start making your product or planning your service.

Knowing your customers could include knowing:

- Geography (Where are they located?)
- Age
- Gender
- Marital status
- Interests
- Income
- Psychographics (How do customers perceive themselves?)

The most important way in which you need to understand your customers, however, is what they need and want. Ideally, you are fulfilling a need that is currently not being addressed—or addressed effectively—by existing products and/or services. These wants and needs should be directly related to your key differentiators (see page 35), which you have already defined.

business
BUZZ
words

"early adopter"

According to communications scholar Everett Rogers' "Diffusion of Innovations" theory, there are five types of people who adopt new products or services at different speeds, ranging from "innovators," who leap into the unknown and are the first to line up when something new appears, to "laggards," who are generally fearful and cautious of trying new things. Early adopters tend to be on the faster end of the spectrum, which also includes "early majority" and "late majority" kinds of people.

High-tech consultant Geoffrey Moore's "Crossing the Chasm" theory builds on this theory and hypothesizes that marketers should focus on one group of customers at a time, using each group as a base for marketing to the next group. The most difficult step is making the transition between visionaries (early adopters) and pragmatists (early majority). This is the chasm he refers to. If a firm can create a bandwagon effect in which the momentum builds from group to group—from innovators down to laggards—its product has a chance of being a market leader.

worksheet: Size of Your Market

Use this worksheet to determine whether your target market is large enough to bring you sufficient sales.

Estimated size of your market:

_____

_____

Is this number growing or declining? By how much?

_____

_____

What are the emerging trends in this market?

_____

_____

worksheet: Defining Key Customer Wants and Needs

Try to come up with the customer wants/needs that you product or service will fulfill. Prioritize them in order of importance to your customer.

Want/Need 1

_____

_____

_____

Want/Need 2

_____

_____

_____

Want/Need 3

_____

_____

_____

Texas Natural Supply:
Growing a Business Organically

In 1999, Hollie Mulhaupt was working full time as a registered nurse in an emergency room in Austin, Texas, and growing increasingly dissatisfied with the philosophy behind most of the traditional medical treatments she saw daily. "The longer I worked in the medical field," she says, "the more I felt we were never fixing the problems, just treating the symptoms."

This motivated Mulhaupt to learn more about Chinese medicine, aromatherapy, and other alternative therapies. The kicker came one day when a child came into the emergency room having seizures that turned out to be caused by ingesting enough off-the-shelf bug spray to induce neurotoxicity. Says Mulhaupt, "I started looking at the ingredients of many of the skin care products I was using and became unnerved by what I was putting on my skin." And thus Texas Herbal Body Solutions was born.

Texas Herbal Body Solutions creates and markets bath and body products, and sells them over its website to customers around the world. Its flagship product is Texas Bug Juice, a Deet- and alcohol-free insect repellant made with 19 essential oils, which a number of other natural skin care product manufacturers purchase and re-label under their own brand names. In 2004, Mulhaupt was able to quit her nursing job and devote herself full time to Texas Herbal Body Solutions.

As she grew her business, Mulhaupt began buying raw materials in ever-greater quantities. Because some of the lot sizes were too big for her needs, she started selling off the excess to other, smaller makers of natural body products as well as to individuals who simply enjoyed making their own soaps and

lotions. "There was such a tremendous response every time I had something extra to sell that it dawned on me that there was a huge hole in the market," says Mulhaupt. With that in mind, she decided to open a new business concentrating solely on supplying makers of natural skin care products with raw ingredients—Texas Natural Supply. Says Mulhaupt, "This is my real baby, and where my real passion lies."

Although Mulhaupt still makes her Texas Herbal Body Solutions products, that business has been folded into Texas Natural Supply, which is growing by leaps and bounds. In 2006, Mulhaupt was able to move her business from her home to a new facility that combines a retail space with backroom storage and a manufacturing facility. Now, the business is growing so fast that Mulhaupt is doubling her space requirements and adding warehouse capacity every three months.

Her biggest challenge: pricing. "We just did it trial and error, and made some mistakes," Mulhaupt admits. "We finally learned to look at what our competitors were charging, add up all of our costs, and test the market to see what it would bear."

Her goal is to build a thriving business that supports a family-centered lifestyle. "You could say that I'm working toward a lifestyle rather than a business goal," Mulhaupt says. She has three young children and hopes that as her business grows, they will be interested in helping out. "I grew up in a family-owned business and worked there as a teenager with my father, my grandmother, my aunt and uncle, and my cousins. We loved it. I'd like to give the same to my kids."

6

Your Competitors

One of the most important aspects of formulating your business concept is being aware of the alternatives available to your customers. In other words, how else can they acquire the products or service you offer? You also need to understand one very critical point: whatever your key differentiator is—that is, whatever you do better than your competitor—it will have to evolve over time. This is because the minute you start to do something different, your competitor will start doing it, too. Thus, you must remain constantly in motion to stay one step ahead of the pack.

That said, although it's important to understand what (or who) your business is up against, it's not necessarily a good thing to obsess over it. Success for an entrepreneur depends much more on what *you* do than on what the other guy (or gal) is doing.

Yes, big businesses spend millions of dollars fighting over each percentage point of market share (just think of Coke vs. Pepsi, Ford vs. GM, and so on). But for small companies, this is not necessarily productive. However, this does not mean that you can just ignore the competition. You need to know who's out there, what they're offering, and what they're charging. If you approach this competitive analysis exercise as an opportunity to learn, you may find ways to enhance your own products or services—or at least improve your marketing.

Types of Competitors

Competition comes in the following forms:

- **Direct competitors.** These are the ones who keep you up at night. They're other companies like yours: close to customers, ambitious, and trying to reach the same target market. In most markets, there's enough business to go around, but you better know what your direct competition is doing.

- **The big guys.** The Wal-Marts, Home Depots, Lawyers 'R' Us—national companies or franchises with huge marketing budgets. Don't just dismiss these as being inferior because they're big—a lot of them have adopted customer service practices that used to be the hallmark of small businesses. These are very real competitors to you, especially if you plan to compete on price.

- **Indirect competition.** It's important to understand that you can face a great deal of *indirect* competition—that is, rather than having another company compete head to head against your product or service, you're competing against other types of products or services that your customers might spend their funds on rather than yours. For example, if you run a lakeside resort for family vacations, your competition would not only include the resort on the other side of the lake, but Disney cruises, mountain cabins for rent, and vacation packages to Hawaii. Likewise, your target customers might decide to remodel their kitchens rather than go on vacation—there are a million ways people can spend their money.

■ **Inertia.** Sometimes your biggest competition is that people just don't have the motivation to change their ways, try a new product, or investigate a new service. In such cases, you may have to devise unique marketing plans to light a fire under them.

In most situations, however, you're going to concentrate your energy on looking at what your direct competitors are doing—who they are, what their competitive strengths and weaknesses are, and how much they charge.

You can identify these direct competitors by looking at directories (Yellow Pages, online directories, trade association directories) and advertisements. You can also ask suppliers and distributors to name the major competition in your area. See if your competitors are exhibiting at trade shows. And you can do a survey of potential customers, asking them to name your competition. Indeed, identifying whom your customers are considering as an alternative to you is one of the best type of market research you can do.

And don't forget that you should always keep an eye open for future competitors as well—those businesses that see an opening for their products and services. You can learn as much from new entrants into the market as existing competitors.

business BUZZ words

"feasibility analysis"

A feasibility analysis is a preliminary study undertaken to determine whether something is viable, and whether to proceed. In the case of starting a new business, all of the worksheets you've been filling out amount to a feasibility analysis of your business concept.

Barriers to Entry

In economics, barriers to entry are obstacles that stand in the way of a company entering a given market. Barriers to entry include:

■ **Investment.** How much money will it take to get on par with competitors? For some industries, the investment required is substantial: think about what it would take to start up a new, low-cost airline, for example.

■ **Government regulations.** In regulated markets like energy the government can make it difficult to jumpstart a new business. Requirements for licenses and permits may raise the investment needed to enter a market. If you want to drive a taxicab in New York, for example, you must purchase a hard-to-acquire "medallion" due to local restrictions on the number of taxis allowed on the streets.

■ **Aggressive prices.** Sometimes companies with a major share of a market will sell at a loss—or even give things away free—to make it difficult for smaller, younger firms to enter the market. Although illegal in many cases, this can be difficult to prove legally.

■ **Intellectual property.** In some industries, the right to use certain patented devices or processes may keep smaller firms from entering the market—either because they lack the funds to purchase rights to use the patents, or because patent holders refuse to license those rights.

■ **Economy of scale.** Larger firms can frequently manufacture products or provide services at lower cost than smaller businesses, making it difficult to compete in a market with entrenched competition.

■ **Customer loyalty.** A common barrier to entry is that customers are extremely reluctant to switch from the company that currently serves them.

worksheet: Your Competitors

Use this worksheet to identify your current direct competitors.

Competitor	Their Advantages/Strengths	Your Advantages/Strengths

Social Responsibility

As you start your business, you'll have many goals. You'll be focused on developing your business concept, getting funded, and making money. So what does social responsibility have to do with any of these?

Just as individuals have responsibilities to their communities, companies likewise have responsibilities and obligations to society at large. Corporations are unique entities with many rights and privileges. Society, through its laws, grants corporations special and favorable benefits, such as limiting the personal liability of a corporation's shareholders. Imagine, if you can, if every shareholder in a company was personally liable for that company's actions: there certainly wouldn't be much of a stock market. Every business, whether it realizes it or not, relies on the continuing support of society.

Moreover, being socially responsible plays a part in the overall health of your company. First, it establishes your company's values and fosters your corporate culture. Businesses that act with integrity and honesty are more likely to see their employees act with integrity and honesty toward the company and their fellow workers. Being a good corporate citizen makes it less likely that your company will get in trouble with regulatory agencies and taxing authorities, or face lawsuits or fines.

In addition, employees themselves get value from being part of an organization that's committed to enhancing the social good. Programs that allow employees to be involved in community causes as part of their company activities are viewed as a valuable employee benefit. Prospective employees often look at a company's values and social commitment when comparing job offers. Being able to attract and retain the kind of people you want is critical to the success and growth of your business, so your social commitment helps the long-term value of your company.

The Triple Bottom Line

How effective you are at being socially responsible can be encapsulated in what has become known as the *triple bottom line.* The *bottom line* is traditionally defined as how much money you've earned (also called *profit)* or lost. The triple bottom line expands on that concept by measuring the success of an organization across three parameters: economic, environmental, and social.

As defined by business consultant and author John Elkington, in the mid-1990s, the major premise behind the triple bottom line is that a business' responsibility is to *stakeholders* rather than *shareholders.* In other words, companies must answer to everyone who's impacted by their actions, not just people who have directly invested money in the business. This includes members of the immediate community in which a business operates, customers, suppliers, the industry, and a host of other individuals and organizations.

Social Entrepreneurship

There's a huge movement underway to do well through doing good. But "social entrepreneurship," as this is called, doesn't mean forgoing profits. Whether it involves coming up with a business that's in business to help the environment (say a "green" company using totally recycled products) or to help financially disadvantaged people (say a high-tech training school for urban youth), social entrepreneurs still want to make money through their efforts. They are not by definition non-profit businesses even though they do have goals that go beyond simply earning money.

Social entrepreneurship is different than running a socially responsible business. Social entrepreneurship occurs when the core mission of the business is to provide some sort of benefit to society at large.

The three components of the triple bottom line are usually referred to as *people, planet,* and *profit.*

- **People.** This part of the triple bottom line means that the business will behave fairly and ethically first toward its employees but also toward the community in which it conducts its business and any person who could be affected by the company's actions around the globe. Thus, a company would take care to deal honestly with its suppliers and customers to ensure that its decisions positively affect the towns and cities where it does business. Likewise, a company would not employ children or sweatshop workers overseas because that would exploit vulnerable populations, even if the financial bottom line would benefit from such actions.

- **Planet.** By considering the planet as a whole a stakeholder in the business, a triple bottom line company will make every attempt to engage in sustainable environmental practices. At the very least, such companies will do no harm by reducing their environmental footprint and paying close attention to the natural resources they consume. They also will not manufacturer or trade in products that could harm the planet, such as toxic materials.

- **Profit.** You know what profit is—the money left over after all of your costs have been subtracted from your revenues. You might think that this is the one "bottom line" that all businesses would have in common, whether they're socially responsible or not. But that's not true. Triple bottom line companies view profit in economic terms but take a broader perspective by considering it as the longer-term economic benefit given to society at large. For example, a company that racked up record financial profits (as measured internally) but which did so at the expense of cutting thousands of jobs would have a disastrous overall economic impact on the community, or even the national economy if the company were large enough. In such a case, the company would not be considered profitable by triple bottom line standards.

What's in It for You?

Your business derives a number of benefits from being committed to social responsibility and involved in community activities and causes. Among the direct benefits that accrue to your company:

- **Visibility.** Being socially responsible gives your company increased visibility in the community and your industry. This can be particularly helpful to small, new companies because community activities can be a very effective way to become known at less cost than other marketing methods.

- **Positive corporate image.** Being seen as a good corporate citizen helps foster positive feelings about your company in the community and in potential customers, employees, and funders.

A Social Responsibility Business Plan

What happens when you include social responsibility in a business plan that you are submitting to potential investors? How will they view such activities?

Some companies find that socially responsibility can be a critical component of their business concept. They may develop a strategic position in the marketplace based on certain of their actions or policies, such as developing organic baby food, non-animal-tested cosmetics, or non-polluting electric cars. Other companies may plan key marketing campaigns around social issues, such as an Internet company drawing traffic to its site by giving a portion of each sale or donating an amount for each visitor to support certain social causes. In companies such as these, including social responsibility as part of a plan is definitely warranted. In fact, it may even be necessary to demonstrate how you will retain your credibility within your market.

■ **Recruitment tool.** Social responsibility can aid your company's effectiveness in attracting employees. Potential employees often choose to apply to those companies whose values and social commitment they respect.

■ **Stronger team.** Having shared values and shared activities helps develop cohesiveness and commitment among all of your employees and management.

■ **More satisfied employees.** A commitment to social responsibility enhances the work experience of employees, not only by allowing them to be involved directly or indirectly in community/social affairs, but also by letting them know they work for a company that acts with integrity in all of its dealings. Employees will never have to lie for a socially responsible employer.

■ **Contacts with other companies.** By being active in the community, you and your employees will meet and work with people from other companies, giving you valuable contacts with potential strategic partners, customers, and suppliers.

Be More Environmentally Responsible

One fallacy is that it costs more to practice environmental sustainability than to operate in a traditional way. Because going green means wasting fewer resources—using less paper, less electricity, and less gasoline—you can actually become more profitable in the long run. There are a number of ways your company can immediately become more environmentally friendly. You can:

☐ Encourage employees to walk, bike, or take public transit to work

☐ Turn the thermostat down or up to save energy

☐ Use energy-efficient light bulbs and turn the lights off when not using a room

☐ Eliminate as much superfluous paper from your office as possible

☐ Recycle

☐ Safely dispose of hazardous materials

☐ Use natural cleaning ingredients

☐ Buy "fair trade" coffee

Part Two:
Starting a Business

8

Identity

Now that you've taken your dream and honed it down to a specific business concept, it's time to think about your business identity. Like your personal identity, your business identity is the set of characteristics that allows people to recognize you as a separate and unique entity. It's what makes your business one of a kind. And it's very important. Your business identity helps attract people to you. Once they become customers, it helps them remember you, understand what you do, and even develop a certain feeling about you. Once you have created it, your business begins to feel "real"—both to you and to potential customers, suppliers, and others. Your identity is your brand image, and once established, it represents a precious asset that you must carefully nurture and protect.

The key elements of your business identity are:

- Name
- Logo
- Tagline
- Colors

In addition, you might have other unique, distinguishing elements that make up your identity, such as clever or unusual packaging.

Once you've developed your identity, you'll use those elements consistently and repeatedly—on your business cards, stationery, signs, advertising vehicles, uniforms, and website.

Creating an identity can be done very inexpensively, or it can cost thousands of dollars. It's so critical to succeeding in business that you may want to use the services of a graphic designer to help you create your logo and other aspects of your company's image. Some entrepreneurs believe their corporate identity is such a competitive differentiator that they pay big bucks to agencies that specialize in branding.

Coming up with a company identity can be a fun, creative, and exciting task. But if you're not careful, it can also paralyze you. You may think that finding the *right* name or logo is absolutely critical for success. Yet although choosing the right name and image for your company *is* important, it doesn't determine your company's future. After all, not many people would consider names like *Microsoft, Safeway,* and *The Walt Disney Co.* to be particularly inspired or critical to the company's eventual success.

And sometimes names chosen for quirky reasons—such as *Starbucks,* after a minor character in *Moby Dick; Kinkos,* which was the college nickname of its curly-haired founder, Paul Orfalea; and *Virgin,* so named after one of founder Richard Branson's early employees observed they were "complete virgins at business"— become top brands despite their obscure origins.

Choosing Your Business Name

Clever company names are everywhere: Curl Up and Dye (a hair salon), All You Knead (a bakery), The Barking Lot (a dog groomer), and The Geek Squad (providers of on-site computer help). A clever business name can serve as an excellent marketing tool, helping make your company memorable, but if it's too cute, it runs the risk of putting people off. It can be difficult to strike the right balance—which is why coming up with a good name can be frustratingly hard work. Big companies spend tens of thousands of dollars researching names, and sometimes even they fail. When successful, a name indicates what your business does in a succinct, and perhaps clever, way. It can help you sell your product/service by clearly telling customers what you offer or what problem you solve.

In small companies, you are the brand, and usually the best name for the company is your own, perhaps with a descriptive phrase to clarify what you do. It can be as simple as Jane Smith: Attorney at Law; or Jason Brown, Child Dentistry. If you plan on growing your business substantially, though, you may not want to use your, or any other person's, name. Having a business name too closely associated with the owner may later make the company harder to sell and can create expectations among customers that they will always be getting personal attention from that person.

Qualities of a good name

A good company name:

- **Communicates the correct information.** Avoid anything in your business name that could substantially confuse potential customers about what you do. Even if you think your name is crystal clear —Smith's Photo Services, for example—people might have trouble easily figuring out what business you are in. Are you a photographer, a film processor, or do you provide digital photo touchups? How could you help them by making your company name less ambiguous?

- **Conveys the right feeling.** Choose a name with positive connotations: a day spa named Haven or Oasis transmits the sense that customers are going to escape the stresses in their lives. Names such as Main Street and Park Avenue tell potential customers something about a business—that it's local or upscale, respectively.

- **Won't get outdated quickly.** You're likely to change the scope of your products over time, so be careful not to choose names that are too closely identified with recent trends or that are too limiting. When Twentieth Century Fox Film Studios was founded in 1935 (merging Fox and Twentieth Century studios), the name "Twentieth Century" was associated with the idea of something young and new. Of course, by the end of that century, it no longer seemed fresh, and the company now uses just the name "Fox" for many of its entertainment units.

- **Is easy to spell and pronounce.** If a name is too hard to spell, it becomes difficult for a potential customer to remember. Spelling becomes even more important when you use your company's name as part of your website domain. In addition, people have a harder time remembering names they can't say easily. They can also feel uncomfortable doing business with companies whose names they can't pronounce. That's why the Ghirardelli company prints a pronunciation guide on the back of their chocolate bar wrappers.

- **Is memorable.** If clients or customers have an easy time remembering your name, they're more likely to do business with you again. However, sometimes simple is a better choice than memorable. In fact, a company with a straightforward name like Des Moines Chiropractic Clinic may develop a more successful business than a company with an overly cute name like Got Your Back, Inc.

In the end, however, one of the most important considerations is whether *you* like the name and feel comfortable with it. After all, you're the one who will be seeing and saying it the most. And don't let getting stuck on trying to decide on your name slow down the start of your business. At some point, you need to make a choice and get on with it.

Great Company Names

NAME	ORIGINS	WHY IT'S GOOD
YouTube	Focuses on the site's origins, which was to allow people to post their homemade videos on the Web for others to see.	The catchy nature of the name perfectly captures the youthful and energetic spirit of the brand.
MySpace	Captures the core mission of the social networking business, which is to give individuals a personal spot on the Web to create an online persona.	Perfectly describes what the site does—succinctly and with style.
7-11	Reflects the company's original operating hours, from 7 a.m. until 11 p.m.	Gives critical information on one of the key things that make a convenience store convenient—that it's open at times when other stores aren't.
Nike	Greek goddess of victory.	Appeals to the competitive instincts of the firm's target market of sports enthusiasts.
Verizon	A combination of *veritas* (Latin for *truth*) and *horizon*.	Good associations for a fledgling telecommunications firm.
Amazon	Named after the river, to indicate the tremendous volume potential of online sales.	Has made the firm's presence and high growth rates synonymous with imagining an unstoppable and fiercely competitive force.
Coca Cola Co.	From the coca leaves and koca nuts of the ingredients making up the flagship drink.	Perfectly describes the ingredients (which were once thought to have medicinal value). The alliteration gives it a pleasant, memorable sound.
Google	A deliberate misspelling of the scientific term *googol,* the very large number 10 to the 100th, to indicate the very large volume of data the firm would be processing	Has a friendly, even goofy connotation that makes the very techie notion of a "search engine" accessible to the general public.

Trademarks

When deciding on a company name, you also must check for trademarks to determine whether anyone else is already using the name under consideration. This is where trademark laws come in. There are two primary kinds of trademarks:

■ **Trademark.** A word, phrase, symbol, or design (or a combination of those) that identifies and distinguishes the maker of a product from makers of other, similar, products.

■ **Servicemark.** The same as a trademark, except that it identifies and distinguishes the provider of a service rather than a product.

When you acquire the rights to a trademark or servicemark, other companies are legally prevented from using your company's name, logos, taglines, or other distinctive markers on competing products or services. Note the emphasis on the word *competing:* two companies that operate in completely different business spheres can have the same name; it's only when there's possible confusion between two entities that trademark law becomes relevant.

Thus, it's important to understand that you don't "own" the name in all instances. As part of the trademark application process, you'll indicate the category or categories of products or services for which you'll be using the name. For instance, if you're using Yummy

Tummy for breakfast cereal, someone else could get the rights to use the same name for unrelated products or services—a weight-loss program, for instance.

But there are limits to what you can trademark. You may be surprised—and frustrated—to learn that you can't trademark the simplest names. That's because the U.S. Patent and Trademark Office requires a mark to be "distinctive" and not just "descriptive." For instance, you can't get a trademark for a health resort called Spa, because it's merely descriptive. This is why the maker of high-end software decided to call itself Cassatt, after the American painter Mary Cassatt (a favorite artist of the founder), rather than a more (or merely) descriptive name like Data Center Automation, Inc..

To begin a trademark search, go to the website of the U.S. Patent and Trademark Office (www.uspto.gov/). Keep in mind that even if the particular name or mark does not show up as being taken, it doesn't mean that you will be able to trademark the name/mark. Some names may already be in use in interstate commerce, but may not have been officially registered. Other names/marks may not be allowed to be registered as trademarks.

Although you can also do a superficial search on the Internet to see if anyone is using your desired name, you probably should do more extensive research to protect yourself. There are many lawyers as well as specialized companies that do nothing but trademark research. Before you hire such a firm, make sure to get references from previous clients.

You may run into difficulty if you use a name that's similar to a bigger, better-known company even if you think you can get a trademark for that name. McDonald's, for instance, has been very effective in keeping others from using the "Mc" as a prefix for many different kinds of products and companies. A juice bar company was able to keep other juice bars from using names starting with the letter "J" just by taking them to court. Often, it's the company with the biggest bank account and most aggressive lawyers, rather than the ones with the law on their side, that controls a name or trademark.

Your Domain Name

In today's increasingly connected world, you must consider what your Internet domain name will be. An Internet domain name is your "address" on the Internet, much like you have a street address in the "real" world. Anyone wishing to visit your site must know your address and enter it into a Web browser before they are allowed entrance to your site. Naturally, it is always best to get a domain name that is as close to your business name as possible. A domain name is so important that many businesses wait to see what domain name they can get before they name their companies.

To find out whether others may be using the name you have selected—or similar names—go to the "who is" section of the Network Solutions website (www.networksolutions.com/whois/index.jsp). (Network Solutions was the first official keeper of the domain name registry worldwide.) Type in the name you'd like to use along with the suffix, or the letters after the "dot." For example, most U.S. businesses have the .com suffix; educational institutions have .edu; and each country has its own suffix—German companies end in .de, for instance, and Australian companies in .au.

Many of the most obvious domain names are likely to be taken. And even if you're able to get a trademark (see page 58) for a name, someone else may legally have the rights to that domain name, especially since many companies can have the same trademark name in different categories. Try to select a domain name that is:

- Identical or similar to your company name
- Related to the product or service you sell
- Easy to spell
- Easy to remember
- Not likely to be confused with another domain name

You may be able to purchase a particularly appropriate domain name from someone who owns it but isn't using it. During the dot-com mania of the late 1990s, "domain squatters" bought up all the domain names they could think of precisely because they anticipated a time when domain names would become scarce. Depending on how much demand there is for a particular name, an owner may ask a couple of hundred or a couple of hundred thousand dollars for it. Some domain names have even been sold for millions of dollars. Business.com, for example, sold for a whopping $7.5 million in 1999. These prices are well beyond the means of the typical entrepreneur! So you may well have to settle for your second, or even third or fourth, choice.

worksheet: **Your Company Name**

Use this worksheet to list and compare the company names you're considering.

	Name 1	Name 2	Name 3	Name 4
List the business names you've considered thus far.				
What aspect of the name tells your customers what you do?				
What aspect of the name tells your customers what they get?				
What aspect of the name conveys a feeling? What is that feeling?				
Is the name trademarked by another business in your market?				

	Name 1	Name 2	Name 3	Name 4
Are there companies with similar or confusing names?				
Is the name trademarked in a different market category? Which one? By whom? Is there any chance you might one day want to expand your business into that category?				
Who likes the name? Why?				
Who dislikes the name? Why?				
What available domain name (Web address) would work well with the name?				
Other comments				

Logos, Taglines, and Colors

Your company identity consists of more than just your company name. The colors you choose, the typeface you use, and the kind of tagline and logo you develop also convey a message to your potential customers.

Your logo

A logo is an image associated with your company that gives the public another way to remember you. All of us are familiar with logos: the Nike "swoosh," Yahoo!'s bright red uneven lettering with the bold exclamation point at the end, and AT&T's blue-striped globe. These are not only utterly unique, they actually define the personality of the company in question.

A good logo conveys something positive about your company. The Target logo, for instance (a bull's-eye), is simple and elegant. It tells customers that Target stores are where they'll find exactly what they want at exactly the right price. The bull's-eye logo also suggests competitiveness, accuracy, and efficiency—traits that shareholders as well as shoppers appreciate. The logo for Tivo—a smiling television with antenna protruding out of the top—is quirky and fresh, inviting the world to view it as innovative and friendly despite being on the cutting edge of technology.

Your tagline

Many companies use a motto or tagline either to better explain the nature of the business or to create a feeling about the company or product. A tagline helps customers remember what's unique about your business. Taglines don't have to be "catchy" to be memorable to your target audience. "Manufacturers of packing materials for technology products," for example, might seem like a boring tagline; however, it could be very effective if what you do is make and sell boxes for computers. It lets potential customers know—and reminds current customers—that you specialize in giving them exactly what they need.

You don't have to have a tagline, and you certainly don't have to choose one before you open your doors. But developing a tagline helps you clarify what makes your business special and enables you to sum up your competitive position in just a few words.

Your tagline can and should appear in many places: your stationery, business cards, website, even at the bottom of your invoices and receipts. And just like your company name, your tagline should be unique. There's even a database you can use (for a fee) to see whether someone else has also thought of that clever slogan you thought so original (www.adslogans.co.uk/).

Great Taglines

COMPANY	TAGLINE
Salesforce.com	"The end of software"
YouTube	"Broadcast yourself"
Gawker	"Daily Manhattan media news and gossip. Reporting live from the center of the universe."
Gizmodo	"The gadget guide. So much in love with shiny new toys, it's unnatural."
Fed Ex	"When it absolutely, positively has to be there overnight"
Nike	"Just do it"
New York Times	"All the news that's fit to print"
M&M's	"Melts in your mouth, not in your hand"
Volkswagen	"Drivers wanted"
Wheaties	"Breakfast of champions"
Avis	"We try harder"
Lay's potato chips	"Betcha can't eat just one"

Your colors

Many entrepreneurs start their businesses without giving colors much thought, and yet most of us intend to use some colors in our businesses—in our décor, business cards, brochures, packaging, websites, and so on. What often happens is that a new business will use one color for one thing (a brochure), another color for something else (stationery), and yet another color elsewhere (website). The result? You've lost the opportunity to develop a strong brand image for your company and perhaps even confused your customer.

Coming up with a consistent use of color—your color palette—gives you another tool to help customers remember who you are and to convey a feeling about your company.

Since you're likely to be using your color palette on your website, keep in mind that some colors do not display well on computer monitors. Check your colors on several different monitors before finalizing your choice.

Be careful about how many colors you use in your business. If you use too many, it can become expensive to print your stationery, business cards, packaging, and so on.

Packaging and Product Design

The design of your products and packaging represents another way to establish your brand identity. Many companies, like Apple Computer, pride themselves on their product design and packaging, and consider it an integral aspect of their brand. Many consumers consider Bloomingdale's famous "Little Brown Bag" a status symbol. And innumerable clothing manufacturers simply incorporate their logos and brand names into their wares as part of the design.

Your Elevator Pitch

An elevator pitch provides a concise summary of your service, business, or product idea that can be delivered in a very short time. The name *elevator pitch* is based on the premise that sometimes you can only catch an

Leveraging Your Colors

Colors aren't just for printed collateral, packaging, or signs. Businesses often use their colors in their décor and in employee clothing and uniforms as well. In general, anything that projects a consistent brand image should incorporate your colors and logo in some way. For example, anyone who has ever visited the Disneyland Hotel in Anaheim, California, can tell you about the ubiquitous black mouse ear graphics that that appear even in the carpeting, wallpaper, and drapes.

influential or powerful person in an elevator—and your pitch should therefore be deliverable within the time it takes for an elevator to move from one floor to another. Since the typical elevator ride is somewhere in the range of 30 to 60 seconds, you should keep your pitch to 100 to 150 words at most.

It's important to have an elevator speech because as an entrepreneur you'll be trying to express your idea to any number of people—friends and family whose support (financial as well as emotional) you'll need to start your business; potential suppliers and business partners; potential investors; and, ultimately, customers. No one is going to listen to a long-winded explanation of what you're trying to do. And if you can't effectively communicate your idea in a manageable length of time, it's possible you haven't thought it through carefully enough.

It takes some thinking to decide which aspects of your business to mention in an elevator pitch. Even more frustrating, you have to decide which parts of your company to leave out. Often, these can be the things you're most excited about—a new technology, a great location, and the fact you get to go to Europe on buying trips. But if they're not central to the core of your business, they don't belong in an elevator pitch.

worksheet: Create Your Identity

Use the space below to begin developing your corporate identity. You may want to draw pictures as well as use words and phrases to develop the look, feel, and message you want to convey.

Business name
Tagline
Logo
Colors
Distinct product design
Distinct packaging
Décor, employee clothing, or other unique identifying features

Your elevator pitch must not only be short, it must be clear. Unless you're in a highly technical field, your neighbor or grandmother should be able to understand your business well enough to be able to describe it to someone else. If you're in an easy-to-understand business, your elevator pitch theoretically could be very short. But you still want it long enough to distinguish you from your competitors. A good elevator pitch offers the following information:

- **What your business makes/does.** This should be very brief: "My company makes water- and weather-proof solar-powered outdoor lights" or "My business does custom upholstering for automobiles."

- **What market you serve.** You should be very specific about this: "Fifteen- to 30-year-old men who regularly play Dungeons and Dragons" or "Small businesses with five to 10 employees."

- **How you plan to make money.** This is very important if you're giving your elevator pitch to potential investors. For all they know, you could be spending more making your special ergonomic computer chair than you're able to sell it for, thus preventing your business from being profitable. For this reason, you need to be very explicit about the business model you plan to employ to bring in more than you pay out. For example, the line "We will set our retail prices by marking our chairs 50 percent above cost" provides a direct explanation of how you plan to achieve profitability.

- **How your business compares to other, familiar businesses.** If you don't compare your business to other similar businesses, people may not understand what your product or service is all about. On the other hand, if you don't show how your business *differs* from familiar companies, you'll have trouble getting anyone's attention. The following examples strike the right balance between both: "Like Facebook for law firm employees" and "Better service than XYZ automotive."

- **Why you will succeed.** This is the most important part of the elevator pitch: what are the market conditions that make your idea a sure-fire success? You need to use all of your powers of persuasion here. If you have any hard numbers to back up your assertions, so much the better. "Census figures show that families with young children are moving into this area at a rapid pace, and those families will require high-quality childcare."

- **Your ultimate goals for the business.** Do you want to eventually run a multinational corporation that provides Fortune 100 organizations with business consulting services? Or a chain of drugstores focused on holistic health? Or do you want to keep it relatively small and contained? You should be prepared to articulate your vision for the business' size and reach.

Sample Elevator Pitches

- I design, install, and maintain landscaping for high-end residences and estates.

- We build high-quality oak furniture in the Mission style for people with traditional tastes.

- My chiropractic practice specializes in treating patients with lower back pain who work in treating physically demanding jobs.

- We create custom software to automate bookkeeping and accounting for the food service industry.

worksheet: **Your Elevator Pitch**

Use this worksheet to develop the main components of your elevator pitch. Then edit your responses to less than 100 words. Remember to keep your pitch short: focus on what customers get, not on what you do, and make it easy to remember

Company name:

_____

Does:

_____

Serves this market:

_____

Makes money by:

_____

Is like these other companies:

_____

But is special because:

_____

It will succeed because:

_____

Aims to achieve:

_____

Final elevator pitch:

_____

_____

_____

_____

_____

chapter 9

Making Your Product or Performing Your Service

You've come up with an idea for your product or service; you've established an identity. Now it's time to start making your ideas and identity real. A first stage is figuring out exactly how you're going to make your product or perform your service for clients.

Your Product Prototype

Your first step in creating a viable product is to actually design and build one. This will be your product *prototype,* and the process of completing it will help you work through a number of critical issues.

- **Is the product viable?** You'll save yourself a great deal of time and money by doing the prototyping before you send an order to suppliers or design specifications out for manufacturing. If you're building a mechanical, electrical, or electronic product in particular, the product has to be functional from an engineering standpoint. If you will be manufacturing the product in bulk, you'll need to judge whether you can ensure enough consistency in the parts so that it can be made efficiently and cost-effectively. Finally, in many cases—especially for consumer products—you need to take into account design considerations that will impact the look and feel of the product. If the tails are the wrong size to fit on the teddy bears you plan to manufacture, or the soldering iron doesn't heat

up to the 400 degrees promised, or the amplifier doesn't integrate seamlessly with the rest of the stereo components you're selling, you need to catch the problem in the prototype stage or risk losing a lot of money after you go into production.

- **Can you create the product on your own?** Although you may think you have the expertise to design and/or create the product yourself, actually attempting to fabricate a prototype will put this notion to the test. If you don't have the skills to do it yourself, you may have to hire an outside design firm to get through the prototyping stage. This will cost you money—and depending on the product in question, sometimes a substantial amount of money. Unless you're a craftsperson turning out one-of-a-kind goods or are making very limited quantities of something you can manufacture yourself using standard or off-the-shelf components, making a product usually requires help at some stage of the process—whether in design or manufacturing.

- **Can you afford to make the product?** You might be capable of making the product, but can you do so in such a way that you make a profit? This is critical information to discover during the prototyping phase and involves doing some initial research into what the market will bear with regard to your product's pricing. If your product is truly unique, you'll have to make your best educated guess as to what price you can command. When in doubt, overestimate your costs and underestimate the price you will get, just to be on the safe side. And, as you'll learn in the next few chapters, your product's profitability will depend not only on the cost of raw goods but also on labor costs (including your own time), overhead (things such as rent, utilities, and so on), and the shipping and distribution costs involved in creating it.

Build, Assemble, or Buy?

If you plan to sell a product, you have to decide whether you're going to build it yourself (or hire a manufacturer to do so to your specifications), assemble it from standard components, or purchase it outright from another manufacturer. If you choose the latter, you must further decide whether to "brand it" with your name and distinctive logo and packaging before reselling it to others. Telephones and computers are often marketed in this fashion. You'd probably be surprised to learn how many brand-name goods are actually made by a single manufacturer—which is obscure to anyone outside the industry. One reason that the tainted pet food incident in 2007 was so widespread was that a single manufacturer made the products sold by a broad range of name-brand pet food retailers.

Some of the things you need to consider whether you build, assemble, or buy:

■ **Materials**. What kind of materials do you—or your supplier—need to make the product? Will you start with raw goods or existing components? For example, if you're making mountain bike frames, you'll need to decide whether you're going

to set up a manufacturing facility to work with the actual raw metal, or whether you'll send the design to a contract manufacturer and merely assemble the frames yourself. If you intend to use existing components, are there standard sizes and dimensions you should employ in your design to keep your costs down? For example, manufacturing super-rugged laptops will be infinitely cheaper if you conform to the dimensions of existing mobile disk drives, network cards, and other components rather than designing your own from scratch.

■ **Sources.** Many businesses are careful to be socially responsible and this means paying special attention to the sources of the materials, components, and products they sell. Whether a supplier conforms to "green" practices is of increasing concern, as is whether it engages in ethical labor practices—especially in third-world countries where labor laws are not as stringent as in developed countries.

■ **Reliability.** The reliability of a product has to do not only with the quality of its components, or the product itself, but also with the suppliers of your materials. Will they ship orders to you on time? Will they have enough inventory for you to meet your customer commitments? Look into the quality of the customer service your suppliers provide: Are they good communicators? Can they respond quickly to changes in your requirements? These are the sorts of things that can make or break a fledgling business that depends on outside suppliers.

■ **Cost comparisons/evaluations.** Naturally, price considerations come into play throughout the manufacturing process. But you might not neces-

business **BUZZ** *words*

"markup"

This is the difference between the cost of goods and the price at which they're sold that creates a profit margin for a business. For example, if a dress costs $15 to buy from the manufacturer, a local women's boutique might mark it up to $45. That $30 is the markup—and the profit. Different industries, and different businesses within industries, have varying markups.

sarily want to go with the lowest-cost supplier. The quality of their materials might be substandard. Or their reliability (see above) might be an issue. Worse, they might not be financially stable and could leave you in the lurch right when you need to deliver to a key customer. Choosing the right supplier thus means evaluating candidates across a broad range of dimensions, including quality, service, reliability, and financial stability. A good way to think about it is that you're not just looking for low cost but good *value*.

■ **Equipment/Facilities needed.** Depending on what aspects of manufacturing, assembling, and/or shipping you plan to handle yourself, you'll need to consider what equipment and facilities you need to get the product out the door and into distributors' and/or customers' hands. These could include woodworking tools for building the custom pine furniture you sell over the Internet or the industrial kitchen appliances required to run your catering business.

Packaging

It's rare that a product doesn't come in some sort of package. Depending on the type of product and the type of market you serve, this packaging can be plain or elaborate. Packaging can even contribute to a company's identity—Tiffany & Company's blue boxes with white bows, for example. In general, consumer packaging falls on the elaborate end of the scale—some companies spend almost as much effort on designing the look of the packaging as they do the product. Business packaging is more often focused on ensuring

New Best Practices in Manufacturing

Manufacturing techniques have dramatically improved over the years to drive waste and inefficiencies, and therefore costs, out of the process. Two of the chief advances in this area are "lean manufacturing" and "just-in-time" inventory management.

☐ **Lean manufacturing.** This is a management philosophy that focuses on eliminating waste to cut costs and, ultimately, deliver more value to customers. Lean manufacturing is based largely on work the car manufacturer Toyota has done in this area. Toyota has identified "seven wastes" that stand in the way of an optimal manufacturing process. These include overproduction, waiting, transporting, inappropriate processing, excess inventory, unnecessary motion, and defects.

☐ **Just-in-time manufacturing.** This is a strategy for minimizing inventory to reduce costs and, by implication, free up money to invest elsewhere in your business. This is generally accomplished by being in very close touch with your distributors, salespeople, and/or customers so that you can pick up on demand signals that allow you to make products as close to the time when you need them as possible without running out. By manufacturing your products "just in time" to deliver them to customers as needed, you reduce expenses by not having product in inventory when it's not needed.

business BUZZ words

"cost of goods sold (COGS)"

An accounting term that refers to all of the direct costs of the supplies and labor involved in manufacturing a product and getting it into customers' hands. Indirect costs, such as rent, utilities, and other overhead, are not included in this category. So a bakery would add up the costs of all the flour, sugar, eggs, and spices it needed to bake its signature chocolate cupcakes to come up with the COGS.

that the product survives the shipping process intact and is in working order when unpacked. Packaging can thus comprise a substantial proportion of the cost of goods sold for a product. The most effective packaging reflects a company's identity, including logo, tagline, and colors. Think of the boxes that Apple's products come in. You'd know who the company is instantly without seeing their name!

worksheet: Making Your Product

Use this worksheet to make a note of your manufacturing plans and needs.

Describe your product:

_____

What do you need to create your prototype?

_____

Will you build, assemble, or buy the finished product?

_____

What materials, and in what quantities, will you need to manufacture your product?

_____

Where you will obtain these materials?

_____

What kind of packaging will you use for the product?

_____

Where will you store your product?

_____

How will you ship it?

_____

Shipping

Finally, you will have to consider how you'll ship your product to your customer—whether that customer is the end user or distributor. These costs include not only of the price of transportation but also the fees for storing or warehousing the product between the time it's made and shipped. Some products also have to be put into an inventory system, be insured, or require special packaging or handling—all of which can contribute to shipping costs.

Performing a Service

If you're performing a service rather than producing a tangible product, you will have some different, and unique, issues to address. Whatever service you will be providing, you should be able to define it simply and in a way that anyone can immediately grasp. This is where your elevator pitch (page 63) will come in handy.

Services that mirror what's already available in the marketplace are easy to describe. Everyone knows what a dog boarding kennel is, for example. But for a service that's new, you will have to find a way to explain the nature of the service and exactly what it delivers to customers. A "dog hotel," for example, might require some explanation for potential customers to comprehend exactly what's being offered—in this case, an upscale kennel that goes above and beyond the typical services found in traditional kennels by offering things like rooms with a private outdoor play area, custom meals, play dates, and so on. Other special considerations for service providers:

- **Will you go it alone, or do you need help?** One of the first things you must consider is whether you can perform and deliver your service solo, or you'll need help—partners and/or employees—to satisfy your customers. Figure this out as early as possible, because it will impact the pricing structure of the service you offer.

- **Can you deliver consistent quality?** Quality is one of the critical factors determining whether people will buy your service—and return for more. What determines the quality of a service is perhaps more subjective than *product* quality, but it's no less critical. A high-quality service accomplishes what the provider of the service promises. For example, a cleaning service that doesn't leave a client's home

clean is obviously a poor-quality service, as is an IT service provider that can't get a client's network back online. It's therefore essential that you guarantee a certain level of quality and provide it consistently. It could be that service quality will depend on things beyond your control. For example, if you run a river rafting company, your customers' experience will depend on the weather, the water level in the river, and the number and personality of the people traveling together, as well as other factors that you simply can't be responsible for. In such cases, you must make it clear to people purchasing your service what their experiences will be dependent on.

- **What materials and/or equipment will you need to perform it?** Some services require more up-front investment in equipment than others. For example, providing personal chef services to homes requires professional-grade cooking implements and utensils, the raw ingredients for the meals prepared at clients' houses, and a large car or a van to transport them. A freelance graphic designer, on the other hand, would need to invest in a powerful computer with a high-resolution color monitor, special software, and high-quality printers and/or copiers.

- **Can you make money doing it?** Just as when making a product, you must make sure that a service can actually be profitable. Generally, with a service, the biggest cost will be labor—yours and that of any partners or employees needed to perform and/or deliver the service. Sometimes the costs will be directly related to a particular job, such as the number of hours spent remodeling a kitchen. Other times, they will be indirect, or more general to your business, such as the rent for the storage unit needed to keep your tools and equipment in, or the signage that you place on the lawn of every house you've remodeled to the owners' satisfaction.

- **Can it "scale" to meet your financial goals?** You may be able to deliver a service profitably, yet not be able to grow it enough to achieve the financial objectives you've established for your business. For example, a string quartet that plays classical repertoire for weddings, parties, and other special events can only fit in so many performances. Since most such events are on weekends, it may be impossible for the group to earn enough money to support all four members even if it is engaged Friday through Sunday each week.

worksheet: Defining Your Service

Define your service by listing its nature, type, and range:

_____
_____
_____
_____
_____
_____

Who will perform/deliver your service? (You? Employee? Independent contractor?)

_____
_____
_____
_____
_____

What materials/equipment will you need to perform/deliver it?

_____
_____
_____
_____
_____

What are your quality standards? (Be very specific.)

_____
_____
_____
_____
_____
_____
_____
_____

Location

How important is location to the success of your business? Depending on your business, sometimes very important, and sometimes not important at all. You need to determine this up front, because a lot of key decisions will follow from it.

If you have a business serving a particular neighborhood or community, you need to be physically located in or near that area. If you're in retail, your choice of location is absolutely critical and may determine whether you have enough customers to stay in business. A factor as seemingly insignificant as which side of a particular street you're on can dramatically affect the amount of customer traffic you'll receive. If you're a manufacturer, you'll need to find a site with easy access to a shipping system (trucks, air, ships, or rail), a good labor force, raw materials, and large buildings that are either low rent or low cost to buy. Then there are lots of companies that provide products or services from a distance (thanks in large part to the Internet)—for them, location simply isn't an issue.

Even if the site of your business doesn't seem critical, keep in mind that your choice of facilities and neighborhood will have an impact on how you and your employees feel about coming to work. A pleasant building in a safe neighborhood with nearby parking and friendly neighbors can make work more enjoyable. It can even help you recruit quality employees.

And many entrepreneurs know exactly where they want to work—at home! Working at home can have great advantages, but it also presents some challenges, especially if you have children or spouses there. Carefully planning your home office—its space, storage, and policies—will help you make the most of this arrangement (see "Home Office," page 79, for more).

Setting Up Your Business Location

First, you must prioritize your needs. How you rank them depends on what kind of business you're in—retail, manufacturing, service, or another type of industry—and your specific business activities. If you will be publishing training materials that teach executives how to use popular computer programs, for example, you will produce lots of heavy boxes of materials, and should look for space on a ground floor or with elevator access so you don't have to carry them up and down stairs.

Don't forget less tangible issues, especially ones important to the quality of life for you and your employees. After all, you aren't starting your own business only to hate the place you go to work! You may want to be able to walk to and from your office, or to create a dog-friendly environment. Things like this will narrow your location choices. You also need to figure out approximately how much space you need and what your budget can handle. You may want to start small with a short-term lease until you are better established.

Most of all, your needs will depend upon how you will use the facilities:

- **Office/Administrative.** Virtually all businesses need at least some office space. Many businesses *only* need office space in the form of professional, sales, or administrative offices. On the other hand, if the main purpose of your business is retail or manufacturing, your "office" may only represent a small portion of your total site.

  If you're just starting out or if your company has just one or two employees, one approach to office space may be to rent an "Executive Suite" office or to find space to sublet from another company. This gets you up and running much faster, since such facilities often include furniture, Internet access, conference room, and the use of office equipment (copiers, printers, fax machines). Some even come with a shared receptionist who will answer phones and direct visitors to your particular office. And frequently, these types of spaces give you the flexibility of a short-term or month-to-month lease. You may even be able to rent an "office" for a few hours—let's say to meet clients—and work the rest of the time from home.

- **Retail.** Location, location, location. One of the most important considerations for a retail business is the choice of location. Do you want to be in a mall? On a popular pedestrian street? In a particular neighborhood? If your business is easily seen by passers-by (in a mall or on a well-trafficked street) you can save considerably on marketing and advertising costs. These locations typically charge higher rent, but paying more to get a more visible and accessible space may be well worth it.

  Customers also have to be able to get to your store easily. If they have easy access—either by walking, driving, or taking public transportation—you have a competitive advantage over businesses that are harder to reach or find.

- **Manufacturing/Production.** What do you make? Toys? Computer peripherals? Packaged organic vegetables? The nature of your product will dictate the kind of facilities you need.

Your production facilities can also have a direct impact on your profitability. Are they set up to save on energy use and costs? Can you design efficient production processes? Are you near your customers or shipping facilities? Are you near enough potential employees? How much does it cost to have waste removed? Understand all costs and benefits as you choose your space. Also consider whether you need your own facilities or if there are contract manufacturing facilities available. Some industries have contract manufacturing/production facilities (such as industrial kitchens) that give you the flexibility to start up without investing large sums of capital.

- **Warehouse/Storage.** Some facilities are used primarily for storage. In these situations, you have many of the same concerns as manufacturing—shipping, docks, utilities, safety, access, security, and proximity to distributors. Be particularly cautious of environmental and zoning considerations that may impact the products/materials you are able to store, or which may affect your product or materials.

- **Virtual.** Perhaps you're one of the lucky ones who can run a business from any location because of technologies, especially the Internet. In that case, your chief concerns will revolve around whether the facility in question can support the technologies you need. For example, is it already wired for high-speed Internet access? Or will you have to do that from scratch (which is common in older buildings)? Likewise, will there be sufficient power and a reliable source of electricity to support an operation that is computer-intensive? If you have special equipment, such as special printers or copy machines, can the facilities handle the energy requirements?

  If all these basic requirements have been met, then you have the luxury to consider issues related to cost, convenience, and comfort. You can locate outside a metropolitan area where leases are much cheaper, or in places that would not be suitable for either retail or manufacturing.

ChardNet:
An Accidental Entrepreneur

Brendan Chard grew up in a family of lawyers. He also had a natural bent for fixing computers. So when he was putting himself through college at the University of Michigan in Ann Arbor, it was a natural thing to offer his technical services to the many law firms scattered around town. "I was doing computer repair work, Web design, pretty much what anyone wanted, at student rates of $30 an hour," he says. "I wasn't really interested in growing a business, but I had about 80 law firms as clients by the time I graduated."

Today Chard is owner and manager of ChardNet, a successful and rapidly growing website design and online marketing firm that serves small law firms, local bar associations, and non-profit legal communities. Although headquartered in Minneapolis, ChardNet has a growing national client base and a steadily increasing reputation in legal circles for understanding the needs of legal professionals.

"We really understand the inner workings of law firms, and how they make decisions, and how they make their money," Chard says. In contrast, Web designers who are more generalists have to learn about the legal business and are reinventing the wheel every time they create a new site for a client.

At the time he finished school, about half of Chard's income came from computer repairs and the other half from Web design. He kept up this mix for a year, before meeting the woman who is now his wife. Together, they decided they wanted to relocate to Minneapolis. "I was basically running two separate companies side by side at that point. I noticed that not only was the computer repair work unpredictable and high stress, but it took up 80 percent of my time and brought in only 50 percent of my income," says Chard. He decided, after he got to Minneapolis, that he would concentrate solely on Web design.

When Chard told his Web design clients he was moving, they refused to give him up—he moved two states away without losing a single client. Today, he has three employees serving more than 200 clients that are increasingly scattered across the country.

In Ann Arbor, Chard worked out of his home. But in Minneapolis the combination of being in a new city and trying to jumpstart a new business felt isolating—"So my wife booted my business out of our house, which was one of the best things that could have happened to me," he says now. He now rents space in an executive suite in an office building with 60 other businesses.

Although the majority of Chard's business comes from word of mouth, he has an interesting marketing strategy that he calls "community blasting." He buys Google and Yahoo search keywords to make sure that if anyone types in "attorney website design" that his firm pops up as the No.1 search result. "And anytime we get a new client in a new city, we go out of our way to do a truly outstanding job, and then ask that client if they will act as an advocate for us in that community." As a result, Chard's client list keeps expanding into new markets.

worksheet: Choosing a Location

Use this worksheet to compare locations you're considering for your business.

Office Space Considerations	Location 1	Location 2	Location 3
Appearance: Will the space make a positive impression on clients? Does the office have a waiting area?			
Privacy: Does the office have sufficient privacy for your business needs?			
Meeting space/Conference rooms: Do you have sufficient access to conference rooms or other meeting space?			
Mail/Shipping/Receiving: Can you receive mail or shipments here? Will they be secure until you collect them?			
Coffee/Kitchen/Eating areas: Is there access to coffee, food preparation, or eating areas? Is water convenient?			
Lighting: Does the space have adequate lighting to avoid eyestrain and fatigue?			
Wiring/Data lines: Is the space wired for high-speed Internet access? If not, will it be difficult or expensive to install wiring?			

Retail Space Considerations	Location 1	Location 2	Location 3
Traffic: Is there good foot or auto traffic that will bring customers naturally?			
History of others in the space: How have other retail or restaurant businesses fared at this location?			
Fellow tenants/neighbors: Are the retail neighbors compatible, with similar market demographics?			
Quality of the space: Does the space feel welcoming? Would it be easy to display your merchandise?			
Limitations on space/ Additional fees: Are there any limits on your hours of operation, or requirements to pay additional fees or participate in certain promotions (common in malls or business improvement districts)?			

Manufacturing Space Considerations	Location 1	Location 2	Location 3
Docks/Shipping facilities: Can your receive/ship my expected materials/inventory here? Does the location mean that you will incur additional shipping fees?			
Utilities: Are there adequate utilities for your production needs (water, electricity, natural gas)? Will the space require particularly high energy use/costs?			
Waste disposal: Is there adequate access to waste disposal, including any hazardous materials resulting from your production process? What does it cost?			
Proximity to suppliers/distributors: How long will it take to replenish materials or to send to your product to distributors and customers? How much will it cost?			
"Green" issues: Is the space particularly eco-friendly? Does it incorporate environmentally friendly materials? Does it use energy efficiently or take advantage of alternative energy sources?			

Home Office

A home office can take many forms. It might simply be one end of your dining room table. It could be the guest room—as long as no guests come to visit. You might claim a section of your garage, in tried-and-true entrepreneurial spirit, by building walls and installing a window, shelves, heating, and air conditioning. Since you're serious about your entrepreneurial venture, you need a good workspace.

One of the biggest challenges of working out of a home is figuring out where and when to meet with customers. If you only meet customers at their place of business, at trade shows, or over the Internet, it's not a problem. But if customers are going to come to you, you need to make sure that you look professional. This means separating your workspace from your family surroundings. If possible, have a separate entrance or at least a path to your office that doesn't go through a playroom or kitchen. If you're meeting clients infrequently or on a regular basis, you may be able to use your own living or dining room as a meeting space. But always be conscious of the image you're projecting.

What if you don't want customers in your home but need to meet them somewhere other than their offices? Look for neutral locations, such as restaurants. If you have an ongoing need, find another company (such as a small law firm) that will allow you to sublet or rent a meeting space or conference room on an hourly basis. Executive Suite services often offer hourly rentals as well.

When you work at home, you face a dilemma: what address should you give out? If you only use your home address, are you comfortable putting it on business cards and marketing brochures that you hand to strangers or putting it on a website where the whole world can see it? On the other hand, if you don't put any address at all on these marketing materials, you might seem less than professional. One alternative is to get a post office box from the U.S. Postal Service. The problem, however, is that your business address will be only a post office box, or P.O. Box, number. That may make your business seem somewhat insubstantial. Moreover, the U.S. Post Office usually refuses to accept deliveries from private delivery services such as Fed Ex and UPS.

The Mobile Office

Many people run their businesses not from an office or from home, but from a car, van, or truck. In some industries and lines of work—contractors, sales representatives, real estate agents, and landscape designers, to name a few—an efficient and workable mobile office is a necessity.

Since people don't tend to think of their vehicles as offices, they often fail to organize the space appropriately. As a result, their workplaces become unworkable, with important notes shoved in glove compartments and valuable equipment rattling around loose in the backs of trucks. If you know you're going to be using your vehicle for business, develop a mobile office plan. There are many products available to outfit cars and trucks for specific purposes, including most kinds of contractors or trades. There are even "desks" for your front seat.

When you vehicle is your office, you'll also want to be sure its contents are safe. Don't store the only copies of valuable documents or records in your vehicle. Consider where you will park your vehicle overnight; you want to make sure it's safe and secure. And when you get insurance, make certain your policy covers not only the vehicle itself but also your "office" contents—especially if you regularly carry expensive tools or equipment. And, of course, talk to your accountant or tax advisor about deductions for your mobile "office."

Another, often better, alternative is to rent a mailbox from one of the many private mailbox providers (such as the UPS Store), also called a "commercial mail receiving agency." A private mailbox gives you a secure place to receive mail, with someone on site who can sign for and receive packages for you. These services generally accept deliveries from private services as well as the U.S. Postal Service. And they often offer other services, such as mail forwarding, calling you if you receive a special delivery, packing and shipping items, and allowing you to call in and check your mail if you're on the road. Best of all, they provide an actual street number and address (123 Main St.), which can be a huge advantage when you're trying to establish your credibility.

chapter 11

Channels

A *channel* is simply the means by which a product or service gets sold to the end user. For instance, if you create custom lampshades, you might sell through a number of different channels. You could sell to high-end home furnishing stores—in other words, through a retail channel. Or you could sell to interior designers who sell to their clients—thus through an agent or intermediary channel. Or you could sell from your website to homeowners, who buy from you directly.

Because many businesses sell through different channels, your customers may not be end users but rather a wholesaler or retailer who in turn sells to end users.

Channels are important precisely because businesses often can't handle all aspects of getting products or services into customers' hands on their own. In many cases, they simply don't have the personnel or financial resources to do it. They need to devote their time, effort, and capital to their core business, whether it's making lampshades, manufacturing computers, or creating works of art or movies.

Often, a series of intermediaries exists between an entrepreneur and the end user, each of which passes the product or service onto the next person or organization until it finally reaches the end user. This is called the *distribution chain.*

Types of Channels

You will have your choice of a range of channels.

- **Selling direct.** This is where you directly "touch" the customer by either selling a product or delivering a service yourself or through a sales force, mail order, the telephone, or over the Internet. When using a direct sales channel, nothing stands between you and the people who use your product or service.

- **Using an agent.** An agent is an individual who sells directly to end users on your behalf. For example, agents are typically used in the financial services and insurance industries. Chances are good, for instance, that you buy your insurance from an agent, who in turn represents one or more insurance companies. But agents are also common in a wide range of industries, including the arts. Agents typically mark up products to higher prices than consumers would pay if they were purchasing directly from the company.

- **Going through a distributor.** A distributor—also called a *wholesaler*—sells to a retailer (see below), who sells to the end user. The distributor is the classic middleman—the person (or business) that stands between you and your end user. If you go the distribution route, you have, in effect, two "layers" between you and your end users. This adds costs to the consumer but saves you the cost and hassle of finding and servicing retail customers yourself.

- **Selling retail (traditional).** A retailer was traditionally an individual or business that sold products or services directly to the end user from a fixed location, like a store. The definition of selling retail has changed with the popularity of the Internet (see below) but most goods in the United States still change hands in traditional storefronts. The business model here is straightforward: the retailer buys the product (or service) from the producer, or from a wholesaler/distributor, and then sells it to the end user.

- **Licensing.** Under a licensing agreement, you grant someone else the right to sell something you own the intellectual property rights to. For instance, you may design T-shirts and decide that you'd like to expand your market. By licensing your T-shirt designs to clothing manufacturers, you could leverage your labor exponentially. Engineering firms routinely license their designs or specifications to other businesses—even competitors.

- **Online.** The fastest growing distribution channel today is the Internet. Many businesses sell direct to end users from their own websites or from the websites of others. It doesn't matter where the businesses (or the customers) are physically located: the Internet makes such things irrelevant. And, of course, online isn't mutually exclusive with other channels. Many

business
BUZZ
words

"big box retailer"

Also known as a superstore or megastore, a big box retailer is a retailer operating out of an extremely large physical facility —usually in excess of 50,000 square feet— which attracts customers through a combination of selection, availability, and price. Some big box retailers such as Wal-Mart and Costco sell general merchandise; others are "category killers" that focus on a particular type of product like Lowe's, Sports Authority, and Best Buy.

wholesalers have websites where retailers can go to purchase large lots of goods. Increasingly, retail businesses, rather than being only store based (bricks-and-mortar) or only online, are a combination of both (bricks-and-clicks).

business
BUZZ
words

"channel conflict"

When two (or more) channels conflict with each other—in other words, sell to the same customers but perhaps at very different prices—you have channel conflict. The Internet created a great deal of channel conflict, as many firms that previously moved goods or services through direct sales forces, agents, or dealers began selling direct to consumers over the Web. For example, auto insurance once was sold almost exclusively by agents. But the Internet forced insurance companies to begin selling directly to drivers. This meant that existing auto insurance agents found their sales dropping off even if the total volume of sales for the insurance company increased over time In general, businesses must be careful to protect their channel partners from these kinds of conflicts, because if members of the distribution chain are unhappy, they might not make as much of an effort to sell your goods or services.

Advantages and Disadvantages of Various Channels

CHANNEL TYPE	ADVANTAGES	DISADVANTAGES
Direct	You keep more of your money because there's no middleman involved. You know who your customers are and "own" them, so you can contact them for future sales or get direct feedback from them on how to improve your products or services. You're in a position to sell the customer additional products and services.	You are completely responsible for reaching and servicing the customer. You have to develop the website, do the marketing, make the sale, and provide post-sale support. You are also responsible for billing and bad debts.
Agent	Agents go out and market you, so that you have more time to spend on your creative and business endeavors. They negotiate for you, getting you a better deal than you could get for yourself. They handle contracts and other business and legal details, and provide you with advice and guidance.	They take a percentage of your income— usually 15 or 20 percent. Because it's usually an exclusive relationship, if they are under-performing, you're precluded from going elsewhere. Their reputation in the industry is your reputation, so if you have a less-than-good one, your creative and business endeavors will suffer.
Distributor	Distributors act as your sales force and can be a very efficient way to reach a large or spread-out market. They perform billing and collections and handle all paperwork. Frequently, they manage warehousing and storage as well. They give you the ability to concentrate on aspects of your business other than selling and distribution.	They take a percentage of your sales income, and they own the customer relationship. If they represent too many companies, your products or services might not be well represented.
Retail	Retailers deal with customers. They also maintain the retail space and are responsible for its costs, merchandising, marketing, and customer service.

They are responsible for unsold merchandise. If you have a good retailer, they can sell your products into markets you would not have been able to enter on your own. | You sell to them at a deep discount, typically 50 percent, and they often also demand good payment terms such as 30 to 90 days. They can be very demanding, and they own the customer. You don't have quality control over the environment. If you're dependent on just a few retailers, their economic well-being can make or break your company. |
| **Licensing** | An additional revenue stream with little or no up-front expense on your part. Licensors allow you to extend your brand to other product lines. | Quality control is always a concern. You run the risk of diluting your brand or hurting your brand image if your licensing partners have different ideas or quality standards than you do. |
| **Online** | A low-overhead way to reach and service customers. Worldwide reach. You are in direct touch with the customer and can try to sell to them again. You can track your customers' preferences and behaviors precisely. | Can be difficult to service customers from all over the world. Can eat up time responding to queries and requests for help. You must build and maintain a marketing-oriented website. |

CASE STUDY

Insider Knowledge Helps Onyx Distribution Company Clean Up

Freeda Muldoon was facilities manager for a movie cineplex owned by Loews Theaters (now AMC Theaters) for more than a decade before she had the flash of insight that became the basis for her own entrepreneurial venture.

Among other responsibilities, Muldoon had to keep all of the supplies needed by her theater well stocked: toilet paper and paper towels, cleaning supplies, light bulbs, office supplies, food service items, and all of the other things required to keep a commercial, public-serving venture operating efficiently. Managing the businesses that supplied all of these products ate up Muldoon's time. "I'd have to buy one product from one company, another product from another," she says. "I was using 15 different suppliers, and keeping on top of them all was always a challenge."

Having always had what she calls the "entrepreneurial bug," Muldoon figured that other facilities managers were probably struggling with the same problem, and decided to go out on her own. "I was working 11-hour days, six days a week anyway. I told my kids, 'If I can work this hard for someone else, I can work this hard for myself,' and I made it happen," she says. She left her secure job in 1999 to found Onyx Distribution Co., a full-service supplier of janitorial, office, and food service supplies.

She worked out of her bedroom and stored her supplies in her garage, and was profitable right from the beginning. Her first client was her former employer—she won a contract to supply 25 Loews movie cineplexes—and little by little she grew. She was able to rent her own warehouse in 2001 with the help of a local business incubator, began hiring employees (she's now up to seven), and in 2006 reaped nearly $1 million in revenues.

Because Muldoon was once a facilities manager herself, she has an intimate understanding of the challenges facing her customers and strives to make their lives easier by providing all of the supplies they need in a one-stop shopping experience. "I'm just doing what I know best—making life easier for people who work my former job," she says.

Muldoon did all of this with her own money—not out of choice, but of necessity. "I tried to get loans, but no one would give me one," she says. "Here I was, a single mother with no income. I remember one loan officer just looking at me and saying, 'Don't even try.'" She used her own 401K as seed capital, and continues to plow profits back into the business to fuel future growth. Her advice to other would-be entrepreneurs: "Do what you know. And tell yourself you deserve to be successful."

Channels for Service Businesses

Distribution channels are used for services as well as products. The same definition applies: the channel is the means by which you deliver your service to end users. For example, those in the hospitality industry—such as tour guides, adventure tour providers, and vacation home rental businesses—often sell their services through a variety of outlets, including travel agents, tour packagers, airlines, and online reservations systems. Although you can go directly to a hotel to book a room for a vacation, many people prefer to go through an alternate channel—either a travel agent or, increasingly, an online travel site—to do their travel planning.

Legal Concerns

Taking care of your company's legal health is like taking care of your personal health: an ounce of prevention is better than a pound of cure. Time after time, entrepreneurs end up in legal battles costing thousands of dollars that could have been avoided with a $300 trip to an attorney.

When starting a business, one of the first questions you need to answer is what legal form your business will take. This may sound like a question that shouldn't be important to a lot of businesses—especially when they're just starting out. After all, if you're going to be a consultant or a graphic designer or an electrical contractor, why bother dealing with the regulations and laws associated with becoming a corporation? Who needs to pay hundreds of dollars in corporation or legal fees to a government agency just to acquire a certain kind of legal structure?

But choosing a legal form affects how much you pay in taxes, who can invest in your company, and most importantly, your own personal financial security. Three things to keep in mind when choosing a legal form are:

- **Liability.** Legally, corporations (and other corporate forms—see following section) are considered individual entities. As such, the corporation—not individual shareholders—is responsible for the actions of the business. In other words, if something goes very wrong and the corporation is sued, only the assets of the corporation are at stake, not the owners' personal assets. (There are some excep-

tions to this rule, but generally, your personal liability is *greatly* limited.)

Obviously, having liability limited to the company's assets is quite desirable, since it means your personal assets—your home, investments, savings—can't be seized if your company has a legal judgment against it.

- **Double taxation.** No one likes paying taxes, and you certainly don't want to pay taxes twice—once on income for the business and then again when that income is distributed as profits to you. Instead, look for a legal form that allows for the profits of the company to "pass through" to the owners, without having to pay corporate taxes first.

- **Ownership.** Some legal forms of business limit the number or type of people who can invest in your company. If you're seeking a large number of investors or international investors, find a corporate structure (for instance, a "C" corporation) that permits such stockholders.

Types of Legal Structures

The legal structures you can consider include:

- **Sole proprietorship.** A business owned by one person with no formal legal structure. Most one-person businesses start out this way, and a majority of these retain this non-formal structure. But you have no protection from personal liability if your business is sued.

■ **Partnership.** A business with more than one owner who actively engages in the management of the company. You can—in the eyes of the law—be a partnership even if you don't write up a partnership agreement. There's also a "Limited Partnership" form of business, in which the General Partners actively manage the affairs of the company and the Limited Partners are passive investors, not permitted to participate in the management of the company (and who have limited financial exposure).

■ **Limited liability company (LLC) or limited liability partnership (LLP).** A legal form that provides liability protection for the company's owners without requiring incorporation. LLCs have become a form of choice for many small companies. These are usually less expensive than "S corporations (see below) and provide pass-through tax treatment. An LLP (not to be confused with a limited partnership, above) is almost the same as an LLC but is used for certain professional practices, such as firms of attorneys or accountants.

■ **"S" corporation.** A type of corporation that provides personal liability protection and permits pass-through taxation. This form of corporation was particularly popular for small companies before the creation of LLCs.

■ **"C" corporation.** A corporate form that allows for the most numbers of investors, foreign investors, and corporate investors, "C" corporations also allow you to issue different classes of stock (typically "preferred" and "common"), enabling the company to give more benefits to some shareholders. Thus, major investors often want companies to be "C" corporations.

There is one other major form of company—a "non-profit, or "not-for-profit," corporation"—for organizations that are formed for the public benefit, such as schools and philanthropic agencies.

Forewarned Is Forearmed

In addition to making a trip to a lawyer's office, you can also consult a number of other resources to help you with legal and licensing issues. These include:

■ **Small business development centers (SBDCs).** Your local SBDC office is likely to be able to help you understand the specific business regulations you'll have to deal with in your community. The SBDC will also have contact information for city, county, and state offices (such as county recorder or city planning departments).

■ **BusinessLaw.gov (www.businesslaw.gov).** This is a website set up and maintained by the U.S. government to aggregate information from various federal agencies as well as from individual states regarding business laws and regulations.

■ **State business portals.** Individual U.S. states all have their own websites. Many have also set up gateways, or "portals," to assist those who want to

business
BUZZ
words   **"DBA"**

The phrase doing business as (abbreviated DBA or d/b/a) is a legal term that simply means that the business name does not contain the legal name of its owner(s), whether they are human or corporate. The distinction between an actual and a "fictitious" name is important because with the latter, the world cannot tell who is legally responsible for the business. This lack of transparency in ownership has the potential to give rise to shady business practices. This is why many local governments require companies operating with fictitious names to file a DBA. To prevent fraud and protect consumers, in many places, you are required to give notice of your fictitious name in a local paper.

Biker Skin Care: Unlikely Partners Make Beautiful Products Together

What do a hard-core motorcycle rider and a podiatrist have in common? In the case of Todd November and Hal Abrahamson, a successful partnership that's married an intimate understanding of a highly specific customer demographic with medical knowledge to come up with an innovative line of skincare products.

November got the first twinge of an idea for Biker Skin Care when people kept complimenting his wife of 30 years on her beautiful complexion. Given that she had spent the last three decades riding on the back of his Harley, this struck him as noteworthy. "Despite all the wind and weather and sun, she still looks magnificent," says November. "I knew she was always putting cream on her face, but I didn't think much about it."

Then, one day in 2004, when on a routine checkup at his podiatrist, Abrahamson, November lamented that he could only ride his bike for a few hours every day because of hand, feet, and skin problems. Simultaneously, they both realized there was an opportunity: to create a line of skin care products by bikers – Abrahamson, too, is an avid motorcyclist—for bikers. The two formed a partnership and immediately set to work formulating their first product: Biker Sun Screen, an SPF 30 sunblock and moisturizer. It took them two years to develop Biker Sun Screen and

get it FDA approved, but the product has been selling well since its introduction. It was November's and Abrahamson's second product, however, that put them on bikers' radar. When brainstorming about what their customers really cared about with regard to skincare, the two men realized the answer was right in front of them: on their arms, to be precise. Tattoos. Once-magnificent tattoos that had faded after too much exposure to the sun. Abrahamson—now the chief medical officer of Biker Skin Care Products—went to work to see if he could solve that problem. Tattoo Boost was the result, and it put Biker Skin Care Products on the proverbial map.

"Bikers are very proud of their tattoos, and this cream enhances and protects new tattoos, and brings old tattoos back to life," says November, who has established a number of innovative distribution channels: tattoo parlors, biking dealerships, local repair shops, doctor's offices, and the Web. He's also started to build a wholesale distribution channel by signing up independent distributors. And, naturally, he's at every major biker show and gathering in the country. "It's hard work, but someone's gotta do it," he says. About what it takes to succeed as an entrepreneur, he says, "Hard work and perseverance. With those two things, your dreams can come to fruition."

do business in that state. These portals compile a great deal of information in one place. Here are a few tricks to find your state's business gateway:

Try www.state.(your state's two-letter abbreviation). us. For California, the website would be www.state. ca.us; for New York, www.state.ny.us. Once at your state's site, look for a tab, button, or menu item that says "Business," "Starting a Business," or something similar.

Type the name of your state and the words *business resources* into any search engine. This may uncover additional state business sites.

■ **City or county websites.** Many cities and counties, especially in large metropolitan areas, maintain business information on their websites. Use a search engine to find the one for your city/county.

Partnership Agreements—How to Protect Yourself

If you're going into business with other people, even a spouse or friend, formalize your arrangement with a written partnership agreement. Take the time to work out as many details as you can. Be certain to include a way to buy each other (or the other's heirs) out of the business. A messy "divorce" from a business partner is as difficult as a messy marital divorce—with potentially greater financial consequences. Drawing up an agreement now will help avoid difficulties if you later decide to go your separate ways.

Use the questions outlined below to discuss the nature of your relationship. Then complete the worksheet "Discussing Partnership Terms," on page 92, to highlight important issues that can later become part of a formal agreement, drawn up with the help of a lawyer.

Questions to ask potential partners:

- [ ] Why are you going into business?
- [ ] What are your personal goals for this business?
- [ ] How much money do you need now? How much money will you need over the next 12 months? 24 months? 36 months?
- [ ] How much money are you able and willing to invest in the company, if any?
- [ ] How big would you like the company to one day be?
- [ ] How much time do you have to devote to the business?
- [ ] What other obligations do you have, both business and personal, that will affect your commitment of time, money, and attention?
- [ ] How do you see decisions being made? By whom?
- [ ] What areas of responsibility do you feel capable of taking on?
- [ ] What areas of responsibility do you want to be in charge of?
- [ ] How formal/informal do you like to be about such things as work hours, dress code, and so on?
- [ ] Is your family supportive of this commitment?
- [ ] Have you ever been in a partnership before? What happened?
- [ ] What are your fears in this partnership?

Legal Forms of Business Organizations

LEGAL FORM	WHAT IS IT?	ADVANTAGES
Sole proprietorship	A business owned by one person that is not incorporated or an LLC. If you don't set up any other legal structure, and no one else owns any part of your business, you have a sole proprietorship.	Simple. No legal forms or costs to establish. No "double taxation."
General partnership	A business with more than one owner in which all partners actively participate in the business.	You have the time and talents of more than one person. No double taxation.
Limited partnership	A business with at least one owner who manages the business (general partners) and other partners who do not participate in the management (limited partners).	Protects the personal assets of limited partners, who are not responsible for the debts and obligations of the business. Enables investors to limit their financial exposure.
Limited liability company (LLC) or limited liability partnership	A legal form which provides much of the protection of incorporating with most of the simplicity of a sole proprietorship.	Protects your personal assets against most business losses. No double taxation. Relatively simple, inexpensive to establish and maintain. Can distribute profits and losses disproportionately to ownership interest.
"C" corporation	A corporation is a legal entity, separate from its owners.	Protects owners' personal assets against corporate losses and obligations. Can issue stock. No limit on the number of people who can own stock. Can deduct cost of benefits for all employees, including owners.
"S" corporation	A type of corporation that allows for pass-through taxation instead of double taxation. S corporations are less popular since the introduction of LLCs.	The personal liability protection of a corporation with the pass-through taxation treatment of a sole proprietorship.

DISADVANTAGES	TAX TREATMENT	WATCH OUT FOR
Provides no protection of personal assets from business losses. The business owner has unlimited personal liability for the debts, obligations, and judgments against the company. The business owner's spouse may likewise be liable.	"Pass through" profits and losses, so the business owner can deduct losses against other personal income, and there is no "double taxation." File a Schedule C with your income tax return.	In community property states, spouses may be liable for business debts as well as having an ownership interest in the company.
Each partner has unlimited personal liability for business losses or obligations. Each partner can sign contracts and incur debts that all partners are liable for.	"Pass through" profits and losses to the partners who pay tax at their individual rates. Partnership pays no taxes but must file a Form 1065.	If you go into business with other people, you have a partnership whether you draw up documents or not, and they will have a share of the business and other legal rights.
Limited partners cannot participate in running the company. General partners are all liable for the company's obligations.	Limited partners can only deduct "passive" losses against "passive income," and they are capped on the total amount of their investment.	If a limited partner participates in any way in the management of the company, they can lose their liability protection.
Each owner can enter into contracts and incur debts for the entire LLC. Must file Articles of Organization with your state; often requires filing and annual state fees.	"Pass through" profits and losses to each owner. LLC pays no taxes but must file a Form 1065.	Be sure to have a written agreement spelling out the percentage ownership of each member to avoid confusion or conflict later.
Double taxation. Must file articles of incorporation with your state; requires filing and annual state fees. Must keep records and have an annual meeting. Requires board of directors in most states if more than one stockholder.	Double taxation: corporation and shareholders each pay tax on income they receive. However, if the corporation will keep significant amounts in reserve, this can have lower tax consequences than pass-through taxation.	Securities rules affect how you sell stock and to whom. Use lawyers to set up a corporation.
Many disadvantages over an LLC, including limits on number and residency of stockholders, requires proportionate distribution of profits and losses, more record keeping required than an LLC.	"Pass through" taxation, but profits and losses must be allocated on same percentage as ownership.	Ask your lawyer if there is any benefit in choosing an S corporation over an LLC.

worksheet: Discussing Partnership Terms

Use this worksheet to determine with your partners the terms of your partnership. Then meet with a lawyer to draw up a formal partnership agreement.

Ownership Division. Who owns what percent?	
Jobs/Responsibilities What jobs and responsibilities does each partner have? Can partners work for any other company or do any other work on the side?	
Decisions How will general business decisions be made? What decisions does each partner have final authority on? Who has the final authority for decisions for the company as a whole?	
Communication How will you communicate on a regular basis? How will serious disputes be resolved?	
Exit strategy and dissolution agreement What happens if one partner wants to leave the business or move? What if one partner wants to sell the company? What happens if a partner dies or becomes disabled?	
Other	

Knowing Your Intellectual Property

An important, and often overlooked, legal consideration for entrepreneurs is intellectual property. You know the value of the PC and printer on your desk. You know how much you paid for the wood you need to manufacture your custom bookshelves. And you can recite the current market value of the three holiday cottages you rent out to vacationers on a weekly basis. But what is the value of the Nike "swoosh"? The design of an iPhone? The content of a Beatles song? We all recognize that these things have a value far beyond just the *physical property* of the running shoes, cell phones, or CDs, because of the value of the ideas behind them—the *intellectual property* (IP) underlying the "swoosh," the iPhone design and interface, or the Beatles' wonderful music and lyrics.

Every company has certain intangible properties that are, or can be, very valuable. Most of them come under the heading of IP—assets that have value because of the knowledge, recognition, and inventiveness they consist of. Some businesses *only* have products composed of intellectual property—software developers, publishers, inventors, consultants, and many more.

There are two ways of protecting your intellectual property: copyrights and patents

Copyrights

If you're creating works that others might want to copy—content, music, art, software, illustrations—you'll want to protect what you've created. This is where copyright law comes in. Copyrights cover any type of work that is "fixed" and "tangible"—even if it's only computer code, words spoken on an audiotape, or images "fixed" on a movie.

Copyrights do not cover ideas, no matter how unique, just the particular fixed expression of those ideas. For instance, you can't copyright your idea for the story of a boy who goes to a school for wizards, but you can copyright your novel telling the story of that boy. Once you have a copyright, you retain the rights to that creation, and no one else can make a movie about your hero without your permission. You also can't copyright "facts." So if what you're creating is purely the compilation of facts, you won't be able to copyright that.

Protecting Your Intangible Assets

Just as you would protect the physical property of your company, you need to protect your intellectual property as well. There are a couple of ways to do this:

- **Non-disclosure agreements.** One of the simplest ways to protect your ideas is to get a signed non-disclosure agreement or confidentiality agreement before discussing your concepts with others. This is a standard business procedure, and you'll often be asked to sign NDAs if you're trying to do business with another company. However, be forewarned: venture capitalists will not sign NDAs because they see too many new business ideas.

- **Non-compete agreements.** Once a trade secret is learned by someone outside your business, it can't be unlearned. So sometimes the biggest fear you'll have is that a valuable and knowledgeable employee will go to work for a competitor. To help guard against this, you may want to have employees sign an agreement limiting their ability to work for a competing firm (or start their own competing company) for a given period of time.

Copyrights are easy to get. Under U.S. law, the rights to your creation are yours *at the moment you create it.* Theoretically, you don't have to do anything to ensure your copyright. But that's putting you at some risk. The easiest thing to do to protect your copyright is to add a simple copyright notice whenever you produce something. Just add the word "copyright," the © notice, the date, and your name. However, for more protection, you can—for a small sum—register your copyright with the U.S. Patent & Trademark Office (www.uspto.gov).

Patents

Patents are designed to protect new inventions rather than creative works.

Copyrights are easy to get; patents are incredibly tough. Copyrights cost little or nothing; patents are very expensive. Copyrights are yours the instant you create the work; patents can take years to get issued. Patents are also difficult and costly to enforce—if someone violates your patent and starts selling a knock-off of your product, it may take a lot of money (in legal fees) and time to put a stop to it. And if the perpetrator is overseas, enforcement will be even harder. So if you're building your business around a new invention, process, machine, recipe, or formula that needs to be patented, it's going to be tough going.

If, however, you have a new invention or a new process that is indeed unique, "non-obvious" (a requirements for qualifying for a patent), and worth a lot of money, then pursue the patent process. The first thing you'll need—after you've come up with your new invention or idea—is a competent patent attorney. A good one will warn you of the costs and pitfalls before you get too far down the road.

Drawing Up the Right Contracts

A contract is an agreement between parties that the law will enforce. Although the days of doing business with just a handshake may not be entirely over, having a written contract or letter of agreement is a normal, advisable business practice.

With a contract, you:

- Spell out all terms, such as what you'll be paid
- Detail the nature of the work to be performed as well as the deadlines for performing it
- Avoid misunderstandings
- Protect your rights

From the start of your business, get in the habit of drawing up contracts or letters of agreement and getting them signed by all parties. Failure to get a written agreement leaves you at risk. Ours is a litigious society, and the best way to avoid ending up in court—or in hot water—is to get things in writing.

You're likely to find you have a number of agreements or contracts that you'll use over and over again. For instance, a consultant may have a simple letter of engagement; an electrician might have a standard contract; and a musician might have a simple written agreement for spelling out the terms of a "gig."

Some of the many types of legal agreements you may need include:

- Contracts
- Letters of agreement or engagement
- Leases
- Employment contracts
- Distribution agreements
- Signed project proposals
- Work for hire agreements
- Non-disclosure agreements
- Non-compete agreements

A lawyer can help you draw up standard agreements to use over and over again—as well as contracts for significant deals. In addition, a number of businesses provide standard templates for these forms, which you can buy or download off the Web. You may be tempted to forgo written agreements—they seem so formal—but when you're in business, it's normal, expected, and prudent to get everything in writing—and signed.

business BUZZ words

"trade secret"

A trade secret is a formula, practice, process, design, instrument, pattern, or compilation of information used by a business to obtain an advantage over competitors. Coca Cola has jealousy guarded its trade secret—its "formula" for mixing the various versions of its flagship product—for more than 120 years. Many manufacturing firms have business processes that allow them to operate more efficiently than other firms, and classify those as trade secrets. Trade secrets are more difficult to protect and defend in court than patents or trademarks.

sample form: **Letter of Agreement**

[DATE] January 15, 2009

[NAME/CONTACT OF CLIENT] Aaron Hill
Telescope Financial Services
3456 University Drive
Chapel Hill, North Carolina 27516

[SALUTATION] Dear Aaron:

[BRIEF OPENING PARAGRAPH]

I am delighted that I will be able to assist you in launching a new website for Telescope Financial Services, and I look forward to working with you on this project. Listed below are the details of our work together. I have enclosed two signed copies of this letter. Please sign and return one copy to me. I am excited about getting this project underway.

PROJECT: Content writing for web pages of relaunch of Telescope Financial Services website.

SCOPE OF WORK: Chris Wong ("Contractor") will write copy for the new Telescope Financial Services' ("Client") website based on materials provided by Telescope Financial Services and interviews with Telescope executives and staff. The contractor will be responsible for editing and rewriting copy on approximately 50 existing web pages and writing new copy for approximately 30 new pages.

TIMELINE AND DUE DATES: The project will begin on February 1, 2009, and continue through March 31, 2009, with the contractor expected to devote approximately 20 hours per week to the project during that period, for approximately 160 hours. Client acknowledges, however, that significant revisions of the text requested of Contractor after completing initial drafts may result in the project extending beyond the due date and add additional hours.

FEES AND EXPENSES: Contractor will be paid a rate of $50 per hour. Contractor will be reimbursed for the following expenses: overnight courier services. Contractor will not be paid for travel time to Client's offices nor be reimbursed for any other expenses.

TERMS AND CONDITIONS: Contractor is engaged by Client as an independent contractor and, and is not deemed an employee of Client in any manner. Contractor acknowledges that this is a work-for-hire relationship in which all work, including but not limited to the content of the web pages, is created for the Client and is the sole property of the client. Contractor further acknowledges that all information provided by Client shall be deemed Confidential and agrees not to disclose such information unless necessary in the scope of the work for the Client and with Client's prior approval.

Upon signing, Client will make a non-refundable deposit of $1,000, which will be applied against the first month's billing. Contractor will then invoice Client for fees at the end of each month. Invoices are due upon receipt. Payment received after 30 days will be subject to a 1.5% per month interest charge. Either Client or Contractor can terminate this relationship by giving at least 30 days notice.

The above is accepted and agreed to by:

_____   _____
For Telegraph Financial Services   By Chris Wong (Contractor)

_____
Title

_____   _____
Date   Date

chapter

13

Taxes, Licenses, and Insurance

Complying with laws and regulations. No one likes it. Yet it's as much a part of doing business as building that widget, designing that line of women's wear, or preparing the daily menu for your organic restaurant. In particular, you will inevitably come to the day when you have to pay taxes—on your revenues, on behalf of your employees, or on the property your business resides upon. You will also have to get insurance to protect your investments in equipment, supplies, and infrastructure. And depending on the type of business you run, you may also have to get special licenses to operate.

Death and ...You Know What

Paying taxes is a part of operating a business. No matter what business structure you choose—sole proprietorship, partnership, or corporation—there are a broad range of taxes you need to pay, and pay on time, or face the penalty.

You may be surprised by the variety of taxes you face. There are income taxes, sales taxes, payroll taxes, property taxes, personal property taxes, inventory taxes, special use taxes, general business taxes, and others. Some taxes incur substantial penalties for late or underpayments, so be certain to keep track of when taxes are due and give yourself enough time to prepare them.

As a business, you will often have responsibility for collecting and then paying taxes owed by others.

For instance, if you are a retailer, you must charge and collect the sales tax on items you sell to consumers. Set up records to keep track of those taxes that you've collected—and pay them by the dates due.

You may want to—or sometimes be required to—set up separate accounts to keep the taxes you collect distinct from your other funds. Governments—whether federal, state, or city—frown on you keeping their money.

Getting an Employer Identification Number

To get started on all of this, you have to get a U.S. Tax ID number for your business.

An Employer Identification Number (EIN)—also known as a Federal Tax Identification Number—is a nine-digit number used to identify a business entity to the IRS (Internal Revenue Service). All businesses that have employees, and many other types of businesses as well, need EINs. You may apply for an EIN in various ways—by fax, telephone, by mail, and in person as well as online by going to www.irs.gov/businesses/small/article/0,,id=102767,00.html. Check with your state to make sure you need a state number or charter.

Your EIN is a permanent number and can be used immediately for most of your business needs, including opening a bank account, applying for business licenses, and filing a tax return by mail.

Sales Tax

How will you know whether you have to collect sales tax? Here's the short answer: You must collect sales tax on most goods and some services that are delivered to a customer in any U.S. state in which you have a physical presence, such as a branch office, a retail location, or a customer service center.

The long answer is much more complicated. Sales tax rates and rules vary from state to state, and even from city to city. There are an enormous number of laws and taxing authorities. According to the National Retail Federation, 45 states and 7,500 cities, counties, and jurisdictions impose sales taxes.

States call these taxes by various names: sales tax, franchise tax, transaction privilege tax, use tax, and more. Some are the responsibility off the seller, others the buyer. But governments figured out that it was easier and more reliable to make the seller collect the tax than to get individual consumers to send in tax on every purchase. This is the reason businesses are typically responsible for collecting sales tax and sending it to the state.

Generally, if you're going to collect sales tax, you must get a license from your state. On each taxable transaction, you calculate the applicable sales tax, collect it from the buyer, keep tax records, and then file a tax return and pay the taxes to your state. You'll pay monthly, quarterly, or annually, depending on your level of sales.

Income Tax

The tax code for businesses, like that for individuals, is complex and well beyond the scope of this book. Still, you have to think about taxes up front as you plan your business venture. In fact, the more successful you are, the more taxes you'll probably pay.

Understanding key tax concerns is critical for most businesses. You will make some decisions—or alter them—based on tax implications. Some business expenses are fully deductible—or "written off"—others are only partially deductible; others have to be depreciated over a number of years; and still others are not deductible at all. You should have at least a fair understanding of those issues as you make choices in your business. If you purchase a very expensive piece of

Do You Need an Employer Identification Number (EIN)?

You will need an EIN if you answer "Yes" to any of the following questions:

- [ ] **Do you have employees?**

- [ ] **Do you operate your business as a corporation or a partnership?**

- [ ] **Do you file any of these tax returns: Employment, Excise, or Alcohol, Tobacco and Firearms?**

- [ ] **Do you withhold taxes on income, other than wages, paid to a non-resident alien?**

- [ ] **Do you have a Keogh plan?**

- [ ] **Are you involved with any of the following types of organizations?**
  - **—Trusts**
  - **—Returns**
  - **—Estates**
  - **—Real estate mortgage investment conduits**
  - **—Non-profit organizations**
  - **—Farmers' cooperatives**
  - **—Plan administrators**

Even if you don't answer "Yes" to any of the above, you may want to get an EIN. That's because most business clients and customers will ask you for a Tax ID number when they pay you. Having an EIN means you will not have to give them your Social Security Number. And that's somewhat safer and more secure than always using your Social Security Number for business purposes.

The Sales Tax Clearinghouse

Founded in 1999, the Sales Tax Clearinghouse (STC) acts as a one-stop shop for businesses to gain access to tools that can navigate the complicated landscape of calculating sales and use taxes in more than 7,000 taxing authorities (states, counties, and cities). STC offers two forms of sales tax calculations: manual, in which subscribers can use either an online or desktop calculator, and automatic, in which an automated service allows businesses to connect their business software systems directly to the STC's servers to calculate rates automatically.

Tax-Free Goods

Each state makes its own rules as to what sales are taxable. Typically, most products sold to end users are taxable. Major exemptions include:

- Prescription drugs
- Food, especially groceries and non-prepared food
- Animal feed, seed, and many agricultural products
- Products for resale, including raw materials, inventory, and other items that are going to be sold, rather than used, by your customers

equipment, for instance, and expect to deduct the total cost of it from your income this year, you may be surprised to discover that the expense has to be spread out over as many as five to ten or even 20 years.

Tax codes are complicated and always changing. Certain tax laws apply to incorporated businesses and not unincorporated ones, or vice versa, and business tax laws differ from regulations for individuals. And, of course, every U.S. state has its own tax laws as well!

So, new entrepreneurs should plan on spending some time with their accountants talking about taxes. Ask them to help you understand which taxes you're liable for, when your taxes are due, and how various transactions and expenses are taxed. (Meals and entertainment expenses, for instance, cannot typically be fully deducted, while other marketing expenses usually can be.) Have your accountant help you plan how to reduce your tax liability.

business
BUZZ
words

"pass-through"

Pass-through taxation allows the income or loss generated by the business to be reflected on the personal income tax return of the owners. This special tax status eliminates the possibility of double taxation. Under current U.S. law partnerships, S Corporations and most LLCs qualify for pass-through tax status.

worksheet: **Your Tax Deadlines**

Use this worksheet to record the due dates for all of you taxes and to estimate the amounts you'll have to pay in each filing period.

Tax	Amount	Where to Send/File	Dates Due
Income tax (federal, state, county, perhaps local)			
Payroll and other employment-related taxes (Social Security, workers' compensation, unemployment, etc.)			
Sales tax			
Personal property tax and use taxes			
Property tax			
Special taxes (hotel, food, transportation, etc.)			
Import/Export, custom taxes and duties			
Transfer taxes			
Capital gains taxes			
Inventory taxes			
Other			

Many businesspeople find it helpful to set up separate savings accounts just for income taxes. With each check they receive, they set aside a certain percentage in this separate tax account, so when income tax time arrives they have the money necessary to pay their bill.

Unlike personal income taxes, which are due once a year (April 14 in the United States), business tax payments must be made four times a year—quarterly estimates of how much you're likely to owe at the end of the year. Generally, this is based on how much you made the previous year. Be sure to ask your tax advisor how to handle your quarterly tax payments.

Payroll Taxes

Payroll taxes are the state and federal taxes that you, as an employer, are required to withhold and/or to pay on behalf of your employees. You are required to withhold state and federal income taxes as well as Social Security and Medicare taxes from your employees' wages. You are also required to pay a matching amount of Social Security and Medicare taxes (together known as FICA) for your employees and to pay state and federal unemployment taxes. In some places, employers may be required to withhold state income tax, or even city income tax.

Licenses and Permits

You may be ready to start your business, but the authorities may not want you to start—at least not without making sure you have the proper licenses or permits. As frustrating as it may seem, you can't just rent an office or a store and set up shop. Although establishing a business in the United States or Canada is far easier than in most parts of the world, you still have to deal with some paperwork

The bureaucratic items you'll deal with fall into three general categories:

- **Identification numbers.** These are used to keep track of your business with government authorities. The Employer Identification Number (EIN) is an example of this.

- **Licenses or certifications.** Cities require that you have a license to engage in any business. Certain types of businesses or professions also have special licensing requirements. For example, you might need a contractor's license, a license to sell alcoholic beverages, or an optometrist certification in order to hang out your shingle.

- **Permits.** These are required for particular, often more limited, actions. Examples include construction and special event permits.

Sometimes the terms *permit* and *license* are used interchangeably. To make matters more complicated, you may need to get licenses, permits, or identification numbers from different levels of government. These may include:

- Federal (U.S.)
- State
- County
- City

"liability"

A liability is an obligation your business has to pay for something resulting from an action—whether that is taking out a loan, settling a lawsuit, or purchasing equipment on a lease—that detracts from the value of the business. For example, balance sheets (see page 114) are composed of assets (what you own) and liabilities (what you owe). You generally want to be careful about the number of liabilities your business incurs: you don't want to owe other people or organizations more than the total value of your company, or your "net worth."

Deductions

A tax deduction is when the government allows you to subtract the cost of a business expense from your overall revenues, resulting in a reduction in the total tax you pay. For example, if you were collecting $100 a week for landscaping services you provided to homeowners, and it cost you $50 to pay your employees to perform the service, plus $10 in gas to operate the various equipment, you would be able to deduct $60 in expenses and only pay taxes on $40 of that income. You'd probably also be able to deduct, or write off, a portion of the cost of your truck and equipment, lowering the amount you'd pay taxes on even more.

Deductions are an important part of figuring out your total income, and they directly affect how much money you'll have at the end of the year. Some people actually start businesses just to be able to deduct certain expenses. For instance, a photography buff may decide to start a business taking photos of weddings or events so that he can deduct the cost of all the latest and greatest camera equipment. Or a person who loves to travel might start an eco-tour travel agency to be able to deduct all of her travel expenses. Talk to an accountant to understand which type of expenses can be deducted and which cannot.

There are many kinds of tax deductions. Some are geared to individuals; some are aimed at businesses. The tax code in the United States has been added to, changed, and overhauled over the decades and is now incredibly complex. Unless you have a specific tax background, it's probably best to go to a professional for assistance preparing your tax returns.

The requirements vary greatly depending on the type of business you're opening, and the state, county, or city in which you plan to do business. That's why it's good to ask your attorney about these types of licenses. Industry associations are also an excellent source of information about the licenses and permits you'll need to operate in different jurisdictions.

Insurance

One of the most frustrating tasks you'll encounter when running a business is shopping for insurance. After all, you can't "see" what you're getting. If this is your first business, you'll be absolutely overwhelmed by the different types of insurance you may need, want, or be offered.

Insurance is a way to protect the value of property, life, or one's person against loss or harm arising in specified contingencies, such as fire, accident, death,

disablement, or the like. Figuring out your insurance coverage will be daunting—guaranteed! So you'll need a good insurance agent, or two or three. Ideally, you'll find an agent who understands business insurance for companies of your size and industry. It's best if they're a broker who can offer you policies from a number of different companies rather than just representing one company's products.

If you don't know any insurance agents, ask for referrals from other business owners or from service providers. You'll want an agent whose advice you can trust because you're likely going to rely on their recommendations for the type and amount of coverage you should have. Check with your industry trade association as well. Many trade associations offer lower-cost insurance specifically for the needs of companies such as yours. But always do your research: just because a policy comes from a trade association doesn't necessarily mean it's best for you.

Consider these three dimensions and types of insurance:

- **Incentive.** Insurance you purchase because your workers (including yourself) desire it—such as medical, dental, life insurance, and retirement.

- **Protection.** Insurance you purchase to protect your business from the unexpected—liability, accident, fire, theft, and business interruption.

- **Legal necessity.** Insurance that others—perhaps your landlord—require (such as fire or liability) or that's required by state law (for example, worker's compensation for those who have employees).

Types of insurance

You need insurance. Period. As tempting as it may be to go without it—especially in the early, cash-strapped days of your entrepreneurial venture—you must have it. Some types of insurance are required by law (such as workman's compensation insurance), while others (like business continuity insurance) are optional but absolutely necessary to protect your investment should something go wrong.

- **Workers' compensation insurance.** All employers are required to have workers' compensation insurance. It provides workers who are injured on the job with some financial payment and protects the business in case of lawsuits due to serious employee accident or death. Although some states allow companies to be self-insured, these companies frequently have to prove they have the financial resources to make payments to workers and cover themselves in case of an incident.

- **Business insurance.** Business insurance (often called *business liability insurance)* provides protection for your routine daily business operations. The exact type of business insurance you will need depends on your business. There is insurance to protect against customers who get hurt on your premises or any harm done by product defects as well as insurance to protect you if a customer sues because a service is perceived to be of an inferior quality.

- **Malpractice insurance.** This is the insurance purchased by professional service providers (such as physicians and attorneys) to pay for lawsuits and any financial awards in the case that a patient or client sues based on a belief they were harmed because the provider was negligent in the way the job was performed.

- **Business continuance insurance.** Business continuance (sometimes referred to as *business continuity*) is insurance to cover any losses from situations that prevent your business from operating. These can include natural disasters like hurricanes, flooding, earthquakes, and fire.

- **Health insurance.** This includes medical, dental, and even such things as elder care. Although fewer and fewer companies pay 100 percent of health insurance for employees, providing health insurance benefits helps attract top-notch workers to your organization.

When shopping around for these various kinds of insurance, make sure you're comfortable with the financial stability and reputation of the company providing your coverage. The last thing you want is to pay expensive premiums over an extended period of time only to have the insurer be unable or unwilling to pay up when you suffer a loss.

Deciding which types and how much insurance to carry is always a juggling act. You want to have enough to cover you in case of problems, but the costs can be discouraging, especially for a young company.

worksheet: Business Licenses and Permits

Use this worksheet to list the licenses and permits you'll need, including where and how to apply, requirements, and fees.

License Type	Agency and Contact Info	Requirements	Fees
Local licenses			
Local permits			
County licenses/ permits			
State licenses			
DBA required			
Federal certification			
Other			

worksheet: Insurance Coverage Comparison

Use this worksheet as you work with your insurance broker to compare the costs and types of coverage you'll get from various companies.

Insurance Type	Option 1	Option 2	Option 3
Health			
Dental			
Vision			
Life/Disability			
Workers' Compensation			
Fire			
Loss/Theft			
Business interruption/ Continuity			
Malpractice (errors & omissions)			
Vehicles			
Unemployment			
Offsite equipment			
Offsite employees			
Other			
Other			

Financial Projections

Now that you've gotten past some of the initial aspects of planning, you'll need to take a close look at how much it will cost you to produce this product or perform this service, as well as how much it's reasonable to expect customers to pay for it, and then see whether the latter figure is larger than the former. One of the most important things on your To Do list at this stage is determining (to the best of your abilities) whether you can actually make money from your proposed business.

After all, even the richest people on the planet will probably only pay you so much to walk their dogs. Likewise, if you plan to sell on-site computer support to small and medium businesses, you need to know how much companies are willing pay for such a service. And if you hope to grow a nationwide chain of one-hour document delivery service providers, you need a good sense of what local carriers are charging so that you can compete and still make a profit. Otherwise, you will work incredibly hard only to fall into debt.

Preparing a Simple Financial Forecast

Entrepreneurs usually fall into one of two categories—those who are fascinated with numbers and those who are frightened by them. If you're in the second category, you're probably intimidated by the prospect of filling in financial forms.

Take heart. Numbers aren't magical, mysterious, or menacing. They merely reflect decisions you've already made in your business planning process. Every decision leads to a number, but numbers in and of themselves do not represent decisions. You cannot pull a number out of thin air because financial forms call for a specific figure on a specific line.

If yours is going to be a very small business such as a boutique graphic design shop, you may only need to prepare a simple budget: a forecast of your estimated sales and a list of how much you plan to spend on the various components of your business. Most other businesses will benefit from preparing at least simple financial forms—especially cash flow projections to help you determine when you'll have money coming in so you can adjust your spending. And if you're seeking outside financing, you'll need a range of financial documents to give to potential lenders or investors.

Besides helping you figure out your spending, there's another reason to draw up financial forecasts—they help you set goals. Writing down specific numbers for your anticipated sales gives you a target to work toward.

"Bottom Up" vs. "Top Down"

Successful financial projections are achieved by budgeting from the "bottom up," not the "top down." Top-down numbers are enticing to work with because they always come out looking good, but they're not realistic. Here's how they work: you look at the big picture—the total market size, growth rate, average sales price, and average profit margins in your industry. You make what seem to be reasonable assumptions, something like achieving a 10 percent market penetration or improving margins by 2 percent. Then you fill in your financial statements to make the total come out to the big numbers projected.

For example, let's say you've invented a new golf club, and you project that you will achieve a 1 percent market penetration within three years. If total annual sales of golf clubs amount to $2 billion, then you'll achieve $20 million in annual sales. With a profit margin of 15 percent, your net profit will be $3 million. Sounds good, doesn't it? Top-down projections result in some very impressive numbers—the kind that make you and perhaps some potential investors excited. But they're just not very realistic.

Instead, the best financials are developed from the bottom up. You do the real business-building legwork: examine different distribution channels, source manufacturers and suppliers, develop a staffing chart, outline your marketing program, and design operations. You plug in numbers from these realistic projections of how much things will cost and then determine how much income you will need to sustain that cost.

So, let's say you're that same golf club manufacturer, and you're building your financials from the bottom up. Here's how it would work:

First, compare distribution channels and then choose one. Let's say you decide to sell through specialty golf retailers and country clubs. This channel has associated costs and impacts on income. You'll need to budget for a sales force to sell to those shops, exhibiting at the annual sporting good trade shows, and advertising in *Golf Retailer* magazine. And you'll only receive 40 percent to 45 percent of the final sales price of the club, since the retailer takes half and the salesperson receives a commission.

Now, you're starting to get some real numbers to plug into each of the lines of your financial forms. You've got numbers for advertising, staffing, and income. It's time to think about your other costs—specifically, your startup and ongoing operational costs.

Startup Costs

So what are your startup costs? How much it will cost you to get your business operational? After all, you don't spring into business overnight. You have to sign a lease, buy equipment and supplies, and pay lawyers and accountants. Among the expenses you'll have to consider:

business
BUZZ
words

"profit margin"

The profit margin is the yardstick by which many businesses measure their success. It is the measure of how much money you actually make compared with the money you take in. You calculate your profit margin as follows:

Profit margin = Net income (sales minus all expenses) <divided by> total sales

The higher the profit margin, the better, because this indicates that proportionally more of what you earn represents profits. This is based on keeping your prices high and your costs low. But you can't compare the profit margins of businesses in different industries or even markets to determine who's doing "better," because different companies operate under vastly different conditions. For example, a supermarket operating in New York is likely to have a different profit margin than one in Peoria, Illinois, because the costs of rent, utilities, and staffing are so much higher.

- Signing a lease (first month, last month, security deposit)

- Cost of raw materials or invention (if making a product or selling goods)

- Cost of initial office supplies

- Equipment (computer, printer, fax, phones, and so on)

- Payroll for help getting started

- Transportation (car, truck)

- Shipping (initial packaging materials)

- Startup marketing (advertising, collateral, and so on)

- Professional services (lawyers, accountants, business consultants)

worksheet: Startup Costs

Use this worksheet to make a list of your actual or estimated startup costs.

Item	Cost
Signing a lease (down payment, first month's rent, security deposit)	
Cost of initial materials or inventory	
Cost of initial office supplies	
Equipment (computers, phones, manufacturing equipment, etc.)	
Payroll (salaries, wages, contract help)	
Transportation costs	
Shipping costs	
Startup marketing (advertising, collateral, etc.)	
Starting professional services (legal, accountant, consulting etc.)	
Travel	
Other	
TOTAL:	

The Importance of Good Cash Flow Management

There's a big difference between being profitable and having enough cash. Some very profitable firms go out of business because they simply run out of ready money. After all, without cash in the bank, you cannot pay your rent (or mortgage), your employees, or your suppliers.

Cash flow problems occur when cash goes out the door faster than it comes in. This can happen for many reasons. You may be slow billing customers, for example, and therefore there's too much delay between the time you have to purchase the materials to make your circuit boards and the time you get paid for those boards. Your suppliers are clamoring for their money, but you simply don't have the funds to pay them because of your billing delays. Or you may have billed promptly, but your customers are dragging their feet paying—not uncommon, especially when the economy is slow.

Your job when running your business is to keep an eye on not only the so-called bottom line, but also on the cash flow statement. There are a number of things you can do to better manage your cash flow:

- Arrange for your payments to suppliers and creditors to be in sync with your payments from customers.

- Keep an adequate cash buffer in the bank at all times.

- Bill customers promptly, and send frequent notifications when an account becomes overdue.

- Give overdue customers the opportunity to make partial payments.

- Give customers discounts for prompt payments.

Operating Expenses

Next, you must consider the ongoing, recurrent expenses that you will experience every month. Note that this doesn't include *just* your cash outlay (which you'll hear about next). It also includes the actual expenses that accrue over time, such as taxes, insurance, depreciation, and maintenance. Here's a list of some of your operating expenses:

- Sales commissions
- Product returns and allowances
- Cost of goods sold
- Salaries and wages
- Employee benefits
- Payroll taxes
- Professional services
- Marketing and advertising
- Rent
- Equipment rental
- Maintenance
- Depreciation
- Insurance
- Telecom
- Utilities
- Office supplies
- Postage and shipping
- Travel
- Entertainment
- Provision for taxes on income

Sales

At this point you also have to make your best estimate of how much money you believe you will bring in every month from selling your product or service. Say you'll be selling high-end home theater systems for $25,000 per installation (including the equipment), and think you can sell five installations per month. That would represent $125,000 in total *sales*. Note that this does not represent *profits*. That's because you have to pay for the equipment you're installing.

Sales—which can also be referred to as *revenue* or *gross income* (income before expenses)—is the total amount of money you make from the products or services you sell. Profits are the amount you have left after expenses.

Cash Flow

If the three most important things in real estate are "location, location, location," the first three rules of business are "cash, cash, cash." It's necessary, of course, to be profitable, but "profit" is a number that shows up on your accounts at the end of the year; cash is money you have in the bank. In a small company, it's cash that determines whether you can pay your bills.

No matter what your business is, you're going to have a lag between what goes out and what comes in. If you're a consultant, for example, you'll have to pay for your phone, computer, marketing materials, and rent before you get your first client.

And if you're a manufacturer, you'll have to pay for raw materials, equipment, and employees many months before money from the sale of your product comes in. Thus, it's vital to create a cash flow projection.

Know Your Financial Forms

You may not have an immediate need to know how to create a balance sheet or income statement, but you certainly should know how to read them. These will be the documents that the world will use to judge you, especially if you have outside investors or bankers. They will eagerly await the quarterly statements that you generate for them.

What is an income statement?

An income statement is a financial document that shows how "gross income" (the money you earn from total sales before expenses are deducted) becomes "net income," or the amount that remains after all expenses have been taken out. The income statement shows whether you made or lost money during the month, quarter, or year in question.

What is a balance sheet?

A balance sheet provides a snapshot of a business that includes all assets (what the business owns) and liabilities (what the business owes). Of all the basic financial statements—income statement, cash flow statement, and balance sheet—the balance sheet is the only one that takes this snapshot of a particular moment rather than reporting financial results over time.

Reality Check

So, what do you do if you realize after filling out these forms that despite all of your research and planning, you won't make money with the business the way you originally envisioned it? You have four options:

- **Change your business model.** Businesses are always experimenting with business models. In the Internet world, for example, many companies switched from for-fee to advertising-supported models that give a product or service away to users for free. When considering your business model, consider that the revenue has to come from somewhere; it's your job to come up with innovative ways to get it

- **Change the pricing.** Another possibility is raising the price of your product or service so that you can make a profit on it. Sometimes this just won't be possible. The market may not bear a price hike because competitive products and services are already out there for less, and you can't justify asking for more than they charge. In such cases, consider trying to reduce your expenses (see the next bullet).

- **Lower your expenses.** The price you charge represents only half of the profit equation. The other half is what it costs you to make that product or deliver that service. If you can eliminate certain costs—either costs directly involved in making a product or delivering a service (such as raw materials or gas expenditures) or indirect costs (such as your energy bills or rent)—then you might be able make a profit without raising the price you charge customers.

- **Change the product or service.** Alter the specifications of the product or service you were going to provide so that you can either raise the price or reduce the cost, or both. For example, you may discover that by adding certain premium features to your high-end home entertainment systems, you can charge considerably more for them.

worksheet: Profit and Loss Projection

	JAN	FEB	MARCH	APRIL	MAY
Sales					
Gross (total) sales					
(commissions)					
(returns & allowances)					
Net sales					
Cost of goods/service supplies					
GROSS PROFIT					
Expensess					
Salaries and wages					
Employee benefits					
Payroll taxes					
Professional services					
Marketing and advertising					
Rent					
Equipment rental					
Maintenance					
Depreciation					
Insurance					
Telecom					
Utilities					
Office supplies					
Travel					
Entertainment					
Other					
Total expenses					
Net income before taxes					
Provision for taxes on income					
Net Profit					

JUNE	JULY	AUGUST	SEPT	OCT	NOV	DEC	TOTAL

worksheet: **Cash Flow Statement**

	JAN	FEB	MARCH	APRIL	MAY
Cash Receipts					
Income from sales					
Cash from loans					
Cash from investors					
Total cash receipts					
Cash Disbursements					
Inventory expenses					
Operating expenses					
Equipment purchases					
Loan payments					
Income tax payments					
Investor payments					
Owner's draw					
Reserve					
Total cash disbursements					
Net Cash Flow					
Opening cash balance					
Net Cash Flow					
Ending Cash Balance					

JUNE	JULY	AUGUST	SEPT	OCT	NOV	DEC	TOTAL

Paying Your Dues: Right Arm Resource

If you regularly tune your radio to stations that play what's called in the music business "album alternative rock" (AAA), or "adult rock," chances are good that you've heard the fruits of Jesse Barnett's labors. These include songs by artists like Avril Lavigne, Barenaked Ladies, Dave Matthews Band, and Sheryl Crow, among others.

Barnett is owner of Boston-based Right Arm Resource, an independent radio promoter that's hired by record labels to persuade radio disk jockeys to play songs recorded by their artists. When Barnett agrees to promote a record—and he doesn't agree to do this for every song he's asked to represent—he gets on the phone and goes down the list of AAA stations around the country, negotiating and cajoling and convincing radio music and program directors to play *his* song.

Barnett agrees it sounds like a sweet gig—he's his own boss, doing what he loves, and getting paid extremely well for it—but he's also quick to point out that he paid his dues in the industry before being able to go out on his own.

Although he majored in advertising, Barnett became enamored of radio broadcasting while attending Emerson College in Boston and graduated with a minor in radio. "Although I followed my major and went into advertising as a copy writer, I got pretty bored pretty quickly," he recalls. "I realized that what I really wanted was to work in the music business." He spent the next year-and-a-half trying to break in. "I sent out more than 120 resumes," he says, "and when

I wasn't getting called back, did a bunch of research and called up prominent members of the community and asked for informational interviews." He eventually began to land some interviews, and on his third try for a job at A&M Records in Los Angeles, landed one in promotions. He lasted two years at A&M before the label went through a major restructuring. Says Barnett, "They let go of my boss, who had been with the company for 22 years, so I saw the writing on the wall and began looking for a new job."

Barnett found one running promotions at Hybrid Recordings in New York and continued to build up his contacts at radio stations around the country. "I really wanted to hang my shingle out, but I wasn't quite ready," he says. "The relationships weren't quite in place." He then took a job at an independent promoter, Outsource Music, where he spent the next four years. In 2003, he did a two-year stint with Vector Promotion, and finally, in 2005, he formed Right Arm Resource and became his own boss. Says Barnett, "It was the best move I've ever made."

He's doing so well and has earned such a name for himself that today he turns down as many clients as he takes on. His advice to would-be entrepreneurs trying to break into a hard-to-penetrate field: "Research it through; talk to as many people as will talk to you; and be prepared to pay your dues." And, he adds, always be nice to the receptionist, "because they're the real gatekeepers."

sample form: **Balance Sheet**

BALANCE SHEET

For ComputerEase, Inc.

For Year Ending: December 31, 2009

ASSETS

Current Assets

Cash	$35,600	
Accounts receivable	17,200	
Inventory	2,100	
Prepaid expenses	780	
Total Current Assets		**$55,680**

Fixed Assets

Land	0	
Buildings	0	
Furniture/equipment	10,000	
Less accumulated depreciation	(2,000)	
Total Fixed Assets		**$8,000**
Other Assets		**0**
TOTAL ASSETS		**$63,680**

LIABILITIES

Current Liabilities

Accounts payable	8,675	
Accrued payroll	3,050	
Taxes payable	295	
Short-term notes payable	5,000	
Total Current Liabilities		**$17,020**

Long-Term Liabilities

Long-term notes payable	15,000	
Total Long-Term Liabilities		**$15,000**

Net Worth

Paid-in capital	31,660	
Retained earnings	0	
Total Net Worth		**$31,660**
TOTAL LIABILITIES AND NET WORTH		**$63,680**

sample form: **Income Statement**

INCOME STATEMENT

Year: 2009 (Actual through 8/31/09, projected 9-12/09)

	Jan	Feb	Mar	Apr	May
Income					
Gross Sales	$0	$2,000	$2,000	$5,000	$12,000
(Sales commissions)	0	0	0	0	350
(Returns and allowances)	0	0	0	0	0
Net Sales	0	2,000	2,000	5,000	11,650
(Cost of Goods)	0	324	324	812	1,946
GROSS PROFIT	0	1,676	1,676	4,188	9,704
OPERATING EXPENSES					
General and Administrative Expenses					
Salaries and wages	2,500	3,700	5,700	6,200	7,700
Employee benefits	275	275	510	510	510
Payroll taxes	210	310	505	505	505
Professional services	2,500	250	2,000	200	200
Rent	0	0	0	0	0
Maintenance	0	0	0	0	0
Equipment rental	250	250	250	250	250
Furniture and equipment purchase	0	0	0	410	0
Depreciation and amortization	2,000	0	0	0	0
Insurance	400	0	0	200	0
Interest expenses	0	125	125	125	125
Utilities	250	60	125	210	160
Telephone service	100	50	100	100	120
Office supplies	450	125	215	185	125
Postage and shipping	210	80	310	65	450
Marketing and advertising	3,200	1,800	4,000	1,500	1,500
Travel	55	150	100	150	0
Entertainment	0	0	110	320	195
Technology	3,000	0	0	0	0
TOTAL OPERATING EXPENSES	15,400	7,175	14,050	10,930	11,840
Net Income before taxes	(15,400)	(5,499)	(12,374)	(6,742)	(2,136)
Taxes on income	0	0	0	0	0
NET PROFIT AFTER TAXES	(15,400)	(5,499)	(12,374)	(6,742)	(2,136)

June	July	Aug	Sep	Oct	Nov	Dec	TOTAL
$16,000	**$20,500**	**$28,000**	**$34,200**	**$41,800**	**$50,000**	**$21,500**	**$233,000**
750	775	1,235	1,500	1,850	2,200	950	$9,610
0	0	0	0	0	0	0	$0
15,250	**19,725**	**26,765**	**32,700**	**39,950**	**47,800**	**20,550**	**$223,390**
2,595	3,449	4,741	5,691	6,926	8,400	3,662	$38,870
12,655	**16,276**	**22,024**	**27,009**	**33,024**	**39,400**	**16,888**	**$184,520**
8,400	6,300	9,900	9,100	10,100	11,100	8,300	**$89,000**
510	510	700	700	700	700	700	**$6,600**
505	505	610	610	610	610	610	**$6,095**
200	200	1,200	200	200	200	200	**$7,550**
0	0	2,100	2,100	2,100	2,100	2,100	**$10,500**
0	0	120	120	120	120	120	**$600**
250	250	2,000	2,000	2,000	2,000	2,000	**$11,750**
0	0	0	0	0	0	0	**$410**
0	0	0	0	0	0	0	**$2,000**
0	200	1,000	350	550	350	350	**$3,400**
125	125	125	125	125	125	125	**$1,375**
200	175	260	220	210	180	150	**$2,200**
130	100	250	200	200	200	200	**$1,750**
85	110	1,100	250	250	250	250	**$3,395**
85	260	60	410	75	300	200	**$2,505**
300	1,500	1,750	2,000	250	2,000	250	**$20,050**
25	100	0	150	150	150	150	**$1,180**
200	75	85	50	50	50	50	**$1,185**
3,000	0	0	0	0	0	0	**$6,000**
14,015	**10,410**	**21,260**	**18,585**	**17,690**	**20,435**	**15,755**	**$177,545**
(1,360)	**5,866**	**764**	**8,424**	**15,334**	**18,965**	**1,133**	**$6,975**
0	0	0	0	0	0	1,046	**$1,046**
(1,360)	**5,866**	**764**	**8,424**	**15,334**	**18,965**	**87**	**$5,929**

15

Financing

Financing refers to how you will fund, or pay for, your business. Sometimes you may be able to start and expand a business simply from the money you make from sales—this is called "bootstrapping." But often, you'll need some money to get started—even if it's just to purchase a laptop and some software—and it's typical to need money, or capital, to grow your business substantially.

Complete the worksheets in Chapter 14 to come up with your startup and operating costs. It's a good idea to have at least six months of cash to cover your operating costs at any one time due to cash flow issues. Your next step is to determine what kind of funding you would like to go for.

What to Look for in Financing

Not all money is equal. When you start to look for financing, you might imagine that you'll take any money you can find, but you should exercise care. Various sources of funding require different amounts of money or other security or benefits in return for helping fund your business. They have varying levels of sophistication and comfort with risk, and provide you with significantly different auxiliary benefits and disadvantages.

Whose money do you want? As you begin your search for financing, first stop and ask yourself these questions:

- Are you willing to give up some amount of ownership of your company?

- Are you willing to have debt that you have to repay even if your business fails?

- Are you willing to risk your personal property or other assets?

- How much control of the direction and operation of your company are you willing to give up?

- What help do you want from a funder besides money?

- How fast do you want to grow?

- How big do you want your company to be?

- What do you see as the long-term relationship between you and your funding source?

Keep in mind that you are going to have an ongoing relationship with your money source; make sure it is someone you can live with.

Being Self-Sufficient

You might be the best source of funding for your business—through personal savings (a common source of money) or by keeping your day job while getting your entrepreneurial venture off the ground. The advantages of doing things this way are that you retain absolute control of your business and all of the profits of your venture belong to you alone. You don't owe anyone a lot of money, and you're not running up a balance on your credit cards.

The disadvantage of this approach is that your growth is likely to be slow; you'll often be short of funds; and you may use up all of your personal savings. If you don't have sufficient savings—or don't want to use them up—you have two major types of funding options:

- **Debt.** Where you borrow money or use credit and almost always have to pay it back—even if the company fails.

- **Equity.** Where you give up some of the ownership of the company in return for cash.

Debt Financing

Debt financing is exactly what it sounds like: you borrow money, which you will then have to repay to a person or institution such as a bank. Typically, interest is charged, and regular payments are required.

Debt financing gives you the advantage of retaining complete ownership of your business. You keep control of all of the eventual profits. You borrow a specific amount, and you have to repay only that amount plus interest, regardless of how profitable your company becomes. Your lender doesn't share in your profits.

There are several types of debt financing:

- **Home equity lines of credit.** Equity in homes is the primary source of wealth for Americans. Many entrepreneurs tap into this wealth to fund their ventures. If you have a great deal of equity in your home, this may be the easiest and least expensive money to get; however, borrowing against your home also means that you could lose your house if your company fails.

- **Bank loans.** Loans from banks and other lending institutions are a great source of financing for businesses. Unfortunately, they can be difficult for new businesses to secure. Many banks will only finance businesses that have been in operation more than three years, and very small businesses may face difficulties at any time. Credit unions may be somewhat more lenient than banks.

- **Credit cards.** Credit cards are probably the No. 1 way most people in the United States fund their business startups. However, you should only use these for very short-term financing—ideally when you know money is coming in—because interest rates on cash advances are extremely high. Credit cards are not recommended for long-term financing because of the hefty debt burden their use places on fledgling companies.

- **Loans from family and friends.** This is a very common way to finance a new business; however, it's also one that can lead to personal complications. You're likely to be nervous about losing money entrusted to you by people with whom you have a personal connection. The prospect of failure thus creates more stress on the already challenging process of starting a business. However, this may be your best—or only—bet for starting your business.

- **Bank lines of credit.** A line of credit is a good way to finance short-term (less than one-year) cash flow problems. You can borrow up to a certain amount of money—typically at better interest rates than credit cards—but you have to pay it all back within a year.

Sources of Debt Financing

	WHAT THEY LOOK FOR	ADVANTAGES	DISADVANTAGES
Banks and lending institutions	Ability to repay; collateral; steady current income from business.	No profit sharing; no obligation for ongoing relationship after repayment; definite preset amount to repay. **Best for:** Established companies needing funding for specific activities; short-term cash flow problems.	Difficult to secure for new businesses; must often risk personal assets; same financial obligation regardless of business' income. **Worst for:** Ongoing operational expenses; new companies with relatively inexperienced management.
Loans from family or friends	Likelihood of repayment; your personal character; other personal considerations.	Easier to secure than institutional loans; specific amount to repay; no profit sharing. **Best for:** Companies with no other option; companies with secure future.	Can jeopardize personal relationships; unsophisticated lender often nervous about money; probably no professional expertise; often get unsolicited advice and frequent queries. **Worst for:** Very risky enterprises; entrepreneurs with difficult family circumstances.
Cash advance on personal credit cards	Ability to repay.	Relatively easy to secure. **Best for:** Businesses requiring small amounts of money for a limited time; short-term cash-flow problems.	High interest rates; limited amount of money; ties up and risks personal credit. **Worst for:** Ongoing, long-term financing.

Investors, or Equity Financing

Equity financing allows you to avoid the personal risk of taking on debt. Instead of committing to repay a specific amount of money, you instead give the investor a piece of the eventual profits in return for their money. This takes the form of stock in the company or a percentage of ownership. If your company is very successful, an equity investor may end up receiving many times the amount originally invested.

However, if the company fails to produce sufficient profits, these investors may never get their money back. Thus, equity investors often want to participate in decision-making to ensure that the company operates in a manner that will produce profits. They may take seats on your board of directors or even play an active role in management. In some cases, you may have to give up so much equity that others actually have controlling interest in your company.

■ **Angels.** A frequent source of capital for entrepreneurial companies is the private, or "angel," investor. Private investors are usually well-to-do individuals seeking investments that provide more personal satisfaction and the potential of greater financial reward than are offered by conventional investments such as stocks and bonds. Private investors can be an excellent source of financing.

They often have business or industry experience that you can call on to help you as you develop your company.

■ **Venture capitalists.** As you search for money, you will frequently hear the term *venture capitalist.* True venture capital firms are among the most sophisticated investors available, typically providing an entrepreneur with more than money. Their knowledge, experience, and connections may prove to be as important to your company as the dollars they bring. However, venture capital firms are looking for big investments and big returns. They're rarely appropriate for companies seeking less than a few million dollars in financing.

■ **Family and friends.** Getting family or friends to invest in your business encompasses most of the same benefits and pitfalls of borrowing from family and friends: These people are the most likely to be enthusiastic and supportive of your endeavor as well as the easiest to reach. However, they're also the least likely to understand if your business fails. And indeed the personal relationship adds another layer of stress. One other issue with using friends and family as investors is that they may not understand that they won't get their money back if you're not profitable.

Find an Angel Investor

There's a huge amount of money available from angel investors for high-growth businesses. In 2005, these private investors contributed more than $23 billion to a range of businesses. To learn more about how to find and attract money from angels, read The Planning Shop's *Finding an Angel Investor In A Day,* available from bookstores or at www.planningshop.com.

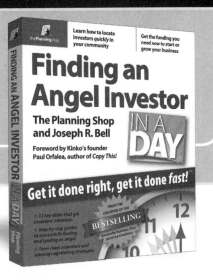

Sources of Equity Financing

	WHAT THEY LOOK FOR	ADVANTAGES	DISADVANTAGES
Venture capitalists	Businesses in their area of interest; companies that can grow to significant size; experienced management; new technology.	Large sums available; sophisticated investor familiar with industry; can bring expertise, connections, and future funding; understand business setbacks and capital risk. *Best for:* Potentially large companies; sophisticated entrepreneur or industry wizard.	Difficult to secure; must have exit possibilities in three to seven years; take substantial, perhaps controlling, equity in company. *Worst for:* Small and medium-size businesses; inexperienced entrepreneurs.
Private, or "angel," investors	Good business opportunities with better potential rewards than conventional investments such as the stock market; appealing concept.	May fund small and medium-size businesses; easier to secure than professional venture capital or bank loans. *Best for:* Smaller companies; those able to locate relatively sophisticated or capable investor; those with appealing business concept.	Often unsophisticated, nervous investor; take equity in company; may want involvement in decisions without having necessary expertise; long-term relationship; expects profits soon. *Worst for:* Companies requiring long development time before profitability; companies needing additional business expertise.
Investment from family and friends	Interest in you and your business concept; chance to make money.	Easier to secure than other investors; no set amount to repay. *Best for:* Companies with no other options; entrepreneurs having friends or relatives with significant business or industry expertise.	Jeopardizes personal relationships; long-term involvement; unsophisticated, nervous investor; makes friend or relative a decision maker in your business; doesn't understand risk. *Worst for:* Very risky enterprises; companies requiring long development time before profitability.

chapter 16

Your Business Plan

If you decide you need to raise money from lenders or investors, you'll need a business plan that tells people precisely what it is they're funding. Few people or businesses will invest or loan money to someone without seeing and taking the time to fully analyze the nature of the business, the strategy for growth, and the plan for operations. And that's what a business plan is.

But don't think of your business plan as simply a document to present to others. The ultimate purpose of developing a business plan is to have a successful business. Thus, it is the planning process rather than the written plan itself that is usually most valuable to a business. Creating the business plan provides a means of crystallizing your ideas and challenging your assumptions. The following factors play the biggest part in business success, so it's key that you use them to guide your planning and thinking:

- **Formulate the business concept.** Your business concept is about meeting needs. In fact, meeting needs is the basis of all business. You can devise a wonderful new machine, but if it doesn't address some real and important need or desire, people won't buy it, and your business will fail. Your business plan should clearly and succinctly lay out your business concept and explain how it will offer the market something it will be unable to resist.

- **Understand the market.** It's not enough to have a great idea or a new invention as the basis of your business. You must also have a market that is sufficiently large, accessible, and responsive. If your market isn't large enough, you can't succeed. If it's too large, you won't be able to reach it efficiently. If it isn't ready for you, your business will fail, no matter how good your concept. Your business plan must contain an overview of the market you intend to enter and an explanation of why it's ripe for receiving your product or service.

- **Investigate industry health and trends.** Generally, your company is subject to the same conditions that affect your overall industry. If consumer spending declines nationally, there's a good chance your retail business—whether it's a neighborhood boutique or an online shopping mall—will also experience poor sales. Thus, as you develop your plan, you need to respond to industry-wide factors that will affect your own company's performance. Although it's certainly possible to make money in an industry that is experiencing hard times, you can only do so if you make a conscious effort to position your company appropriately. For example, if you plan to start a construction business and the number of new-home starts is down, you may want to target the remodeling market or the commercial real estate market rather than the new-home construction market. But you need to be aware of industry conditions.

■ **Create a consistent business focus and clear strategic position.** Key to creating any successful business is developing a clear strategic position that differentiates you from your competition—and then maintaining focus on that position. All too often businesses fail because management loses sight of the central character of the enterprise. Defining a clear strategic position enables you to capture a particular place in the market and distinguish yourself from your competitors. Different companies may sell a similar product, but each may have a very different sense of what its business is really all about.

■ **Hire capable management.** Perhaps more than any other factor, competent management stands out as the most important ingredient in business success. The people in key positions are crucial in determining the health and viability of your business. Moreover, because of the importance of capable management to business success, many investors and venture capital firms place the single greatest emphasis on this factor when evaluating business plans and deciding on loans or investments. They'll review the management section of a business plan with special scrutiny. Your business plan must inspire confidence in the capabilities of your management, and you should put your management team together carefully.

■ **Attract, motivate, and retain employees.** A company is only as good as its people. The ability to find, attract, and retain outstanding employees and managers is crucial to a company's long-term viability and competitiveness. Demographic trends indicate a tight labor market in the United States well through the early part of the 21st century. This means that companies will have a difficult time competing for the relatively limited number of outstanding job applicants. Your company's reputation for treating employees well directly enhances both the number and the quality of job applicants and your company's ability to retain employees once hired.

■ **Take control of your finances.** Key to any business is the way it handles money. Not fully anticipating startup costs can immediately place impossible pressures on a new business. And poor cash flow management can bring down even a seemingly thriving enterprise. Things always take longer and cost more than anticipated. Build financial cushions into your plan to allow for unanticipated expenses and delays.

■ **Anticipate and adapt to change.** Change is inevitable, and the rate of change gets ever faster. In today's world, your company needs to anticipate and respond to change quickly, and train its employees to

Writing a Business Plan

A business plan outlines your business strategy and describes your competition, market, staffing, future developments, and the steps necessary to achieve your results. If you do not yet have a business plan, it's time to develop one. The Planning Shop has two books to help you do this:

▪ *The Successful Business Plan: Secrets & Strategies*, and its accompanying Electronic Financial Worksheets, is recommended if you're starting a new business—especially in a field that's new to you—or are seeking $10,000 or more in financing (particularly from investors).

▪ *Business Plan In A Day*, which can also be used with the Electronic Financial Worksheets, is helpful for established businesses seeking bank loans, simple startup businesses, or those seeking less than $10,000 in financing.

Both books are available at bookstores or online at www.planningshop.com.

be adaptable. Companies that are nimble and able to quickly evaluate and respond to changing conditions are most likely to be successful.

■ **Emphasize company values and integrity.** Every company must make money. You can't stay in business unless you eventually earn a profit. However, studies of business success have shown that companies that emphasize goals in addition to making money succeed better and survive longer than companies whose sole motivation is monetary.

As you develop your business plan, keep in mind those values you wish to characterize the company you are creating or expanding. These values can be aimed externally, at achieving some business, social, or environmental goal, or they can be aimed internally, at achieving a certain type of workplace or quality of product or service, or both.

Components of a Business Plan

When you prepare a business plan, be sure it contains all of the following sections:

■ **Executive summary.** This is the most important portion of your business plan if you're seeking financing. Only a clear, concise, and compelling condensation of your business right up front will persuade readers to wade through the rest of your plan. No matter how beneficial your product, how lucrative your market, or how innovative your manufacturing techniques, it is your executive summary alone that persuades a reader to spend the time to find out about your product, market, and techniques.

■ **Company description.** Before you can discuss the more complex aspects of your business and the meatier sections of your business plan, such as marketing strategy or new technology, you must first describe the basic details of your business. The object of this section is to convey information such as your legal status, ownership, products or services, company mission, and milestones achieved to date.

■ **Industry analysis and trends.** No company operates in a vacuum. Every business is part of a larger, overall industry: the forces that affect your industry as a whole will inevitably affect your business as well. Evaluating your industry increases your own knowledge of the factors that contribute to your company's success and shows potential investors that you understand external business conditions.

■ **Target market.** Essential to business success is a thorough understanding of your customers. After all, if you don't know who your customers are, how will you be able to assess whether you're meeting their needs? Since success depends on your being able to meet customers' needs and desires, you must know who your customers are, what they want, how they behave, and what they can afford. Moreover, if you're using your business plan to secure funding, defining the nature and size of your market is critical. Many investors look for companies that are aimed at substantial-size markets and are market driven. In other words, they seek to fund companies whose orientation is shaped by the demands and trends of the marketplace rather than the inherent characteristics of a particular product or service.

■ **Competition.** Famed baseball player Satchel Paige used to say, "Don't look back; someone may be gaining on you." But in business it's imperative to see who's gaining on you. It is far better to know what you're up against than to be surprised when your sales suddenly disappear to an unexpected competitor. If you think you have no competitors—that the product or service you are offering is utterly unique—make no mistake about it, you're wrong! Thus, it's important, first of all, to be able to recognize that you have competition (even if it's not direct) and then be able to identify who it is. Investors like this, because it shows a sophisticated, rather than naïve, view of the marketplace.

■ **Strategic position and risk assessment.** In today's highly competitive and constantly changing business environment, it's no longer enough just to know *how* to run a business; you also have to know *what* business you're really running. While you must, of course, attend to the basics of operating your business, you also have to see exactly where you stand in the marketplace, what makes you compelling to customers, and what advantages you have over the competition. You need a clearly defined strategic position.

Presenting to Investors and Lenders

Once you begin to circulate your business plan to potential funders, you will inevitably begin to worry about the confidentiality of your information. Obviously, you don't want your competitors, or potential competitors, to know you strategy and technology. However, many professional investors—particularly venture capitalists and bankers—do not sign non-disclosure agreements (NDAs). They see so many plans in so many related industries that they would inevitably have the possibility of a conflict. But it is part of their business to respect the confidentiality of entrepreneurs.

Your plan should look as good as the business really is. It's a shame to have an outstanding business overlooked or turned down by investors because the plan doesn't represent the company well. You may want to use the services of a professional writer to help make your language clearer or a graphic designer to help you lay out your plan or create graphs and charts to enhance its impact—especially if you're seeking large sums of money (say, more than a million dollars)

For most sophisticated investors, such as venture capitalists, you will want to—or need to—prepare a computer slide presentation, outlining the highlights of your business plan, especially if you are invited to meet with them. A computer slide presentation is an excellent way of conveying the most important aspects of your business in a short time. The most common software used to prepare such presentations is Microsoft's PowerPoint.

The key points an investor will want to learn from your presentation are likely to be:

- ☐ The business concept

- ☐ The size and nature of the market

- ☐ What's happening with the competition

- ☐ What kind of growth you project

- ☐ Who's on your team

■ **Marketing plan and sales strategy.** You have to have customers to stay in business: it's the most basic business truth. That's why an effective marketing plan to communicate with, motivate, and secure customers is vital for your company's success. Since reaching customers costs money, and money is always limited, your marketing strategy must be carefully and thoughtfully designed. If you are developing a business plan to seek outside funding, remember that many investors read the marketing plan portion closely. They want to know you have a realistic and price-conscious strategy to get your product or service into the hands of customers. In your marketing plan, you define what your overall strategy will be to reach potential customers, the marketing vehicles you choose (see Chapter 18), and your budget.

- **Operations.** How are you actually going to run your business? The operations section of your business plan is where you begin to explain the day-to-day functions of your company. This is where you translate your theories into practice by specifying where you will be located, who your suppliers will be, and so on.

- **Management and organization.** People are the heart of every business. Overwhelmingly, the quality of the people determines the success of the business. Many investors base their investment choices entirely on the strength of the people involved in the enterprise. They know that the experience, skills, and personalities of the management team have a greater impact on the long-term fortunes of the company than the product or service provided.

- **Community involvement and social responsibility.** As you start your business, you have many goals. You're focused on developing your business concept, getting funded, and making money. What does social responsibility have to do with these? Just as individuals have responsibilities to their communities, companies have responsibilities and obligations to society at large. Moreover, being socially responsible is part of the overall health of your company. It establishes your company's values and fosters your corporate culture. Businesses that act with integrity and honesty are more likely to have their employees act with integrity and honesty toward the company and their fellow workers. Being a good corporate citizen makes it less likely that your company will get in trouble with regulatory agencies and taxing authorities or face lawsuits or fines.

- **Development, milestones, and exit plan.** If a business plan serves as a roadmap for your company, then to use it properly you need a sense of your ultimate destination. What do you want your business to look like in three, five, or seven years? You can't hope to just stumble across success; you have to figure out how to get there. One of the most important aspects of the business planning process, therefore, is the examination of your long-term goal. Moreover, in the course of your planning process you will find it useful to establish markers—milestones—to keep you on track. By developing specific objectives, you will have signposts to measure progress along the way.

- **Detailed financials.** Every business decision leads to a number, and taken together, these numbers form the basis of your financial forms. But numbers themselves are not decisions. You cannot pull a number out of thin air because the financial forms you are completing call for a specific figure on a specific line. Rather, your numbers should always be the result of careful planning.

Crafting a Winning Presentation

If you're new to presenting or could use a few tips on how to improve the organization, content, and delivery of your presentation, as well as how to create more interesting PowerPoint presentations, check out The Planning Shop's *Winning Presentation In A Day*, available at bookstores or online at www.planningshop.com.

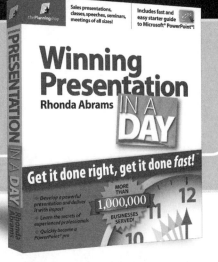

Part Three:
Marketing, Pricing, and Sales

Marketing

Marketing consists of all those activities you undertake to make potential customers or clients aware of you and your products or services. If you put up a sign with your business name, send a brochure to potential customers, or place an advertisement in a magazine, that's marketing. If you run ads alongside online search engine results or on a social networking site, that's marketing. Likewise, if you network at local chapter meetings of an industry association, donate to a local public radio station, or perform volunteer work in your community, that's marketing as well. Anything that gets your business' name out into the world—and promotes the advantages of buying from you—falls into this category.

Marketing is a critically important business function, so having a well-thought-out marketing plan is vital. After all, if no one knows about you, no one can buy from you. To stay in business, you need customers. And since reaching customers costs money, and money is always limited, your marketing strategy must be carefully and thoughtfully designed.

What's more, effective marketing doesn't just increase the chance that customers will think about you, it encourages them to think about you in a particular way—the way *you* choose. This is your marketing "message," and it's vitally important to your marketing efforts.

Marketing vs. Sales

Although the two are often confused, marketing is quite distinct from sales. Marketing is designed to increase customer awareness of your business and service, and communicate the benefits and advantages of what you offer—your marketing message. It includes activities such as advertising, branding (think of McDonalds, Nike, Coke, Nintendo, and Verizon), direct marketing (all those cards and catalogs your receive in the mail), online marketing, and public relations, as well as numerous other activities, including networking, which is a fancy term for meeting potential customers and referral sources through informal activities, such as joining organizations, attending industry events, or taking people to lunch. In smaller companies, networking may be the major marketing activity.

Sales, on the other hand, are direct actions you take to secure customer orders. The term *sales* encompasses face-to-face sales (when a salesperson meets with customers to tell them about the company and asks them to commit to buying their product or service), online sales, and cold calling (or telemarketing), which is when a sales person calls potential customers, pitches the offering, and asks for an order.

Sometimes the line between marketing and sales can be blurred. For example, if you place a coupon in a local paper, is this marketing or sales or some hybrid of the two? Likewise, if you put on a special promotion where existing customers get discounts or rebates by recommending you to new customers, it can be difficult to separate marketing from sales. For the most part, however, anything that spreads the word about your company, products, or services can be categorized as marketing, whereas anything that causes your cash register to go ka-ching is sales.

What Creates Effective Marketing?

A successful marketing strategy possesses three key attributes: it fits your target market; it repeats your name and message frequently; and it gives you a return on investment (ROI) from your marketing efforts.

- **Fit to market.** You have to reach the right people with your marketing. No matter how well, or how many times, you explain why your product or service is the best, if your message isn't reaching the right eyes and ears, your marketing efforts will be in vain. If you're selling software programs that help businesses track sales, but you're not reaching the key decision maker, your marketing won't be effective. Although this sounds obvious, many businesses spend money—a lot of it—on marketing without considering who's paying attention.

- **Repetition.** You might be surprised to learn how many times a potential customer needs to be exposed to a company's name and marketing message before it sinks in—as many as nine or ten times, by some accounts. This is why you see the same ads again and again. You have to repeat the same message to the same market over and over and over and over. …

- **Return on investment.** If you're not careful, marketing can be a big hole into which you pour cash without getting much of a return. Although it might seem like a great idea to buy a full-page ad in the *New York Times*, the cost could outweigh the benefits you would receive, based on who your target market is. If you have limited resources—and most startup companies do—you'll have to plan and analyze the best places to put your marketing dollars so they'll reap the greatest reward.

Your Marketing Message

Every business sends a message through its marketing. Your message is based on the strategic position your company stakes out for itself, such as "low-price leader" or "one-day service." Your message could also specify a particular market niche: "Specialists in estate planning," for example, or "Software for residential architects."

Most marketing strategists agree that people buy *benefits*, not *features*. Customers are more concerned about how a purchase will affect their lives than about how the company achieved those results. No matter how cool you think your new improved business process is, your marketing message should concentrate on the *benefits* customers receive.

What messages do you send customers to motivate them to purchase your products or service? Traditional marketing experts emphasize including the elements known as the "Four P's" for influencing customers to buy:

- **Product.** The tangible product or service itself.

- **Price.** The cost advantage of buying the product.

- **Place.** The convenience and attributes of the location where the product or service will be acquired.

- **Promotion.** The amount and nature of the marketing activities.

But because these elements leave a lot out of the marketing picture—especially as customers look for products or services not just to fill an immediate need but to enhance their overall sense of well-being—you can take a more customer-centric approach to thinking about marketing through the following categories:

- **Function.** How does the product or service meet customers' concrete needs?

- **Finances.** How will the purchase affect your customers' overall financial situation? This is not just about the price of the product or service, but about the other savings it will engender and the increased productivity that will result.

- **Freedom.** How convenient is it for customers to purchase and use the product or service? How will they gain more time and less worry in other aspects of their lives?

- **Feelings.** How does the product or service make customers feel about themselves, and how does it affect and relate to their self-image? Do they like and respect the salesperson and the company?

- **Future.** How will they deal with the product or service and company over time? Will support and service be available? How will the product or service affect their lives in coming years, and will they have an increased sense of security about the future?

Customers, of course, would like to receive benefits in all of these areas, and you should be aware of how your product or service fulfills the entire range of their needs. But your primary message must concentrate on one or two of these benefits that can effectively motivate your customers.

You must be able to succinctly convey the benefits of your product or service in a brief message. For instance, a mobile dog grooming service might say, "Saves you time and money," or a musical group could indicate the following in its marketing material: "You have enough things to worry about when planning your big event. Don't let your musicians be one of them: we'll show up on time, play great, and look good!"

worksheet: Your Marketing Message

In the space below, write a brief message that explains the benefit to the customer of buying or using your product or service.

_____
_____
_____
_____
_____
_____
_____
_____
_____
_____
_____
_____
_____
_____
_____
_____

chapter 18

Your Marketing Vehicles and Tactics

It's not enough to simply have an effective marketing message. You also need to find the right vehicle or tactics to spread it. This means choosing the right way to reach the right people at a time when they will pay attention and take actions that result in sales. This can be challenging. Many entrepreneurs spend a great deal of money experimenting before they find the right marketing vehicles for their businesses. And it's not just one—most companies use a number of different vehicles simultaneously.

Search Engine Marketing

One marketing vehicle that has seen an explosion in growth is online search engine–based advertising—also referred to as *search engine marketing,* or SEM. Search engine-based advertising, as the name implies, is based on the results of Internet searches that people perform using Google, Yahoo, Microsoft, and other search technology. The way it works is very straightforward: businesses simply buy keywords and phrases that are relevant to their products or services. For example, an organic caterer in the Atlanta area could buy the phrase "organic catering Atlanta" and other similar phrases such as "organic party planning Atlanta" or "fresh catering Georgia." Then, anytime someone typed those words into the search engine, up would pop that catering company's ad. The reason SEM makes such a great marketing vehicle is that it sends marketing messages to people who are searching for products or services right at the point when they're ready to make a purchasing decision. Thus, as a marketing vehicle it represents a good fit both for finding the right people and getting to them at the right point in the buying cycle.

Of course it takes some work to find the right words to make your ad come up high in search engine results. If you don't have a very specific product or service, or if a lot of competition exists for the key words you want, you may end up paying a lot for every person who "clicks through" an online ad to get to your website.

Traditional Advertising

Traditional advertising—that is, advertising that appears in the places you've been seeing and hearing ads for most of your life, namely newspapers, magazines, radio, and TV—is effective at reaching both a large mainstream audience and a very targeted selection of consumers. It can put your company, product, or service in front of a sizable audience while they're reading the news, listening to a talk show, or watching their favorite programs on TV or cable. It can also bring your message to a specific group as they read a magazine or watch a show about their hobby, profession, industry, or special interest.

To advertise effectively in these traditional venues, you need to find out which media attract the attention of your target market—that is, what sections of the newspaper they read, what magazines they subscribe to, what radio stations and programs they listen to, and what channels their TVs are tuned to—and then be present there as often as your company can afford. (For more on how to find your target market, see the "Media Kits" sidebar, page below.)

Frequently, repeating an advertisement with the same message is the key to success. Most people need to see or hear an ad a minimum of three to five times before they remember it. Repetition helps people remember your company, product, or service, whether your message is a general introduction to a new company or a specific announcement about a grand opening, a new product, or a sale. Say you've just opened a new jazz club. Buying an advertising spot every half-hour during the local jazz radio station's drive-home commute hours for the next few months guarantees that a segment of the population very likely to be interested in your club is going to hear the ad. If they don't hear it one day, or week, or month, they will hear it the next.

There are a number of advertising options to suit any budget or goal.

Print

Advertising in print—in newspapers, magazines, or newsletters—is a time-honored method of marketing. Some benefits of print advertising include:

- **Shelf life.** A radio or TV ad lasts for a minute or less, and then is gone. A print publication on the other hand can stay around for days, weeks, even months, offering more opportunities for a customer to see an ad.

- **Pass-along readership.** People share print publications with others, who may also be your target customers. "Pass-along readers" expand an ad's reach and increase your exposure.

- **More specific audience.** In general, it's easier to target your customer using print publications. This is particularly true if you advertise in magazines geared toward readers with special interests (like fashion, yoga, or home improvement) or those with "controlled circulation," which are distributed only to a highly targeted list of readers (such as doctors, executives, or human resources professionals).

Media Kits: Your Key to Customers

The best way to find out where the eyes and ears of your target audience are pointed is to ask for media kits from the various publications, radio stations, and channels you think they might be interested in. Media kits are materials produced by publishers and broadcasters that describe the demographics—common characteristics such as age, gender, income, and ethnicity—of their audience. (Media kits also include information about how much a publisher or broadcaster charges for the different advertising opportunities they offer.) The demographic data available is quite specific, often including Zip codes, age, job titles, income, interests, education, and other relevant information about their audience. You'll get a much clearer picture of who, exactly, is watching, listening to, or reading a particular publication or station by studying its media kit. This information will help you determine if the publication or station actually attracts or "reaches" the kind of people you're looking for. Your ads will be most effective when you make the right match between what you're promoting and whom you're promoting it to.

Comparing Print Media

PUBLICATION TYPE	COST	BENEFITS	CHALLENGES	BEST FOR	TIPS FOR EFFECTIVENESS
Newsletter	$	Tightly focused target readership; usually inexpensive to place an ad	Low circulation; exposed to fewer numbers	Targeting a particular community or group	Take advantage of low price to run larger ads; repeat often
Community Newspaper	$–$$	Reaches a general group of local readers; inexpensive	Limited reach; won't be read by potential customers not living in the area	Targeting an audience who live in your immediate business area	Feature larger, well-placed ads; appeal to local concerns
Regional Newspaper	$$–$$$	Reaches a larger group of prospective mainstream customers in your general region	More expensive than community papers; advertising here may be overkill if you're trying to attract a very local audience	Advertising to a general regional audience	If you can't afford big ads, advertise frequently in sections your target customers are likely to read
Regional Business Paper	$$–$$$	Reaches local and regional readers with common business interests	Can be costly, and you'll be vying for placement with savvy business advertisers	Targeting a regional business-to-business market and business executives in general	Advertise frequently, even if your ad is small, and try for placement near content related to your business offering
National Newspaper	$$$–$$$$	Reaches a very broad national audience	Ad space is very expensive; may be overkill for reaching your target customers	Getting your message out to as many people as possible	If you have the budget to advertise here, try to place your ads near content related to your business
Regional Magazine	$$$	Reaches targeted subscribers in a particular area; sometimes these magazines appeal to residents or business people with particular common interests	Ads can be expensive, and there tend to be a good number of these competing with each other for the same readership	Targeting a regional audience, especially when the magazines serves area readers with special interests	Advertise in a special-interest regional magazine, or a section of the magazine that will appeal to your prospective customers
National Magazine	$$$$	Reaches the widest possible mainstream audience or national audiences with special lifestyle interests and hobbies	Probably the most expensive print ads available	Targeting either a huge mainstream audience, or a large audience of readers with particular lifestyles and interests.	Unless you have a huge budget, do small, regular ads as close as possible to a content area that might interest your customers

Cost Key* $: Relatively Inexpensive $$: Moderately Expensive $$$: Fairly Expensive $$$$: Expensive

* These symbols represent general rate estimations. Ad rates will vary by circulation of publication; quality of publication; and region, target market, and type of audience. A four-color newsletter aimed at physicians will likely command higher ad rates than a black-and-white community newsletter.

Newsletters

Although newspapers and magazines are the print media that are likely to come to mind immediately, print newsletters also offer excellent opportunities to reach an extremely targeted audience—often at a very low price. Newsletters are small print publications—generally four, eight, or 16 pages long—that provide news updates to a defined niche of people who share a common location, profession, or interest. If you rely on local customers, community newsletters can serve as an excellent place to advertise your business. Likewise, newsletters for professional groups or industry associations can work well if your target customers are associated with specific businesses. A newsletter's readership is generally smaller than that of most newspapers and magazines, but because newsletters reach such a specific audience, you can be sure that your advertisements will reach the eyes of those most interested in what you have to offer.

Radio

Like magazines, radio stations cater to specific audience segments—usually in particular geographical areas—and tailor their content to reach them. This makes them ideal for reaching out to targeted groups in targeted locations. Whether your potential customers are married white-collar workers in your city between the ages of 25 and 45 or local retirees with second homes, there's a radio station where you can find them. Radio stations know exactly who their listeners are (their business depends on it!), and they are eager to share this information with potential advertisers.

Radio offers some distinct advantages over print and TV advertising. The main one is that messages are broadcast to a semi-captive audience, primarily people in cars. When someone is driving, they're less likely to change stations when commercials come on. TV watchers, in contrast, do more channel surfing, wander out to the kitchen for a snack during the commercials, or even record shows and skip the commercials entirely on playback. Print has a similar downside. People only peruse the ads that interest them and then skip the rest. Other benefits of advertising on radio include the following:

- Radio is typically the last media your customers come into contact with before making a retail purchase, since ads reach them while they're driving—on the way to or in the vicinity of a store.

- Radio is targeted and segmented. Young urban listeners will tune into very different stations than people over 60. Because it caters to well-defined niches, radio is a good medium for reaching a specific target market.

- Radio can be a very effective way to promote a product or service that doesn't require too much description because listeners already know what it is. Everyone understands what dentists, print shops, and restaurants provide. These kinds of businesses can use the radio time to focus on the specific benefits they offer and what makes them different from others in their markets.

- Radio listeners are often fiercely loyal, keeping their dials locked on a particular station, so if you find one that appeals to your target market, it will give you many opportunities to reach them.

- Since radio broadcasts to a limited geographical range, it is ideal for reaching potential customers if your company relies on business from your local area.

Comparing Radio Outlets

MEDIA VENUE	COST	BENEFITS	CHALLENGES	BEST FOR	TIPS FOR EFFECTIVENESS
College Radio	$	Young audience; inexpensive	Content can be edgy	Targeting a young, educated demographic	Produce ads in a voice that mirrors the tone of the station
Local Public Radio	$–$$	Moderate fees; educated audience; good community image	Sponsorship spots (as opposed to ads) limit format for message	Building positive brand associations; targeting educated, often financially secure listeners	Create a line that demonstrates your philanthropic nature while still delivering your message
Local Commercial Radio	$$–$$$	Medium to large listener base; can target audience by music/radio show preference	Can be pricey; good amount of competition; ads can get lost if not well placed and frequent	Targeting a large segment of your regional customer demographic	Check to see when (and on what stations) your competitors are advertising, especially if they've been doing it for a while
National Public Radio	$$$–$$$$	Can reach a large national, educated audience, and create a positive image of brand on a national scale	Expensive; limited message format	Enhancing brand image nationally	Same as local public radio above

Cost Key* $: Relatively Inexpensive $$: Moderately Expensive $$$: Fairly Expensive $$$$: Expensive

* These symbols represent general rate estimates. Ad rates will vary widely by station reach, region, and time of day.

Billboard Advertising

A billboard is a large outdoor advertising structure usually found alongside highways or busy roads. They display oversized advertisements designed to catch the attention of drivers quickly and make a big impact in an extremely short period of time—that is, the time it takes to drive by, often at high speed. Billboards are also used in large cities and urban areas to catch the attention of pedestrians.

There's an art to an effective billboard: they have to be easily read and absorbed, and remain in the observer's mind long after the billboard has been glimpsed. That's why most billboards typically use few words in large print, and feature graphics or designs that are especially eye-catching and distinctive. Humor plays a large role in billboard advertising.

Generally, billboard advertising works best if you have a message that doesn't need to be changed often—since putting up new billboards is an expensive proposition—and is targeted at a general, rather than highly specific, audience segment.

When to Advertise

Advertising on a consistent basis helps establish your company and products and keeps them in front of existing and potential customers. Since many companies can't afford to advertise all the time, it's important to know that advertising is particularly critical at certain points in the development and growth of your business. When you're just starting out, you'll want to build awareness about your company. If you have a big event going on and want to draw people to your establishment, or if you're introducing a new product and want potential customers to be aware of it, advertise as often and in as many different media as you can afford to help spread the word. Critical times to advertise include:

- The start of your businesses (such as a grand opening)

- When you launch a new service or product

- When you improve an existing product or service

- When you change location

- When you're having a sale on products or offering a discount on services

- When you want to announce a special community event (such as a food drive your business is sponsoring)

- When you want to boost dwindling sales

TV

People tend to remember TV ads because they tap into two senses—sight and hearing. You can show and tell, reinforcing your brand message on two levels. What's more, your potential customers can hear your message even if they're not in the room with the TV, and see it even if the volume is off. A good TV ad campaign can put your product or service on the map for your target audience. TV's other benefits include the following:

- It enables you to show how a product or service works. You can demonstrate how it will make life easier, or simply better, for your potential customer.

- TV advertising reaches customers right in their living rooms, bedrooms, and other areas of the home where there's a TV, and where they're usually relaxed. In most cases, they're on their home turf, where they have easy access to a pen and paper to write down contact information if they're interested in what you're selling.

- Unlike a newspaper ad, your TV ad isn't competing for viewer's attention with several other ads on a page. People only see one TV ad at a time.

- Appearing on TV gives your business credibility. Being on the medium raises your status because it puts you on the same plane as huge national advertisers (even if you're only paying local rates). That's why many businesses include the phrase "As Seen on TV" in their print ads and other marketing materials.

- Based on station range and programming, TV ads enable you to target a range of geographic audiences. This runs the gamut from small local populations to larger, more mainstream national audiences. You can also target customers by interest, based on what shows they're watching.

Comparing TV Outlets

VENUE	COST	BENEFITS	CHALLENGES	BEST FOR	TIPS FOR EFFECTIVENESS
Local	$–$$	Inexpensive on many stations, access to a local audience (in a small geographic area)	Limited reach	Targeting neighborhood, local customers	Repeat frequently on the same shows; choose shows your audience is likely to watch
Local Public (PBS) TV	$–$$	Not too expensive; positive community associations	Offers sponsorships, not ads, with limited formats and time lengths for your message	Building positive brand image with local community/customers	Include an effective tagline in your announcement and contact info
Local Network Affiliate TV	$$–$$$	Good for reaching large numbers of potential customers in your geographic region	Can be expensive; audience not as targeted as cable	Broadcasting to a large, regional, less targeted base of potential customers	Work with the station to find ad deals; look for co-op ad opportunities; choose programs time slots/programs carefully
National Public (PBS) TV	$$$–$$$$	Reaches a national audience of often educated, financially stable listeners	Offers sponsorships, not ads, with limited formats and time lengths for your message; can be expensive	Large audience; positive association with a respected national entity	Include an effective tagline in your announcement and contact info
National Commercial Cable	$$$–$$$$	Reaches a highly targeted audience of local or national subscribers	Limited space for local ad spots; national ads can be expensive; audience size for niche stations may not justify ad price	Targeting a local or national niche audience	Try to find stations that target your customer base and are willing to offer deals on local ad spots (unless there's a compelling reason to broadcast to a national audience)

Cost Key* $: Relatively Inexpensive $$: Moderately Expensive $$$: Fairly Expensive $$$$: Expensive

* These symbols represent general rate estimates. Ad rates will vary widely by station reach, region, and time of day.

Public Relations

The best publicity is often free publicity. A story about your business in the local newspaper or on TV can be more powerful than a paid advertisement. Public relations involves getting your business or product mentioned in publications—online as well as printed—and in other types of media, such as television or radio.

But even though you won't be spending money on ads, this free publicity will cost you. You'll have to pay someone in your company, or hire a public relations specialist, to send a press release and "pitch" various media outlets on your products, services, or other significant event such as new product launch.

A press release is a document that provides the public with detailed information about a particular event, such as the introduction of a new product or service, or a milestone in the development of a company (the thousandth customer, the 25-year anniversary). A press release should include all of the info that a media representative needs to write a story about the event, including all of the details (dates, names, prices—whatever is relevant). A good press release will also include quotes for the media writer to use. These quotes might come from customers praising the product or service, an industry analyst placing the company or its products or services in a market context, or a representative of the company. Press releases should *always* have contact info that the media can use to get further information about the event.

When designing your press release, remember that most people in the media are overworked. Thus, the easier you make it for them to understand the *who, what, where, when,* and *why* of your product or service, the better your chances of getting publicity. The most successful press releases have an interesting "hook"—an aspect of your story that "hooks" readers in, the thing that makes your news compelling. Perhaps you're launching a new line of heart-shaped chocolates around Valentine's Day. Or maybe new tax laws are about to be put into effect, and your team of accountants can find more deductions than last year. Find an angle for reporters that shows them how your story is timely, amusing, or informative—in other words, don't make them work to cover it.

Product and service reviews are an increasingly important component of a successful PR campaign. A positive review from a trusted source will lead customers to you. In addition to the traditional places where experts review and/or compare products and services such as *Consumer Reports* and industry specialty or trade magazines, there are an increasing number of online sites where users can submit their own reviews. Such sites are very influential, because the ratings on them come from actual users of a product or service. Generally, if other customers say that your architecture firm is terrific, it's much more credible

Finding Media Contact Info

It's usually easy to find contact information for media representatives. First, check the website for the publication or station. Newspaper sites often list the email addresses and/or phone numbers for section editors and key journalists. Do a search for a reporter's past articles and make sure they cover your kind of story before you pitch them.

Contact information is also listed in newspapers and magazines within their first few pages (in staff boxes). If you can't determine who edits or writes for a particular section, call the publication and ask. Do the same for radio and TV programs. While you're on the phone, ask for an editorial calendar, which will tell you what topics are going to be covered by the publication or station in the next few months. This will help you figure out the best time to make your pitch.

than if *you* declare this in an advertisement. And success breeds success. After getting publicity in one venue, it is common for it to follow in another.

There are drawbacks to depending on public relations, however. Public relations takes time. Writing the press releases, making the media contact, calling that person, sending out products for review, and doing all the necessary follow-up can take hours. And it can take considerable time for PR to be effective. As well, PR is not controllable. Unlike an ad, where you pay to specify the conditions it will run under, you have no control over how your PR efforts will turn out. You may get products into reviewers' hands only to get negative reviews. Or your efforts could simply be ignored.

Word of Mouth

Word of mouth marketing is exactly what it sounds like: your goal is to generate "buzz" about your product or service that will spread naturally and ignite interest in your offerings. Word of mouth is powerful because people trust what their friends, associates, and family members tell them. However, you have to come up with ways to make people not only remember you but also be motivated to spread the word about you. And this can take time. *Word of mouth,* however, is a bit of a misnomer because it implies that the buzz about an offering just happens spontaneously. Nothing could be further from the truth. Your customers will forget you even if they're satisfied with your business and services. You must constantly be thinking of ways to encourage them to spread the word. The following represent some effective methods of generating word of mouth:

- **Onsite events.** Host an event at your business that brings potential customers in and gets them talking about your business. A service business could hold a grand opening with wine and cheese and offer discounts on services; a retail business could hold hourly drawings for prizes.

- **Offsite events.** Participate in an event that will attract your target market. A job placement service could buy booth space at a job fair, offering free résumé consultation. Or the company could also help sponsor the fair, which would entitle it to place its logo on the main entrance banner and receive a public thank you from fair organizers on the fair website. This public acknowledgement not only increases the placement service's exposure, but also enhances its image among job seekers and businesses looking to hire.

- **Referral programs.** Create a program that provides incentives for your customers to tell others about you. Offer them discounts on services if they bring in friends or colleagues. Health clubs often offer "Two for One" specials or let you sign up a friend and get your first month free. Promote these specials in your ads and hand out flyers to existing customers.

- **Blogs.** If you have a product or service that would interest readers of a particular blog, contact the blog coordinator, send a free sample, and ask them to mention it on the blog if they like it. A recommendation will be much more powerful coming from a trusted blogger.

- **Message boards.** Visit message boards of interest to your target customers and participate in the discussion *without* directly promoting your business. Include your company name (with email and website) in your signature. If you consistently offer good advice or valuable input, participants will come to trust you and be more inclined to try your product or service—and then tell the other participants about it.

- **Public testimonials.** Testimonials from satisfied customers make a big impact. Put testimonials on your website and in your marketing materials. If you participate in a professional network and have done work for any of its members, ask them to give a testimonial to the group through an announcement at an event or over the network's group email (often called email list-serves). Testimonials through group emails, where other members chime in with their own kudos for your talents, work particularly well for service providers such as graphic artists, marketing and PR professional, and lawyers.

- **Product placement/Associative marketing.** Everyone's seen celebrities using brand-name products such as computers, soft drinks, and cars in movies in moves or on TV. These kinds of high-profile product placements can take a lot of effort, time, and money to procure. But you can do a low-cost version of this by getting your products placed in well-respected venues where your customers will see them. A florist could put a beautiful bouquet in a hotel lobby with a "Flowers provided by …" placard or business cards nearby. Or a graphic design firm could donate the design of a flyer for an industry conference in return for having the words *Designed by …* on the flyer. In some cases, you'll pay to get your goods in these venues. In others, you'll donate your products and services in exchange for the exposure.

■ **Influencers.** This form of marketing involves seeding products among well-respected members of a particular demographic, group, or network (whether social or business) as a means of influencing others to try the product. For example, if the members of a high-tech industry association see their chairperson using your new hand-held device, they're more likely to start up a discussion about it and perhaps purchase it themselves.

Online Marketing

Online marketing is just what it sounds like: marketing that strives to influence the online world to think highly of—and hopefully purchase—your product or service. Just about any type of product or service can benefit from online marketing—from dentists to massage therapy, veterinary services, restaurant supplies, and more. Anything that people search for online is fair game for online marketing initiatives.

Online marketing falls into three main categories:

■ Search engine optimization

■ Search engine marketing

■ Banner ads

Search engine optimization (SEO) encompasses techniques for trying to improve the "page ranking" your website gets from the major search engines. (The ranking is simply the order in which the results of a search for a particular topic appear on the screen.) You want to be as close to the top of the first page that shows up after a potential customer types "graphic design for physicians" or "coffeehouses in Austin" into the search engine. Doing SEO is tricky business—so much so that a whole industry has sprung up around helping businesses of all sizes improve their page rankings. This takes time and an ongoing commitment. The reason it

is so difficult is that the major search engines (Google, Microsoft, and Yahoo) keep their algorithms, or mathematical formulas, for determining page ranking secret and are constantly changing them so that people can't manipulate them.

Search engine marketing (SEM) is when you buy keywords so that your advertisement appears when a user searches the Internet using them. For example, if you design and manufacture original upholstery textiles, you might purchase the keyword phrase "original designs upholstering fabric" so that when someone typed in those words, your ad would have a good chance of appearing at the top of the page.

The great advantage of SEM is that it is *contextual.* Your ad shows up when a potential customer does a search on keywords directly related to your product or service. And because you don't pay unless someone actually clicks on your ad, it can be very cost-effective. You can see and measure how many of your "click-throughs" result in actual sales. With other kinds of advertisements, you're paying for what's called *eyeballs*—the total number of people who receive a publication or watch a show—whereas with SEM you're generally paying for actions, which can be tremendously effective. Another advantage is that the ads appear in front of users at the exact right time—that is, when they're actually researching products and services with an eye toward making a purchase.

The downside—and it's a big one—is that keywords can be expensive. That's because there's no flat fee for keywords: you bid on them against other people who want to place their ads when those keywords are used. Depending on your business, and the keywords you want to use, SEM might be priced *way* out of your budget. Try and bid on the keyword "wooden toy" for example, and you'll see that a beginning entrepreneur making wooden toys may still have to compete against the likes of Toys R Us.

Banner ads. These were the first click-through ads to appear on the Web. In many ways, these resemble traditional ads in print magazines: you typically place them on a website that appears to have the correct "readership" for your product or service. Thus, if you sell tennis rackets, you'd probably want to advertise on www.tennis.com rather than www.baseball.com! If a Web user clicks on your banner ad, they land on your website (or anywhere else you want to take them) to watch a video, read the information presented there, listen to a Webcast, fill out a form, or proceed to a checkout counter to purchase a racket.

Purchasing terms

The three most common ways in which online advertising is purchased are CPM, CPC, and CPA.

- CPM (cost per thousand) is where advertisers pay to have their messages exposed to specific audiences. CPM costs are priced per thousand impressions. (The *M* in the acronym is the Roman numeral for 1,000.)

- CPC (cost per click) and PPC (pay per click) are where advertisers pay every time users click on their listings and are redirected to their websites. Advertisers don't actually pay for the listing but rather for each time the listing is clicked on. Thus, CPC is the amount an advertiser pays per click. This does not, however, mean that all of those people coming to your website are actually buying your product or service

- CPA (cost per action or cost per acquisition) advertising is based on actual results. You pay only for the amount of users who complete a transaction, such as making a purchase or signing up for a service.

Networking

People like doing business with people they know. Networking is seeking out and interacting with people who are gathered for the purpose of building their businesses. It usually takes place at a venue such as a meeting, conference, or other event, and involves a mutually beneficial exchange of goods and services or information. For certain types of businesses (for example, consulting and professional services), networking represents *the* single best way to build a customer base.

If you choose your networking group well, you'll come into contact with people who can help you strengthen your business by:

- Buying what you sell

- Connecting you with others who will buy what you sell

- Providing a product or service you need

- Partnering with you in some aspect of your business venture

Although your main goal in joining a network is to enhance your business, keep in mind that in many

Social Networking

One aspect of word-of-mouth marketing (see page 141) that's been receiving a lot of attention is online social networking. The popularity of MySpace, Facebook, LinkedIn, and other social networking sites has resulted in a grass roots spreading of the news about a broad range of products and services, particularly music. By putting the names of their favorite artists and tracks on their Facebook or MySpace pages, young people—and they are mostly young—spread the word about new artists in a much more organic way than was possible before the advent of such sites.

In addition, all sorts of websites exist today for users to weigh in on specific products and services. For example, TripAdvisor has become an extraordinarily important site within the travel industry because of the huge volume of user-contributed reviews of hotels, restaurants, local businesses, and other destination details. Likewise, Yelp.com solicits reviews on everything from dry cleaners to dentists to corner grocery stories. Some people predict that these user reviews, in aggregate, will soon have more influence than even the most highly respected critics at major media outlets.

cases *getting* involves a willingness to *give* first. The best and strongest networks are created by professionals who respect the reciprocal nature of doing business.

Networking is relatively affordable, since it generally takes the form of getting involved in groups like a local chamber of commerce or chapter of an industry association. Not incidentally, while you're networking, you can pick up a lot of useful information about an industry or market, and make valuable contacts within the business community. Every community has its share of organizations. Some types of groups you can join include:

- **Entrepreneur's groups.** You're likely to find lots of entrepreneur's groups, both formal associations and informal get-togethers.

- **Industry associations.** With more than 37,000 industry and professional associations in the United States, there's likely to be a local chapter of interest in your community. For a list of industry associations go to www.planningshop.com/associations.

- **Group-specific entrepreneur associations.** You'll find business organizations aimed at minorities, women, religious groups, youth, immigrants, and more.

Look Before You Leap

The best way to determine whether a trade show is a good fit for you and your business is to go first as an attendee, not an exhibitor. You'll discover what the atmosphere is like and who attends and exhibits, and you'll get a better feel for how business is done at the event. And as an attendee, you'll still be able to take advantage of having so many industry contacts in one place. Without being tied to an exhibit, you'll also be able to attend even more meetings and events.

To find out if there's a group that's right for you in your town, check:

- **Business section of your local newspaper.** Look here for a calendar of meetings or events put on by entrepreneur's groups.

- **Small business development centers (SBDCs).** Go to these to obtain lists of local entrepreneur's groups. (To find a contact for an SBDC office in your area, go to www.asbdc-us.org.)

- **Websites of trade associations.** Find an appropriate industry association and join it. Many associations run members-only forums on their websites, and this is the first place to look for a forum that will be useful to you.

- **Yahoo groups (http://groups.yahoo.com).** Yahoo hosts all sorts of online groups. There are plenty for people with particular interests, but there are also a fair number of professional groups, so find one that fits your business.

- **Google groups (http://groups.google.com).** You'll find discussion groups here on just about every topic under the sun. Spend some time on the Groups home page looking for topic areas that relate to your industry or business specialty.

Trade Shows

Trade shows are exhibitions where companies in a particular industry congregate to showcase their latest products, services, and developments. At trade shows, bookstore buyers can meet publishers to discover the hot new authors; auto manufacturers can view a variety of suppliers under one roof; and clothing designers can show off their wares to retailers of all sizes. Trade shows are sponsored by trade associations for specific industries and are generally not open to the public. They are usually several days long and are attended by people from the industry, company representatives, and members of the press.

Not only are all of these key prospects gathered under one roof, they're eager to see what you have to offer. Trade show attendees have an interest in looking at your products or services. That's why they're there. Trade shows are a great way to meet potential new customers and for them to meet you. This is especially helpful if many of your potential customers are located outside your immediate area but will be attending the same show as you. A face-to-face meeting makes doing business a lot more inviting—and the trade show setting makes it easy for you to showcase your product or service and for potential customers to ask you questions about your company.

At the right trade show, with the right approach, you can:

- Land a big customer

- Launch a new product

- Develop a mailing list of hot leads

- Find a strategic partner

- Enhance relationships with your existing customers

- Learn about new trends and developments in your field

- Find out what your competitors are up to

The type of trade show you choose to attend will vary depending on what you're selling and whom you're selling it to. Let's say your company makes gourmet salsa. If your goal is to sell the salsa directly to as many new customers as possible, your best bet is to exhibit at a broad food show with thousands of attendees and hundreds of exhibitors, like the annual Internal Fancy Food and Confection Show. But if you want to posi-

Community Service

Being a good member of the community can work wonders for your marketing efforts. Whether this involves volunteering at the local pet or homeless shelter, being an active member of the chamber of commerce, or running for the school board, being visibly involved in your community puts you, personally, in a positive light; creates positive feelings about your business; and increases word of mouth about you and what you do.

tion your salsa as leader in the Hispanic food market, a smaller, more targeted conference might be a better choice—one like the Expo Comido Latina.

Trade shows can be expensive—the costs of being an exhibitor, preparing your booth, creating marketing materials (including catalogs and brochures), and bringing enough personnel to staff the booth will add up. If you don't choose the right trade show for your needs, you may have spent the money for nothing. And frequently your competitors are in the next booth. Despite all of this, a trade show is often one of the best places to reach your target market and can give you an excellent return on investment (ROI).

business
BUZZ
words   **"cost per conversion"**

Cost per conversion describes the cost of acquiring a customer, typically calculated by dividing the total cost of an ad campaign by the number of conversions to actual sales. Thus, if you paid $1,000 for a search engine ad and ended up selling 100 tennis rackets, your cost per conversion would be $10 per racket. Depending on the price of your rackets, and your profit margin, this may or may not be a good deal.

Direct Mail

Direct mail is also called, unflatteringly, *junk mail* because it arrives unsolicited and is often immediately thrown away by recipients. Many people so despise junk mail that services even exist to help people reduce the amount of junk mail they receive.

Two things distinguish direct mail from other types of marketing: First, it's sent directly to the consumer (hence its name)—which means there's no media or other intermediary between you (the business) and the end customer. And second, each piece of direct mail has a specific "call to action"—that is, it's very specific about the next step the consumer should take, whether it's to call a toll-free number, clip out a coupon, visit a website, or provide some other measurable "response." In fact, this is one of the advantages of direct mail: you can immediately and concretely measure the results—and therefore how much it costs you for each sale made as a result of the marketing push. The downside is that direct mail has a very negative connotation among many consumers and businesses, and is perhaps even perceived as a "lower class" type of marketing than other possible vehicles.

Sampling

Another time-honored way of getting the word out about your products or services is to offer samples, freebies, or free trials. The idea, of course, is that once customers sample your goods or services, they'll be eager for more—and willing to pay for it! By eliminating risks, sampling breaks down the barriers to buying. And because people are creatures of habit, once they start using something, they're less likely to switch to another product or service.

Food sampling is the most common form of sampling. You've doubtless noticed the people cooking up enticingly flavorful samples of food in grocery stores and giving out bite-size portions to lure you into purchasing a particular item. But there are many other products that can be sampled. In the cosmetics industry, for example, it's standard practice to give away samples of perfume, eye makeup, lipstick, and powder with purchases of full-size products. And thirty-day trial versions of software are typically available for download free. Even service businesses can offer samples: by giving a free five-minute massage or answering a question about gardening or law at a street fair or shopping mall, service providers can reap the benefits of sampling, "hooking" someone into purchasing their services.

The drawbacks of sampling are that it's costly—you have to produce the good or perform the service without getting paid—and it can be hard to reach people and get them to take a sample or agree to a free trial.

At the end of the next chapter, you'll find a Marketing Plan worksheet on pages 152 and 153. In that worksheet, you will outline which of the marketing vehicles and tactics discussed in this chapter you plan to use to make prospective customers aware of your products or services. Refer back to this chapter as you complete that worksheet and sketch out your marketing plan.

19

Your Marketing Plan

A marketing plan is a written document that details the actions necessary to achieve one or more marketing objectives for your product or service. Some marketing plans are short term (covering the next three months, six months, or a year), and some are long term (covering a period as long as five years). As part of your overall business plan (see page 125), your marketing plan covers everything from your goals and actions to your budget and message.

Your marketing plan is essential. Rather than throwing money at various marketing activities in an ad hoc manner, you should create a marketing plan that allows you to systematically analyze what will work best for your business—and carefully track the results. The following sections outline the components of a good marketing plan.

Goals

Precisely delineated goals represent a key aspect of your marketing plan. After all, if you can't articulate what you hope to achieve, you won't know if and when you've succeeded. Goals can be for the near or long term, or both. Most marketing plans will set milestones for achieving their goals. For example, a three-month goal could be to get mentions of your company and/or products and services in local newspapers through a carefully targeted public relations campaign; a six-month goal might be to establish relationships with at least a dozen media contacts in your industry. And your yearly goal might be to increase sales by 20 percent.

There a number of marketing goals you might wish to achieve, from increasing your sales numbers to increasing the number of names in your database. No matter what your marketing goals, they will fall into two main categories: quantitative and qualitative:

- **Quantitative** goals are usually tied to numerical measures, like sales figures, income, and other quantifiable factors. The following represent some typical quantitative goals:

  — Increase sales by $100,000 per year

  — Get 2,010 new customers by 2010

  — Get 750 people to sign up for special trial offers

- **Qualitative** marketing goals are more subjective. They focus on factors like brand influence, positive press, and favorable customer feedback. The following represent some common qualitative goals:

  — Introduce a new company or product to a market

  — Increase name recognition

  — Increase prestige with prospective employees

  — Generate positive press coverage

Smaller companies often lack the budgets to measure the impact of their marketing activities accurately (beyond sales figures). That's why their goals tend to be more qualitative. Having—and achieving—both kinds of goals is important for business growth. A qualitative goal like increasing positive customer feedback may not be something your accountant can enter into a financial statement, but it's as vital to your bottom line as your sales figures.

Target Market

Unless you are very clear about *whom* you're targeting, your marketing plan simply won't be helpful. And the more specific you can be, the better. Rather than simply targeting women aged 35 through 60, for example, to sell your line of sports clothes, you could aim to reach women aged 35 through 60 with an annual income of more than $75,000 who play golf more than twice a week. You could then advertise in golf magazines and exhibit at trade shows that attract managers of golf pro shops. Unless you can identify precisely whom you're trying to reach, you won't be able to find the vehicles that will reach them best.

Marketing Message

Your marketing message is the impression of your company and/or products or services you want to convey to your target market. Your message might be "the highest-quality and most environmentally sensitive drapery cleaning service in town" or "the low-price leader in premium-name brand luggage." You should be as pointed and precise about your marketing message as you are about your target market.

Quantitative vs. Qualitative Goals

QUANTITATIVE	QUALITATIVE
Gain a 10 percent share in the Boise, Idaho, dry cleaning market.	Become Boise's most popular dry cleaner.
Generate trade show leads that result in $30,000 in sales.	Increase exposure for your company and its new products at the trade show.
Get your new organic jams on the shelves of Boulder, Colorado's top five organic markets.	Create buzz in Boulder about your new jams.
Attract 10 new dog sitting customers through newspaper print ad discount coupons.	Build awareness of your luxury dog sitting service throughout the Boston area.

business **BUZZ** *words*

"CRM"

CRM—which stands for customer relationship management—is based on the idea that rather than keeping information about sales, marketing, and customer service in three different databases, you can store it in one integrated system. This allows you to track all "customer activity"—from first contact to a mass mailing to a personal call made by a salesperson to actual sales made to an after-sales request for support. By simply looking up a customer name, you thus get what CRM experts call a "360-degree view" of customers. You've probably experienced this yourself if you call a company with an effective CRM system in place: by giving the representative your name, phone number, or customer ID, that person knows about every contact you've ever had with the business. This is considered a hallmark of stellar customer service and can be a key competitive differentiator, especially in crowded markets.

Marketing Savvy: Giving It Away

Dana Cox had achieved her dream of many years: she had finally hung out her shingle on her own personal chef business. Her challenge: How to find customers?

Based in Chicago and serving the surrounding suburbs as well as the city itself, Cox had her "Aha" moment when working for celebrity chef Wolfgang Puck's catering service. "I had firsthand experience of going into affluent people's homes and putting on parties, and I realized I could do it—and in many cases, do it better," she said. Cox, who graduated from the prestigious Kendall College School of Culinary Arts with honors in 1997, listened when customers told her they wished they could have every meal catered. "I said, 'Why not?'" Cox recalls. "The idea that I could provide that caliber of restaurant cuisine, customized to the tastes and dietary needs of individual households, in people's homes took hold."

Today, Cox's business, Old Stove Gourmet, is going gangbusters. She has steady customers all over the Chicago area, and her work has been featured in *Gourmet* magazine, on Chicago's WGN News, and on the "Oprah Winfrey Show."

Her business model is straightforward: she meets with clients, asks them a detailed list of questions about their likes and dislikes and special needs, and presents them with a menu of dinners covering a two-week period. Once the menu is approved, Cox does everything: she shops for all the ingredients, shows up at the client's home on a designated day, and prepares all two weeks' worth of meals, which she

then freezes for them to use at their convenience.

But in the beginning, it was difficult to find clients. Cox knew she had to find a marketing strategy that worked for her specific market niche. She printed up business cards and flyers and distributed them to everyone she knew. She tried advertising in local media outlets, but that proved to be a bust.

Finally, Cox had a brainstorm: to donate her services as raffle prizes for local charity events. She found out when and where such events were taking place, and offered to donate a package of a three-course meal for 10 people—at a personal cost of $1,500—in exchange for setting up a table at the event itself. It worked. Her first event was in her own neighborhood, which every year sponsors a charity ball, and "it was phenomenal," she says. People crowded around her table, eager to hear about the raffle prize and in the process got her sales pitch. She also received a lot of free press for her donation. Calls started coming in. Since then, she's continued this strategy at other charity events, and has learned that by doing this, her marketing dollars have a triple impact: First, there's the free advertising she gets just from the publicity over the much-coveted raffle prize. Then there's the repeat business she gets from the winners of the raffle. Finally, there's the word of mouth that results from giving successful parties for the winners. "It's a winning strategy all around," she says.

Developing Your Marketing Plan

To develop a thorough marketing plan, check out *Successful Marketing: Secrets & Strategies*, also from Rhonda Abrams and The Planning Shop. This volume includes an in-depth discussion of the pros and cons of various marketing tactics, identifies the most affordable marketing techniques, and provides a full set of marketing budget worksheets. The book is available at www.PlanningShop.com

Budget

The most important aspect of your marketing program is that you can afford it. Every marketing vehicle costs money, so carefully plan how you intend to spend your marketing dollars. Often the best marketing vehicles are not the most obvious or even the most expensive. An inexpensive ad in a specialty or trade publication read by your target customers may prove far more effective than a more costly one in a general newspaper.

And don't forget that the money you spend on marketing is money you won't have to spend elsewhere. If you spend a ton of cash on a huge advertising campaign, but it leaves you without the money to pay the rent or make payroll, you'll be in trouble.

Marketing Vehicles

The bulk of your marketing plan will be devoted to detailing which marketing vehicles—and what mix of vehicles—will be used to carry your message to the world. You'll outline the tactics and techniques you plan to use and these will become your marketing plan's "game plan."

Repetition/Frequency

Pay special attention to how frequently you plan to repeat your marketing message in the marketing vehicles you choose. This is critical because you want to be sure you repeat your message enough times to the same market to make an impact and see results.

Creating Your Contacts Database

As your business grows, you will need an easy and organized way to store and retrieve the contact information for your customers, suppliers, professional service providers, and other business partners. The best way to do this is through an electronic database. Although this may sound complicated, it doesn't have to be elaborate, difficult, or expensive. There are many inexpensive contact manager software packages and a growing number of online services that allow you to manage your contacts from anywhere you have an Internet connection. Such software allows you to get your hands on exactly the right person—and the contact info for that person—in a flash. For example, you will naturally want to capture customers' names, addresses, phone numbers, and email addresses; however, you will also want to track when—and why—you've contacted them in the past and store notes about what happened as a result of that interaction. Most contact management software packages today allow you to program in "alerts" that remind you that you need to follow up on action items after an interaction with a customer.

worksheet: Your Marketing Goals

Use this worksheet to make note of your key marketing goals for the next year.

List your top three quantitative marketing goals:

1) _____

_____

_____

2) _____

_____

_____

3) _____

_____

_____

List your top three qualitative marketing goals:

1) _____

_____

_____

2) _____

_____

_____

3) _____

_____

_____

worksheet: Your Marketing Plan

On this page and the following one, outline the beginning aspects of your marketing plan. Refer back to Chapters 17 and 18 to help you complete the questions below.

GOALS, TARGET MARKET, MESSAGE

List the major goals of your marketing efforts. Be sure to include both qualitative and quantitative goals. Use numbers! _____

Describe your target customer, including specific demographics such as age, income, and education level. If your customer is a business, be specific about the industry and size of business:_____

What are your customers' key wants and needs as they relate to your product/service? _____

What are the key benefits you offer to customers? Why would they prefer your product or service to those of your competitors? Sum up those benefits in a "marketing message": _____

BUDGET

Before you can choose your marketing vehicles, you need to know how much money you have to spend. If you know how much money you can spend on your marketing activities, list it here; if not, estimate a range for the amount of money you'll have available for marketing: _____

MARKETING TACTICS & VEHICLES

Traditional Advertising

Will you be using traditional advertising such as newspapers, magazines, radio, and TV to get the word out about your company? If so, list the names or types of advertising media outlets you'll use: print (newspapers, magazines, newsletters, etc.), radio and/or TV stations: _____

What products or services will you advertise in these traditional media outlets? _____

When will you advertise (for instance, time of year, during special sales, at your grand opening)? _____

What will you offer or say in your ads? _____

How frequently will you advertise? _____

Online Marketing:

Note the ways you plan to use each of the following online marketing tactics to help build awareness of your company: _____

Search engine optimization (writing/coding your Web pages to rank high in search results): _____

Search engine marketing (paying for ads that appear adjacent to search results): _____

Social networking sites (building company pages, starting groups, buying ads, etc.): _____

Blogs: _____

Email newsletters: _____

Banner ads: _____

Other online activities: _____

Networking, Word of Mouth, and Public Relations

Describe how you will "network," or build referrals and awareness, through person-to-person contacts. List the organizations/associations you could join to meet prospective customers or referral sources: _____

What will you do to help generate and maintain positive word-of-mouth marketing about your business? Detail some of the tactics you'll use, such as referral programs, events, getting testimonials, etc.: _____

Do you plan to use PR to get media coverage of your company, products, or services? If so, who will manage your PR efforts? Who in the media will you target? Will you try to get product/service reviewed? _____

How can you get involved in community service or in socially responsible causes to increase your company's visibility while you contribute to the common good? _____

Sampling, Direct Mail, Signs, and Trade Shows

How can you make "samples" of your product or service available to prospective customers in order to lower their sales resistance? If you're offering a product, how and where could you distribute samples? If a service, software, or web-based application, how much of a trial could you offer? _____

Do you plan to use direct mail to make prospects or customers aware of you or of specific offerings? If so, when will you use direct mail? What mailing list will you use? Who will handle the logistics of preparing and sending the mail piece? _____

Will you use any signs to make people aware of your company, location or offerings? If so, what kind and where (for instance, billboards, at your place of business, on vehicles)? _____

Which trade shows can you exhibit at to reach a large number of prospective customers at one time? _____

Frequency & Repetition

Recognizing that repetition is crucial in getting your marketing message to stick, how will you ensure that both current and prospective customers are exposed to your marketing message many times? _____

chapter 20

Pricing

ere's an old joke: A storeowner purchases pencils for 10 cents each and then sells them for a nickel each. Noticing this bizarre behavior, his partner asks, "How do you expect us to stay in business that way?" The man replies, "Volume!"

Surprisingly, many novice entrepreneurs choose a relatively similar business strategy. They imagine all that's necessary for success is to price their products or services lower than the competition's. Low prices, they assume, will generate sufficient sales to more than make up for smaller profits.

But competing on price alone is risky. Some discount outlets do build thriving businesses on low prices, but this strategy almost always means narrow profit margins, which in turn means less cash for your company. With a small financial cushion, you're vulnerable to every slight increase in cost. The landlord raises your rent 5 percent? That may be your entire year's profit. And you're also at risk from competitors. If you become a serious threat and they have deeper cash reserves, they can just undercut your prices and wait until you're squeezed out of the market. Moreover, customers attracted solely by price are notoriously fickle. If they shopped around a lot before choosing you, they're probably going to shop around continually. And as soon as someone has a lower price, you're history!

Of course, when you're just starting out in business, you may want to set your prices lower (even much

lower) than the competition's. This gives you a chance to build a customer base and get some experience. Especially if you're in a service industry, you're going to be learning a lot while working for your first customers, so it's only fair to charge them less.

You've already done some research on the prices competitors are charging). This should help you get an idea of the market as you establish your own prices.

Your Pricing Strategy

Although pricing is a complex issue, there are some things you can do to lessen the time—and pain—of getting it right. Here's a four-step process you can follow to get to your optimal price point.

1. **Do your research.** You need to know what's happening in your market before you set your prices. After all, if the custom leather upholstery store across town is offering to re-upholster antique chairs for $500 each, it probably won't work to charge $2,000 without good reason (such as providing higher quality or quick turnaround).

2. **Test the market.** But that doesn't mean you should take the existing pricing structure for granted. Especially when you're new, you should try to see what prices the market will bear. There might be a reason for you to charge four times as much as your nearest

competitor—for example, the grade of leather you offer might be significantly higher, or your workmanship is such that people will gladly pay a premium. Alternatively, you might find that by undercutting your competitor by even a little bit, you can capture a good percent of the market (although for many reasons, this can be a risky strategy).

3. **Try different pricing models.** Don't just assume that traditional means of pricing your products and services are your only options. For example, the innovative new software you've written that increases the speed of transferring documents over home networks might sell better as a service rather than as a for-purchase product. Or you might consider offering your gardening service as a subscription rather than on a per-use basis.

4. **Offer a range of features and price points for your products or services.** Product segmentation is a good way to offer customers a range of prices on what are essentially the same products or services. For example, you could offer a base model hand-designed and hand-made aluminum bicycle frame that you sold for $1,000, but one made of carbon fiber you could charge $5,000 for. Or if you videotape weddings and other special occasions, you could do so at a base price but offer special add-on services like posting the clips on a secure website for authorized viewers for an additional fee.

Pricing Goods

If you're a retailer or a reseller of products or services produced by others, it's often relatively easy to figure out how much to charge. Most industries have generally accepted mark-ups over the cost of goods (for example, 100 percent in department stores; 200 percent for jewelry).

Understanding normal prices in your industry will help you figure out how much you want to charge. If you're a retailer, ask your supplier what the typical mark-up is on their goods by other retailers (but be careful: there are some laws limiting suppliers from setting the final prices of their goods). Of course, you may want to price your goods more aggressively, especially in the earliest days of your business.

Fees for Professional Services

Setting fees is more of an art than a science when what you're selling is your own expertise. After all, if you're smarter than the lawyer down the street but he has more experience, should you charge less or more? What if you work faster? Why does one management consultant charge $50 an hour and another $250? Is the second really five times better than the first?

Clearly, setting professional fees is a challenge. Nevertheless, there are generally accepted practices and ranges. The two primary ways of pricing services are on an "hourly" basis or on a "project" basis.

- **Hourly.** Most professional services can be charged on an hourly fee. This rewards you appropriately when you are performing long, complicated tasks for a client. However, you may find yourself shortchanged when what you're selling is your existing knowledge or expertise, and it doesn't take as long to convey that to your client as a less experienced person.

- **Project.** On a project, or task, basis, you establish a set or minimum fee for an entire project. Clients often like to pay on a project basis, because they like knowing what they will be charged before they commit. Project fees reward you when your knowledge enables you to finish projects quickly but penalize you if you've badly misjudged the amount of time a given project will take.

One way to establish fees is to determine typical fees charged by others for similar services. Contact an industry association, ideally located in your geographic area, to get a sense of typical fee structures and ranges. In the final analysis, the appropriate fee is always the same: whatever the market will bear. Time and experience will help determine what that is.

If you manufacture or produce goods or services sold by others, the reseller will set the final price for the end user. They, in turn, are going to base their prices, in large part, on what you charge them. If your costs to the reseller are too high, they won't be able to make money and won't purchase from you. That's why it's critical to know what retailers typically sell similar products for and, if possible, what your competitors are charging those same resellers.

Of course, when setting prices, you have to cover your costs and make a profit. And that's typically how manufacturers and others set prices. This is "bottom up" planning: figure your costs for raw materials, labor overhead, shipping, returns, and so on, and then set a reasonable figure for profit.

Some brilliant businesspeople have built great companies by knowing how to maintain ultra-low prices or convince customers to pay premium prices. Most of us, though, need to stick to the normal range.

Subscriptions vs. Per-Use Fees

If you plan to provide a service—especially, as is increasingly the case, if you can do so virtually, over the Internet—you have the option of choosing whether you want to provide it as a subscription or on a per-use basis.

Let's say you're a CPA providing tax preparation and consulting services. Typically, CPA services are priced on an hourly basis; however, it's becoming increasingly common for such professionals to offer clients an annual service for a flat fee that includes all document preparation for state and federal authorities, as well as any advice they might need over the course of that year.

Another example: a growing number of publications that have put their articles and other content online offer readers the option of paying every time they want to read a particular article—a per-use basis—or instead paying a monthly or annual subscription rate (just as they would with a traditional print magazine) to access all of the content anytime they want, as many times as they want. A broad range of businesses offer subscription models instead of or in addition to per-use pricing models to expand their markets.

Discounts

Discounting regular prices is a time-honored way of attracting new customers or encouraging existing ones to buy more products or services. You can use discounts as a means of getting rid of older merchandise as well. There are a number of different kinds of discounts you can offer to encourage sales.

- **One-time sales and promotions.** The most common type of discount is a special price on an item or service for a limited time. This can be an introductory price on a new product or service, a discounted price on an old or overstock item, or limited-time discounts (for example, "Back-to-School Savings Week").

- **Volume discounts.** Another common form of discount is simply offering a lower cost for the more products or services a customer purchases. Thus, if you make your own organic cosmetics, you could offer customers 10 percent off for every $100 of products purchased to encourage current customers to purchase more items. Even a "Buy One, Get One Free" offer is a form of volume discount.

business BUZZ words

"loss leader"

By offering a product or service for little more or less than it actually costs you, you can get customers in your door, or into your office, with the goal of eventually up-selling them or encouraging them to purchase more profitable products or services.

■ **Customer loyalty programs.** An increasingly popular, and effective, form of marketing is offering special discounts or promotions to people who sign up for your company's loyalty—or frequent buyer—program. If you run a coffee house, for instance, you might hand out loyalty cards that you mark or punch each time a customer buys a coffee drink. After buying so many drinks, the customer can then get a freebie.

Whether you charge a nominal fee for your loyalty program or offer free enrollment, this encourages customers to purchase from you instead of competitors. What's more, if you use a computerized database to keep track of purchases, a loyalty program allows you to collect information on buying patterns of repeat customers.

■ **Rebates.** Rebates are a sales promotion where the customer gets money back after purchasing an item. There are several advantages of using rebates: first, there aren't any negative perceptions or backlash from customers, who can feel resentful and resist buying at full price when an item is on sale and then returns to its regular price. Second, because many purchasers never actually mail in the documentation to claim the rebate, the manufacturer and/or retailer has the advantage of getting the customer's attention—and making the sale—without actually forfeiting any profit.

Freebies

Sometimes the smartest marketing move you can make is to give products or services away. This is especially true in mature or crowded markets where you're having trouble getting customers' attention. In such cases, allowing potential buyers to sample the goods or services can pay you back in spades. Whether this involves sending out free samples in the mail, putting a coupon in the paper entitling the first 50 respondents to a free manicure in your salon, or offering a free 30-day trial of a new Internet service that automatically backs up all files on users' hard disks every night, this can often serve as the best hook you can devise to make your company stand out from the pack.

worksheet: Pricing

What do you intend to charge for your product or service? _____

What are competitors charging for similar products or services? _____

If you are selling a service, what is your pricing model—for example, by the hour or project, a per-use fee, subscription? _____

What different features, services, or product variations can you offer at different price points? _____

What kinds of discounts, rebates, or other special offers do you intend to use? _____

chapter 21

Sales

If your marketing strategy is successful, soon potential customers will be interested in buying products or services from you. Now, you just have to make the actual sale.

Any action you take that involves making direct contact with people with the goal of placing an order or securing a client falls under the category of *sales*. Sales are critical for your business—indeed, everything in your business must be geared toward sales if you want to stay in business. And although the quality of your product or service is important, your ability to sell is just as critical.

Some entrepreneurs view the prospect of making a sales call with the same fear and loathing as a tax audit. After all, your talent lies in your ability to make mouth-watering apple tarts, create compelling logos, or build software, not in trying to convince people to part with their hard-earned cash. Sorry: that's no excuse. If you can't picture yourself in the role of salesperson, it's essential that you get someone on board who can.

Recognizing Good Customers

Any customer is a good customer, right? After all, as long as someone wants to purchase your product or service, they've done what you want. What more do you want from a customer?

Lots.

There's a huge difference between good customers, not-so-good customers, and downright bad ones. Believe it or not, you may even find yourself wanting to get rid of customers! Some customers cause problems, are more work than they're worth, or will cost you money. In such cases, you will need an exit strategy to get out of the relationship. So what makes for a good customer?

- **They keep coming back.** The very best customers are looking for a relationship, not a single product or one-time service. Because it takes so much time and energy—not to mention money—to acquire new customers, you'll want to hold onto existing customers whenever possible. Targeting potential customers who are most likely to return time and again is an important way to keep your marketing costs down and allows you to focus on other aspects of your business.

- **They buy a lot.** Having a few customers who buy in large quantities is almost always better than selling small amounts to large numbers of customers. Sure, there are certain risks—if one of your major customers goes away, you could be in financial difficulties—but in general, your costs will be lower and your ability to satisfy your customers much greater if you have a contingent of loyal customers who buy in volume.

- **Their purchases are profitable.** This is a major point, especially if your margins are relatively low and you have to watch your costs. A sale might look good on paper, but if a customer is too demanding or takes up too much of your time with unnecessary questions and service requests, your profit could well evaporate. For that reason, it's always critical to continually calculate the profitability of customers.

- **They know what they want.** By being clear about their wants and needs, and communicating them effectively to you, customers can help you do a good job of serving them. There's nothing worse than trying to please people who don't understand what they want.

- **They pay on time.** For any business that sells products on account (on credit) or any service in which payment is collected in arrears of the service being performed (which is the case for the vast majority of services), prompt payment is critical to keep cash flowing and your company in business.

- **They are ethical.** Everyone wants to do business with people they like and respect. The last thing you want is to be constantly watching your back to see if someone is trying to take advantage of you in some way.

- **They are not litigious.** Any individual or business that immediately turns to legal action to solve problems is not someone you want to be in a business relationship with.

- **They are financially stable.** You don't want to have to worry about whether your customers can pay their bills every month. Having customers who can easily make their financial commitments is therefore critical.

Managing Bad Customers

Once you understand what good customers look like, it's time to consider the reverse. In most cases, bad customers represent the antithesis of good customers: they purchase once, and you never see them again. They fail to pay or are late paying. They threaten to sue over minor problems that arise. And so on.

You can usually measure the degree to which a customer is not worth having in two ways: financially and emotionally. Financially, you can just do the math. When you're spending so much time selling to or servicing a client (or selling at a price so low) that you can't make a profit—either in terms of products, supplies, or employee time (including your own)—that client is not worthwhile.

But bad customers can also take an emotional toll. And even when a customer is profitable, they can be so problematic that they're simply not worth it. If you dread dealing with certain customers—if they're constantly making things difficult or are even outright abusive—it might be time to let them go.

business
BUZZ
words   **"up-selling and cross-selling"**

You should always be looking for opportunities to make more money from each sale. This involves *up-selling* (selling a pricier and more function-rich version of a product or service) and *cross-selling* (selling complementary products or services). Say you just booked a series of 10 hour-long massages for a new client, to be fulfilled over a 10-week period. You might want to up-sell that package by convincing the customer to extend the standard hour to a more expensive 90-minute massage. Or you might want to cross-sell by offering body lotions to complement the massages.

But how do you do that? Sometimes the most direct way is the best: simply tell the customer that the relationship is not working out for you, and that you'd like to terminate it. Sometimes, however, this is difficult, if not impossible. For example, your customer might depend on you for a key component or service—say a widget they can't manufacture *their* product without or a Web hosting service that keeps their e-commerce site up and running. In such cases, you will have to give notice, just as if you were firing an employee, to give them sufficient time to line up a new supplier or service provider. In some cases, you can raise the product price or service fee sufficiently to either make it worth your while to keep unprofitable or otherwise poor customers, or to prompt them to seek similar products or services elsewhere. In either case, it's best to take action sooner rather than later so as to reduce the financial and emotional toll on yourself as well as your business.

A Successful Sales Call/ Interaction

Whether you're using a direct sales force, hiring salespeople to stand in your retail store, using a telesales service, or employing the Internet, what makes a sales call successful? You might think it has to do with being prepared, having a good sales pitch, making a good impression—perhaps by demonstrating how your product or service works—and distributing impressive collateral or sales materials. It does; however, it's actually a little more complex than that.

First, you have to be able to close the deal. It's not enough to make a convincing argument on behalf of your services or product. You must turn that pitch into an actual sale by asking or directing the customer to buy the product or service you're trying to sell. In person, this can be uncomfortable, but your potential customer is waiting for you to say, "Can I ring you up?" or "Let's discuss the terms of the contract." If you don't practice asking for the money, you'll walk out of many sales calls wondering what happened. Many a sale has been lost because the salesperson omitted to take this very basic but important step.

Even on the Web, you have to close the deal and direct customers to make the purchase. That's why you see so many "Buy Now" buttons on websites.

Next, the product/service has to provide a clear benefit for the purchaser. Success has two sides. True, your goal is to profitably exchange your product or service for money. Yet if you fail to satisfy the customer by meeting their wants or needs, you're only halfway to a successful sale. That's why an important part of any sales call is to *listen* so that you can learn what the customer is really looking for and what's important to them.

Finally, the transaction has to be profitable. This means that if you add up everything it costs you to produce and deliver a product or service—including your sales expenses—you still end up actually making money on it. Thus, as you negotiate price—and you will have to do some negotiating—make sure you can make a profit.

"sales pipeline"

The sales pipeline represents the number of potential transactions currently in progress. This includes everyone from very strong prospects to customers in the final stages of negotiation.

The Sales Pitch

Many people wrongly believe that a good salesperson is simply someone who can talk well. But that's only half of it. It's equally important—perhaps even more important—to be able to listen well. By listening to customers, you find out which issues are important in their purchasing decision.

At some point, though, you will need to make the pitch—that is, actually ask a prospect, or prospective customer, to buy your product or service. A sales pitch can come in many forms, but it has three distinct stages:

- Your pitch (describing your products or services, company, customer benefits, and competitive advantage)

- The customer's concerns and objections

- Your rejoinder, or reply, to those concerns and objections

After you've been in business for a while, you'll have heard the objections or concerns that keep most prospects from making the decision to buy. Work on responding to those so you'll sound confident should they arise in the course of a sales call. It's generally best to anticipate objections and respond to them before they're raised. This way, you can address whatever shortcomings or problems the prospect may be thinking about but doesn't want to mention out loud.

business
BUZZ
words

"sales cycle"

A sales cycle is the timing or stages customers go through when deciding to buy a product or service. They must recognize a need for a product or service and then begin investigating possible ways to fill that need. In the final stage, the customer actually purchases the product or service. Different types of products and services, and different types of customers, have different sales cycles, ranging from very short (hours or days) to months or even years. For example, if you are selling janitorial services, the small business moving in down the street might be able to make a decision quickly because it has a short sales cycle. However, a huge corporation might take a year deciding on a new janitorial service.

Jim Bell Skateboard Ramps: Skating to Riches

Jim Bell was just a skateboarder and punk rock musician who drove from the Midwest to move to California with only $50 in his pocket. He wasn't sure what he wanted to do, but he knew he loved skateboarding. Needing money, he took a job at a Los Angeles skateboarding manufacturing company. It wasn't glamorous—he was doing telemarketing sales—but at least he was able to remain involved in the world of skateboarding.

That job alone, however, wasn't enough to support him. So on weekends, Bell worked at a skateboard shop at the beach to earn extra cash. One day a customer came in, and Bell and the man began talking. The customer asked Bell if he knew where he could get a skateboard ramp for his son. Recalls Bell, "I'd been building skateboard ramps since I was a kid, so I offered to do it for him." After building the ramp and delivering it to the customer, Bell was actually startled to receive a payment. "When he handed me the check," says Bell, "I sort of looked at it. I had viewed it as a favor, not a business transaction." But the fact that he could earn money building skateboard ramps gave him the idea for his company. "The next day I went into work and gave my two-weeks notice," says Bell, "and the following day registered my fictitious business name."

Suddenly, Bell was in business—the business of making skateboard ramps. Because Bell was a passionate skateboarder himself, he understood what skateboarders wanted, and he built ramps that immediately appealed to avid skaters.

But Bell still needed to make sales. Fortunately, he had some sales experience and he wasn't afraid to go out there and begin making sales. To get customers, he started out on the cheap—specifically, by hanging up posters and signs at skateboard shops and passing out flyers to skateboarders. He knew that business wouldn't just come to him. So Bell was persistent. Word of mouth about his ramps spread quickly, and soon Bell had a thriving business.

In fact, by 2005, only his second year in business, Bell was pulling in just under $100,000 in revenues from building custom skateboard ramps for residential backyards and driveways. In 2006, he more than doubled his revenues, moved to a new 4,000-square-foot building, and expanded his staff to help grow his business even further. He then started building larger custom ramps, even skateboard parks.

As Bell looks to grow beyond the custom skateboard ramp business—which requires employees to do the work—he's excited about his latest endeavor: a skateboard ramp kit that enables skateboarders to build their own ramps. This offering allows Bell to serve a much larger market than his current Southern California operation without adding locations, since his ramp kit can be shipped anywhere in the world. Bell has already been featured on national TV—Fox News, the "Ellen DeGeneres Show," MTV—and is adding more employees. Not bad for a skateboarder and punk rocker.

Sales Vehicles

The sales vehicle you choose will depend on a number of factors, including your personality/personal preferences, budget, and target customer base. If you're selling high-end customer-made jewelry, hiring a telesales force probably isn't your best option; however, if you're selling a highly proprietary and complex product that requires expertise to sell, you would probably choose to keep your sales force in house so that you could provide ongoing training and ensure the quality of your sales force. If, on the other hand, you have a commodity product that is easy to comprehend, using a contract sales force might be the optimal choice.

Just as there are a number of possible marketing vehicles, or ways to get your marketing message out into the world, you can choose from a variety of vehicles for making sales. Sales vehicles include:

- **Meeting in person.** Depending on what you're selling, a face-to-face encounter might be your best bet for picking up new customers. If you're an investment advisor looking for high-net-value clients, taking prospects out to an impressive lunch or dinner might be the best way of selling them on your services and expertise.

- **Telephone calling.** Another way of making direct contact is over the phone. By calling up potential customers, whose names you've collected through your marketing activities or purchased as a part of prospect marketing list, you can make your sales pitch directly to potential customers.

Phone calls work best when you have a terrific hook, or pitch, that will immediately grab someone's attention, or if you already have a relationship with someone. Because you've interrupted

---

Personnel Options for Sales

If you're not inclined, or able, to sell your product or service yourself to prospective customers, you have a number of options for making sure this critical business function is covered.

- **Staff employee(s).** The most common solution is to simply hire salespeople to do the job for you. You can either pay such people a flat salary or, as is more common, a base salary plus commission for each sale made. It's also standard practice to set quotas, or require a minimum number/dollar value of sales made, and to provide bonuses or other incentives for meeting quota.

- **Contractors or sales reps.** Another possibility is to hire contractors or sales representatives, who are not actual employees, to sell on your behalf. Cost is the primary advantage of this approach: you don't have to pay benefits or accrue other expenses that come with having someone on payroll. The disadvantage is that these "hired guns" probably have other clients, which means you won't have their undivided attention.

- **Outsourced sales force/telesales service.** A third option is to make use of the myriad third-party sales/telesales services that exist. This can be a costly, though highly effective, choice, depending on the quality of the service in question.

- **Wholesalers, distributors, or other third parties.** These are people or companies with their own sales forces who sell your products to consumers, retailers, or other businesses. As such, they are part of your sales channel. They typically take a hefty percentage of the sales price but save you the hassle of selling to and servicing customers.

Spam

Spamming is the practice of sending identical (or nearly identical) email sales or marketing messages unsolicited to a large number of people. A whopping 88 percent of all email messages sent are spam, according to security vendor Postini, which monitors spam volume. Spam is such a problem that a whole industry has been created to find ways to protect against it. (Anti-spam methods include filters, "black lists" that block emails originating from specific domains, and special programs that ask email senders to verify that they are legitimate before their messages will be forwarded.) In addition, laws have been passed to strictly limit sending unsolicited email. Even if you avoid criminal prosecution, sending spam can cause more harm than good by annoying potential customers. The last thing you want is to be perceived as spamming potential customers. The one sure way to avoid this is to only send marketing and sales emails to those individuals who specifically "opt in" or indicate that they want to receive promotional materials from you via email.

organic dog food, you might want to purchase the subscriber list for *Pug Fancier* subscribers. Likewise, if you've just opened up a new sporting goods store, you could purchase the member list of the local swim club. Again, direct mail works when you have a specific "call to action" that will spur the recipient of the advertisement to take immediate action (see page 146).

- **Direct emailing.** Increasingly, instead of sending out traditional paper mail delivered by the U.S. Postal Service, businesses send out email messages that have a similar "call to action" for recipients to buy a product or service. When sent indiscriminately, email sales messages risk being considered spam (see "Spam" sidebar, this page) by recipients—which means not only are such messages likely to be redirected to spam folders (where recipients won't necessarily have to seem them), they can also be against the law. If sent judiciously, however, direct emails can be very effective. The most effective email is that which recipients have specifically told you they *want* to receive by "opting in" to receive special promotions or newsletters or sales info. Existing customers are also often happy to receive periodic emails from you notifying them of new or enhanced products or services, or promotions. Online services make it easy and inexpensive to email customers regularly.

- **Third-party sales.** Rather than selling goods or services directly, you might consider having third parties sell for you. This can take the form of value-added resellers (VARs), solution providers, independent sales representatives, and agents.

- **E-commerce.** A common way to make sales is online, via websites. Using this vehicle, customers actually purchase your products or services online using a credit card, PayPal, bank account debiting, or some other form of electronic payment. At this point, there are few businesses that *don't* do e-commerce, since it has quickly become a requirement for competing not only with businesses that sell similar products and services to yours in your immediate geographic region, but also those that offer competing products from around the world.

someone's day, and they're unlikely to have much time to spare, you have to make it worth your prospect's while. Offering something they already routinely buy—say office supplies—at an obviously more attractive price, or accompanied by additional services that none of your competitors are offering, is the ideal situation in which to do cold calling.

- **Direct mail.** This is where you use a reduced bulk postal rate to send mail to all postal customers in a specific geographic area or all individuals or businesses on a list. For example, if you're selling

Comparing Sales Vehicles

SALES VEHICLE	PROS	CONS
Meeting in person	Personal, builds relationships. Can listen to customers' needs and address their concerns directly, on the spot.	Time consuming and expensive. Must be prepared for a lot of rejection.
Phone calls	Reach customers directly. You can make your sales pitch without involving an intermediary. Much less expensive than calling on prospects in person. If carefully targeted, can be effective.	Telemarketing and telesales have bad reputations. Many people won't listen to sales pitches when called. Others have put their names on "do not call" lists, and you can be fined high fees if you call them.
Direct mail	Reaches a lot of potential customers very efficiently. A good way to communicate sales and discounts.	Much of it is ignored. Can be expensive. Response rates are very low. Bad for the environment.
Email	Inexpensive. If targets are carefully selected and have "opted in" to your list, your emails are welcomed and can be a good way to communicate new products and/or services and promotions.	The vast majority is ignored. Spam filters prevent most such email from being seen by targets. If classified as a spammer, you could be prosecuted.
Third-party sales	Professionals handle the very important job of sales for your firm.	Expensive. Little or no control over agents and/or representatives.
Website transactions	Low overhead, very efficient for the customer.	Must have effective sales pitch. Must maintain and update website. Have to drive traffic to your site. Some customers are still nervous about doing business over the Internet.

The National Do Not Call Registry

The National Do Not Call Registry is a way for consumers to request that they not be called by telemarketers or telesales personnel. Once you're on the Do Not Call list, telemarketers are prohibited from calling you. There are, however, some exceptions. A telemarketer or teleseller may call a consumer with whom it has an established business relationship for up to 18 months after the consumer's last purchase, delivery, or payment—even if the consumer is on the National Do Not Call Registry. In addition, a company may call a consumer for up to three months after that consumer makes an inquiry or submits an application to the company. Or if a consumer has given a company written permission, the company may call them.

If you engage in telemarketing, you must honor the Do Not Call Registry scrupulously. Starting in 2005, businesses were required to search the registry at least once a month and drop any registered consumers from their call lists. A consumer who receives a telemarketing call despite being on the registry will be able to file a complaint with the FTC, either online or by calling a toll-free number. Violators can be fined as much as $11,000 per incident. For further information pertaining to businesses engaging in telemarketing or telesales, go to www.telemarketing.donotcall.gov.

Successful Sales Techniques

Selling is a craft, not an art. It is a skill that can be learned. Here are a few keys to successful sales.

- **Listen.** No skill is more important to making a sale than listening. A great salesperson hears what customers want—their concerns and priorities. When calling on a customer, it's tempting to immediately launch into a sales pitch, especially if you're nervous. But by listening, you can better understand how your products or services meet the customer's needs and desires. If a potential customer of your house-sitting service is concerned about the safety of property, don't try and sell how well you and your employees will take care of the plants. Don't just tell the customer what you think they'll be interested in or stick to your standard sales patter, find out what their concerns are and address them.

- **Ask questions.** You can't listen to a customer unless you get them talking. Ask relevant questions to draw them out. "What are you especially worried about when you go away? What's the first thing you check when you get back home? What's your chief concern about entrusting your home to a service?" Don't just ask questions to qualify customers as hot prospects, such as "Do you have any plans to go away soon?"

- **Tell them what they get, not what you do.** This is a common mistake. You work with your product or service every day, so it's natural to focus on details of your work. But customers don't want to know the ins and outs of your business; they want to know how you will meet their needs. So don't bore your potential customer with excruciating details of how you manufacture the widgets by hand. Tell them what the widgets do—and focus on their *benefits* rather than their features.

- **Appreciate the benefits of your product or service.** Genuine enthusiasm is contagious. If you truly believe you're offering the customer something worthwhile, you'll be a more effective salesperson. On the other hand, if you don't believe in your product or service, you shouldn't be selling it.

- **Don't oversell.** It's tempting to land a sale by telling customers everything they want to hear, but that's almost certain to lead to their being dissatisfied or disappointed. One way to avoid this is to actually underpromise and overdeliver to make customers delighted with what you have sold them and extraordinarily pleased with its value.

Talking About Price

Finding the right time and method to talk about price can be tricky, especially if you offer products or services with a broad span of possible price points. Professional services—such as consulting, legal, engineering, architectural, and the like—can be particularly difficult to discuss from this perspective because their cost depends on the size and demands of a particular job.

There are three critical skills when discussing price: getting the timing right, estimating price, and negotiating to fit a potential customer's budget.

- **Getting the timing of mentioning price right.** The *timing* of mentioning a price to a potential client depends on a lot of factors, such as how your pricing stacks up against competitors' pricing and whether it will cause "sticker shock" in your prospect. A general rule of thumb is to lead with your price if it is much lower than the competition and will be a pleasant surprise, and to wait until after

Do Your Homework

As with so much else in business, research can be the key to success. Before approaching potential clients gather as much information as you can about them. Google them, go to their website, do everything you can to learn as much about their businesses and needs as possible before giving them your sales pitch.

you have described all the benefits of your product or service if it is the same or higher than that of your competitors.

The one hard and fast rule you *must* follow is to provide the estimate and get the customer to agree to a price *before* starting actual work. This might seem obvious, but you'd be surprised how many fledgling entrepreneurs are so eager to get business that they omit this very important step! Even if you charge by the hour, it's critical to give an approximate estimate of how many hours you think a job will take and to get clients to sign an estimate or letter of agreement. If the scope of the job changes over time—for example, if the client for your musical ensemble decides to have you play at the reception as well as during the wedding—make sure to provide a new estimate and have the client sign off on the changes.

- **Estimating price accurately.** Your kitchen remodeling business is finally taking off, and you have a number of potential clients asking you for bids. Key to your ultimate success—whether you will actually make money from your work—is being able to accurately predict how much work is involved. This includes costs for materials you will need to complete the job as well as the time it will take—both yours and that of any employees or contractors you use. This is a skill you will hone over time. It is almost inevitable that you will make mistakes at first, which is why it is a good idea to build in a healthy buffer when providing an estimate—whatever you can get away with while still remaining competitive.

The best way to learn how to estimate accurately is to keep track of your time and expenses, so that you can see—over time—how much any job truly costs you.

- **Negotiating to fit customers' budgets.** An essential skill in setting prices is negotiating. Often, customers have unrealistic ideas of what they can get for their money. (They may even gasp in horror when you name your price!) Rather than walking away without a sale, attempt to work with them. Ask the customer what their budget is—most of the time they'll to tell you—and instead of just saying, "I can't do the job for that amount," let them know what you *can*

Don't Oversell

Although you might think the best thing you can do is up-sell and cross-sell to the max, this may in fact not be the case. You might make more profit in your digital camera emporium from selling the high-end digital cameras with all the bells and whistles, but what happens when customers who succumb to your sales pitch go home and realize they didn't need all of those features? You may have put a potentially lucrative long-term relationship with them in jeopardy. Although in the short term you might have made more dollars, over the long run you'll actually lose money, since the next time that customer needs a piece of photographic equipment they'll go to someone they can trust not to oversell them.

provide within their budget. This might involve cutting back on volume or eliminating certain features. In effect, you are making a counter offer, letting them know how much you can provide for the money they're willing to pay.

For example, if a homeowner wants to add an additional room and they say their budget is only $5,000, instead of just saying, "That can't be done," say something like, "For that amount of money, we could add a deck or change some windows. It would take a minimum of $30,000 to add even a small room." By laying out a range of choices, you help them learn about costs; you can still make the sale; and everyone can leave the negotiating table happy.

Your Formal Proposal to the Client

A proposal is a document, typically used in professional services, that lays out exactly what you will deliver to a client and what it will cost. The proposal should include the following components:

- **Background/Statement of need (for professional services).** Explain why the client is coming to you, show that you understand the reasons the work is being undertaken, and outline the needs.

- **Scope of Work/Description of work to be provided/Deliverables.** Outline exactly what work you'll be doing for the client and what "deliverables"—such as reports, designs, and materials—you'll be providing. This should be fairly detailed.

- **Bio of provider/Description of company.** Provide a short description of yourself and/or your company so that the client knows why you're well suited for the work. Even if the client has already decided to use you, this section reinforces that decision.

- **Delivery date/Timeline/Due dates.** Detail the due dates for the various stages of the project and/or the final completion date; indicate if there are any known contingencies that may change the timing.

- **Delivery terms.** If you're selling a physical product and there are details relating to the delivery (such as who pays freight) delineate the conditions under which the delivery must be paid and so forth.

- **Fees/Price and payment terms.** Clearly list the fees for the project. If you're charging by the hour, list both your hourly fee and the estimated total for the project. If you're charging by the project, list an hourly fee if the client adds additional work. Describe who's responsible for which expenses—for instance, who pays for travel or out-of-pocket costs. List any payment terms as well when the payment is due and any late charges for late payments.

- **After-sales support/Tech support.** If any, list them here.

- **Returns policy/Warranties/Satisfaction guarantee.** If applicable, include it here.

- **Acceptance/Date.** Include a line for each party to sign and date

Closing the Sale

A "closing" occurs when you come to an agreement about the price, scope, and other terms of the sale. The sales cycle has been completed, and you can now move into the next phase, which is actually performing the work or delivering the product. The closing is essential because no matter how good your sales pitch is, or how proficient you get at estimating the scope and price of a project, if you can't get the customer to actually agree to purchase your goods or services, you have not been successful. There are several elements that characterize an effective closing:

- **The customer agrees to the sale.** This is the primary requirement of a closing: that you and the customer come to an agreement of the exchange of goods or services for money.

- **You arrange a time to deliver the goods or start the project.** Make sure you are very clear about when the customer will actually receive the products, or when you will begin providing the service. If your customer is not located locally, specify when you will ship your product and by what method—that is, courier, next-day air, postal service, or other.

- **You establish how the goods/services will be paid for—and when.** Payment terms are almost as critical as the actual price you're charging. Will the customer be paying in cash, by check, a credit card, or on account? If the latter, how much time do they have before they must pay? Thirty days? Sixty days? Ninety days? All of this must be clearly spelled out.

- **You formalize the agreement with a written document.** Although many successful entrepreneurs believe this step is optional and prefer to rely on "handshake" agreements, it's always best to have things in writing. Whether it's your proposal or another kind of contract, document all of the key aspects of the agreed-upon deal. Don't leave anything ambiguous or up to chance. It's always best to be very clear about everything related to your sales agreement.

worksheet: Creating a Proposal

Background/Statement of need:

_____
_____
_____
_____
_____
_____
_____

Scope of work/Description of work to be provided/deliverables:

_____

Bio of provider/Description of company:

_____

Delivery date/Timeline/Due dates:

_____

Delivery terms (if any):

_____

Fees/Price:

_____

After-sales support/Tech support (if any):

_____

Returns policy/Warranties/Satisfaction guarantee:

_____

Acceptance/Date:

_____

Making the Customer Feel Good

One of the smartest things you can do after the sale is to provide some sort of evidence to customers that they have made the right decision. Head off buyers' remorse at the pass by sending them a follow-up email congratulating them on their choice of products or commending them for choosing your service. Include quotes from previous customers or other accolades you've received for your goods or services. All of this is just as important as providing compelling evidence before the sale that you were the right choice.

Follow-up: Reinforcing the Sale

So you've made the sale—congratulations! But your work doesn't stop there. In fact, many people believe that what you do *after* the sale is just as important as what you've done to secure it. Think of this as the beginning of a relationship rather than the end of a transaction, and proceed accordingly. Send follow-up letters or emails, or make quick phone calls once you've judged that the customer has had a chance to use your product or experience the quality of your service. Ask if you can include them on future mailings announcing specials, promotions, or new developments at your firm. And keep checking back with them regularly. If you deliver a quality good or service and, without being too aggressive, follow up with communications that keep your name in front of them, chances are good customers will come back or spread the good news about your company through word of mouth.

worksheet: Sales

Customers and Sales Cycle

Who are the customers you're targeting, and why do they need or want your product/service? What time of year are your customers most likely to make a purchase? _____

How long will it take between the time you present your product/service to a customer and the time that customer makes an actual purchase decision? _____

Sales Call

What compelling benefits, features, and reasons for purchasing will you highlight in your sales pitch? _____

How will you make sure you're listening to the customer explain their needs and wants? _____

What objections or hesitations might a customer have about purchasing your offering? _____

What can you honestly say to counter those hesitations? _____

How and when will you bring price into the discussion? _____

If a customer is hesitant about the price, what terms can you negotiate (for example, providing a slightly different product, service, features, timing)? _____

How much are you willing to lower your price if necessary? _____

What additional products/features/services can you offer the customer to increase your total sale and profitability? _____

How will you "close" the sale? What can you say to direct the customer to make a decision and purchase? _____

How will you follow up your sales call—follow-up letters, emails, or phone calls? If the prospect has not yet made a decision, how many times—and when—will you contact them again? _____

Once someone is a customer, how will you reinforce their purchase and make them feel good about doing business with you? _____

Sales Vehicles

How will you actually make a sale to a customer? _____

In-person, face-to-face sales? _____

Online? _____

Telephone sales? _____

Direct mail? _____

Email? _____

Third-party sales (through a retailer, distributor, independent sales rep, etc.)? _____

Proposals, Estimates

Will you have to submit proposals or estimates to prospective clients/customers? If so, have you created a proposal template? _____

When estimating, have you considered all expenses and costs, and made proper allowance for a reasonable profit? What factors will go into your estimate of the price? _____

Once you have finished making a sale and supplying the product/service, how will you evaluate whether the sale has been profitable? How will you keep track of time and expenses? _____

Part Four:
Running Your Business

Operations

Where will you make or sell your products or perform your services? What kind of equipment will you need? How will you keep track of paperwork? Which chair or desk is best suited to your office and the work you do? All of these questions (and more) fall under the category of "operations."

Operations represent the infrastructure, equipment, processes, and procedures you've put into place that allow you to produce and deliver your product or service in a way that enables you to run a profitable business. Operations are important because without them, nothing could get done: You wouldn't have an office or manufacturing plant, much less one with electricity, running water, and networking capabilities. You wouldn't have the machinery to make your products or a warehousing facility to store them or a trucking fleet to get them to market. Operations can be categorized in a number of ways and include the following:

- **Facilities.** These include anything having to do with purchasing or renting a location, as well as maintaining it—buildings, office space, utilities, janitorial services, repairs, and landscaping, among other things.

- **Production/Manufacturing.** This includes not only your equipment but also the cost of maintaining it, raw materials and supplies, labor, and everything else you need to actually create the goods you sell.

- **Information technology.** Technology has come to play an increasingly important part in just about every business. Information technology, or IT, covers everything from your computers and networks to the software that runs on them to everything else technology related that keeps your operations humming along smoothly.

- **Customer service.** This is just what its name implies: the provision of after-sales support to customers who have purchased your products or services.

- **Supply chain operations.** These include anything having to do with moving from the initial supplies that make up your products to getting the product into customers' hands. Among other things, they include:

  —Purchasing

  —Inventory management

  —Order fulfillment

  —Distribution

  —Packaging and shipping

Why Are Operations Important?

How you handle the day-to-day operations and administration of your company directly affects your success. While operational details may seem mundane, they can make all the difference in whether you're profitable, have sufficient cash flow to pay your bills, or stay out of trouble with authorities. The wrong location can doom a retail business; a poor manufacturing process can result in higher costs, lower quality, or too much waste.

Operations are so critical that they can either give you a competitive edge or drag you down. Because they comprise such a major component of overall business costs, they directly impact profit margins.

Best Practices in Operations

The sign of well-managed operations is *efficiency*: everything that needs to be done gets done, on time, and without waste. Some questions you should ask as you're setting up your operations:

■ **Will I be profitable given how I run my business?** This is the critical question because the efficiency of operations can make or break your ability to actually make money. If your overhead is too high because you order too many raw goods, or

Operations in a Service Business

For service businesses, operations are just as critical. Have you set up efficient processes for marketing your services, providing the service, and billing for your services? Do you have the right technology tools to help you perform your service effectively? If you have employees, do they understand the flow of work through the organization and how they fit into it? Think of operations as anything that needs to be done using a step-by-step process, and you'll have a better understanding of how to improve them.

because you aren't preparing your products for shipment in the most efficient fashion, you're wasting money and time—both of which directly impact your bottom line. In a service business, do you have too many employees because you failed to calculate the division of labor appropriately? Again, this can mean the difference between being profitable and not.

business BUZZ words

"just-in-time inventory"

Just-in-time—or JIT—inventory refers to a way of reducing inventory, and therefore the cash that's tied up when products sit in a warehouse. The premise of JIT inventory is that you manufacture your goods as close to the point of sale as possible. There are obvious trade-offs between waiting until you have an actual customer order in hand before manufacturing it and having products waiting for customers to purchase immediately. But the trend in business as of late is to keep inventory to an absolute minimum while still providing customers with ready access to products.

Outsourcing

Outsourcing is when you take some aspect of your operations and give it to an outside party to perform. Usually, this is done for what are called "non-core competencies," or the functions that do not distinguish you from competitors. Thus, if you derive your competitive edge from the uniqueness of the lamps you create, you probably wouldn't want to outsource lamp design to a third party. However, you might want to outsource manufacturing, IT, or some other essential aspect of operations that another company might do more proficiently and efficiently.

The primary reason for outsourcing is to save money. By hiring a business that specializes in a certain aspect of operations—say, manufacturing, distribution, or even customer service—you eliminate waste within your own four walls and drive your costs down. Another reason to outsource is focus. You want to concentrate on the things about your business that matter rather than those that are peripheral.

Contract manufacturing is one type of outsourcing that specifically relates to production of goods. The way this usually works is that you provide the design specifications for the product to a company that specializes in manufacturing a certain kind of good—metal automotive components, for example—and the contract manufacturer takes care of everything from procuring the basic supplies to manufacturing and shipping to a warehouse or even, in some cases, the retailer or end customer.

- **Are my operational tasks repeatable?** Say you produce a new kind of headset: if every time you receive a customer order, a different person processes it in a unique way, or there's no standard procedure for packing and shipping your headset, you'll end up wasting a great deal of time. One of the keys to efficiency is *not* reinventing the wheel every time you do something. By making routine operational tasks easily repeatable, you stand a much greater chance of minimizing costs and maximizing profits.

- **Am I wasting anything?** This applies to everything from supplies used to make products to pens and paper and other routine office supplies to the space you've leased or bought to the capacity of the equipment you've purchased or the people you've hired. Waste can occur at any time or place in your operations. Waste not only eats up money, it's bad for the environment. Eliminating waste is an important part of your operations.

business
BUZZ
words
"supply chain management"

Supply chain management is the process of planning, implementing, and controlling the operations of the entire life cycle of a product as efficiently as possible. Supply chain management spans all movement and storage of raw materials, work-in-process inventory, and finished goods from point of origin to point of consumption.

U Dirty Dog:
Efficiency Experts

Back in February 2004, Nancy Baio, a medical product sales rep, decided she wanted to start her own business. Not one to waste any time, she checked out the 50 fastest-growing franchisers listed in a business magazine to see what was hot. "Not that I was interested in buying a franchise," she said. "But I thought it would give me ideas."

It certainly did. Baio noticed that mobile dog grooming weighed in at No. 39. "It had three things going for it," says Baio, who is based in Madison, Wisconsin, and a pet owner. "It sounded like fun; it was something I could believe in; and there was only one competitor in my market."

Using her own funds, Baio bought two full-size vans customized for mobile dog groomers, recruited local dog groomers, and began advertising her services under the name of U Dirty Dog Mobile Pet Groomers. Today, she serves a client base of 700, has two full-time employees as well as a number of part-time contractors, and is profitable enough to begin thinking about taking her business to the next level.

Key to her success: operational efficiency. She has documented everything about running her business, from the amount of cleaning products to use when grooming a particular size dog to how long her groomers should spend on each animal. She's programmed QuickBooks to contain all of her customer histories, including contact information, names of animals, dates serviced, and all interactions with them. "Every time a new invoice is created, it adds to the customer history," she says. When her groomers are on the way to a customer, she makes sure they have everything they need to get to the appointment on time. "Unlike many services, we never cancel, and if we're going to be even slightly late, we notify our customers," she says. She's equipped her groomers with Palm Pilots and synchronizes them with her Microsoft Outlook calendaring program at the beginning of every week so they have a full list of all appointments along with all customer histories before they begin their workweek. If there are any last-minute changes to the schedule, she text messages them from her Palm Pilot.

"In a way, I run this like a franchise," she says. "Every procedure and process is documented. It's almost a turnkey system—I could sell it tomorrow, and someone could step right in and not need any training."

For marketing her business, Baio's found that traditional Yellow Pages advertising has worked best for her, as well as some online search engine keyword purchases. She also spends a lot of time out in the community, visiting veterinarian offices and handing out dog treats along with her business card.

Baio is currently considering her options for growing the business. She's at the point where she could expand it, but she'll need outside funding. "I'm about to start looking for investors," she says, although she admits that her ultimate "exit strategy" is probably to sell the business and move on to another entrepreneurial venture.

worksheet: Operations

Use this worksheet to outline your key operational procedures.

What are the key steps in making your product/service?

_____

What supplies do you need?

_____

Where will it be made?

_____

Who will make it?

_____

What key equipment is needed?

_____

What are the sources of those supplies?

_____

What are the sources of that equipment?

_____

What vehicles are needed?

_____

What key facilities are required?

_____

How will your product/service be packaged and shipped?

_____

Other operational issues:

_____

_____

_____

Customer Service

Providing stellar customer service is one of the most critical aspects of operations. The sales transaction is just the beginning of what you hope will be a long-term relationship with the customer. And one of the things that will determine the quality of that relationship is what happens *after* the sale has been made. Time and again, companies with excellent products or services, profitable pricing structures, and efficient operations fall flat on their faces when it comes to customer service.

There are three key elements to superb customer service:

- **Be honest in all of your dealings.** Honesty truly is the best policy—not only because it's the right thing to do ethically, but because your reputation for being straightforward with customers will directly impact your ability to make sales, retain customers, and (ultimately) stay in business. In an age of user-created reviews where any customer can log on to a specialized website and rate your products or services, you must treat each and every customer with care, respect, and—yes—honesty.

- **Promise only what you can deliver.** This has a direct impact on how satisfied your customers will be with what they've purchased from you. If you make and sell handcrafted chef's knives and promise that they are of comparable quality to the top Swiss-made brand, make sure that they fulfill that promise. It's much better to underpromise and overdeliver than risk routinely disappointing customers.

- **Follow through with commitments.** If you say you're going to do something, do it. Period. If you promise to be on call to customers seven days a

Offshoring

Offshoring is a subset of outsourcing in which operations (or certain aspects of operations) are delegated to firms located outside of the country in which your business operates. If you've ever called a computer manufacturer for help with a technical problem or contacted the customer service department of a major airline, chances are you actually talked to someone who lives on the other side of the world.

The reason for offshoring is, again, cost savings. Because labor and supplies are frequently cheaper in other parts of the world, companies can save significant money by purchasing raw materials or having services performed elsewhere.

week, 24 hours a day (24/7) to fix any problems that arise with the website you've designed for them, then make sure you do exactly that.

Technology

Technology has made it possible for small companies to compete with huge corporations and has dramatically lowered the cost of performing many business functions. But dealing with technology can be an immense headache—decisions can be confusing and expensive to make and difficult and costly to change.

business
BUZZ
words   **"service-level agreement"**

Service-level agreement (SLA) is a term frequently used in service industries—particularly in the IT field—where the degree and quality of the after-sales service is actually included in the contract. Thus, you might promise customers 24/7 service or that all phone calls will be returned within one hour. An SLA is the service company equivalent of the warranty that typically comes with products.

The Customer Is Always Right

Not always. Sometimes the customer is flat wrong—they want more than they have legally contracted for or claim something is defective when in fact it isn't. In such cases, you have to decide what it's worth to you to keep that customer happy. Some businesses have a policy of going out of their way to satisfy customers, even under the most dubious circumstances. One example is the retail chain Nordstrom, which will accept almost any return, even without original tags or receipt. You don't have to go this far. What's important is that you have a policy of listening to the customer and trying to do the right thing.

Whether you love technology or hate it, you've got to deal with it. You don't need to become a geek, but you do need to learn some basics. Just as you couldn't run a business without knowing what "accounts receivable" are, you can't run a company without being comfortable discussing Internet connections or databases.

But with technology changing as rapidly as it does, how do you buy something that fits your budget today yet will continue to meet your needs as your business grows and changes? Should you buy an economy model, realizing you may quickly outgrow it, or should you buy the latest, fully loaded version?

You Don't Always Need the Latest and Greatest

Before you start shopping for technology, get a good idea of what you'll be looking for. Outline your critical business needs and then look for solutions that fit them. Otherwise, it's easy to get enamored of "gee whiz" technology, even though you don't have a real need for it.

In new companies every dollar counts. That means you often have to settle for less than you'd ideally desire. Fortunately, many low-cost technology products—printers, copiers, and some computers—offer excellent features that may meet your needs until your business has time to get established. When comparing your options in choosing technology products, ask yourself:

- **What features do I absolutely need?** If you can't do the things you need—send faxes, download image files, make copies—you've wasted money, even if you got a bargain. Consider what functions you need to perform and make certain your technology can handle them.

- **Are my needs basic or complex?** Complicated tasks require more powerful equipment and software. Most inexpensive computers can handle word processing, simple bookkeeping, and basic email. A low-cost inkjet printer may suffice for a one- or two-person office with minimal printing needs. But if you're creating high-end presentations, you may need a more powerful computer and higher-end printers.

- **Does my new equipment have to be compatible with other equipment and software?** With stand-alone machines (such as copiers and fax machines), it may not matter if you buy an unknown brand, but with a computer or printer, you'll probably want to avoid the hassles of making an off-brand work with other equipment.

- **Do I want single-purpose or multi-function equipment?** Many pieces of equipment now handle multiple functions, such as the all-in-one fax printer/copier/scanner. These can be a good value, especially for a young company with limited demands.

- **Are replacement supplies readily available—and how much do they cost?** Office and discount stores usually carry only the best-known brands of printers, fax machines, and copiers. Look at the cost of "consumables" such as ink and paper. Sometimes bargain hardware can cost you more because of the price of these consumables.

- **How cool do I want to be?** Ever since Apple introduced the iMac, the computer industry has started catching onto the importance of design. Consider design and ergonomics as you shop for technology.

chapter 23

Managing People

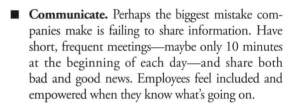

Entrepreneurs like to be in charge. You don't start your own company to have someone else call the shots. But if you want to grow your business, you're going to have to work with others. And if you want employees who are productive and motivated, you're going to have to learn how to manage them effectively.

Managing employees is all about attracting, hiring, motivating, and retaining good people to help you build your business. Being good at managing them is important because you probably won't be able to do everything yourself. And the quality of your people determines the quality of your organization. There are a number of ways to be effective at this:

■ **Choose the right people.** If an employee is smart and capable, they'll help your business grow. Hire for attitude and adaptability rather than merely for skills. Look for the ability to learn quickly, common sense, good work habits, and a willingness to take on any task.

■ **Train them well.** It's hard to take time away from your own work to train someone else, but you'll save time in the long run. If you have to, train after regular work hours when you can give the new employee your undivided attention. In a small business, employees should be able to pitch in on just about any job, so don't just train for specific tasks. Instead, teach them about the whole business and emphasize problem solving.

■ **Communicate.** Perhaps the biggest mistake companies make is failing to share information. Have short, frequent meetings—maybe only 10 minutes at the beginning of each day—and share both bad and good news. Employees feel included and empowered when they know what's going on.

■ **Motivate them to be productive.** Your attitude toward work goes a long way in determining your employees' attitude about their jobs. Think of this parable: Three men are working in a rock quarry. A passerby asks each of them what they're doing. The first one, working slowly and badly, stops and grunts, "Digging up stones." The second one, working well but unenthusiastically, pauses and says, "Feeding my family." The third one continues working diligently, smiles, and replies, "Building a cathedral." People who share a common vision work harder and feel a greater sense of purpose. Share your vision and enthusiasm.

■ **Empower them.** Give your employees the ability to make certain decisions. Nothing is worse for morale, or for the bottom line, than an employee who is only allowed to follow narrow rules. Most employees will learn how to do their jobs better than you can teach them. Let them use their brains, not just their backs.

■ **Provide feedback.** You can't expect employees to improve if you don't give them regular, constructive feedback. Employees are better able to meet your needs if you let them know when they do well and how they could have done better. And give specific suggestions, don't just complain.

■ **Acknowledge their contributions.** One of the least productive things an employer can say is, "I don't need to thank employees; they get paid." We all need to be thanked and recognized. Find opportunities to get the staff together to acknowledge jobs well done. Give small acknowledgements—plaques, certificates, T-shirts—to recognize even modest achievements.

■ **Reward them.** Pay people decently, reward them when you're successful, and give them as much security as you legitimately can. Employees don't work well when they're worried about how they'll pay the rent or whether they'll have a job next month. Job security, good pay, and decent benefits will help make your staff much more productive.

Leading the Troops

You may want to be the kind of laid-back boss who's always approachable and ready to discuss alternative ideas. Or you might want your word to be law, no questions asked. It's your choice. Keep in mind, however, that management philosophies have evolved considerably over the past few decades, and that these days, people—younger people in particular—want a more collaborative work environment and more responsibility. Your real challenge is discovering how to give employees the responsibility and authority they crave while maintaining standards and guarding the organization against problem employees.

■ **Hierarchical vs. flat management.** You may choose to impose several "layers" of managers or supervisors between yourself and the lowest person on your organizational totem pole, with many clear delineations of rank and salary between each. Or you might eschew this traditional hierarchical arrangement in favor of a "flat" organizational structure in which everyone interacts like peers (although there will inevitably be differences in salaries and responsibilities) and collaborates on important decisions. This latter approach has become much more prevalent in recent years, especially among entrepreneurial start-ups, and there are many potentially very valuable

employees who would refuse to work anywhere that doesn't operate in this way.

■ **"Open door" vs. authoritative management.** Another way to think about your management style is how accessible you want to be. Some firms have documented "open door" policies in which managers are encouraged to take the time to listen to employees' ideas, concerns, and complaints. Others prefer a more authoritarian style in which decisions are made at the top and passed down through the ranks, and which are not meant to be questioned or challenged. But although some old-style authoritatively inclined managers still exist—especially in larger, more established firms—the trend over the past decade has been toward a more open and relaxed management style that encourages innovative thinking and initiative- and risk-taking among employees.

Being a boss is a skill you have to learn—and relearn. Just like any other business skill, perfecting it takes practice, thought, and input from others. Bad bosses seem to fall into one of two categories: they're either too lenient or too tough. But those aren't the real problems. You get into trouble as a boss, just as you do as a parent, when you fail at five basic requirements: setting standards, acting fairly, listening, respecting, and rewarding. Regardless of the management philosophy or model you use, you should be able to cultivate good employees if you keep in mind the following basic guidelines:

■ **Set standards.** The best way to set standards is by being an example to others. Employees resent being held to higher standards than the boss. Clearly state your expectations, and try to be consistent. Develop and distribute clear policies. Even a small company should have a basic manual outlining benefits, holidays, sick leave, and such. Let employees know on what basis they will be judged and stick to that.

■ **Be fair.** Make certain your standards are reasonable and fair and that the goals you set are actually reachable. Don't change the rules constantly—one of the worst things you can do is want things one way today and another way tomorrow. Be careful not to play favorites, and never use benefits to manipulate employees.

■ **Listen.** Learn to talk *with* and not just *to* your employees. Many employers fail to use one of their most important resources—their employees' minds. Enlist their suggestions and set goals together. Have problem-solving sessions where employees help devise solutions to company problems. Make it clear, however, that decisions usually lie with you. Before reprimanding an employee, seek their explanation of why they failed to perform. Share information with your employees so that they understand some of the constraints on the company.

- **Respect.** Recognize the unique skills and talents of each person who works with you. Demonstrate to them that you believe they are capable of doing their jobs, even if it takes some time for them to learn. People generally live up to the trust—or mistrust—that others show them. As employees gain experience, allow them to make independent judgments and decisions.

- **Reward.** Everyone wants acknowledgement for a job well done. Give credit to all employees who do their jobs well and reward those who perform exceptionally. Rewards don't have to be only monetary; find fun or creative ways to congratulate people publicly. Recognize and reward teamwork, not just individual performance. Never criticize or discipline employees in front of others.

Your Employee Needs

One of the first things you need to do is decide whom you need to hire. Do you need full-time workers? Part-timers? Contractors or consultants? You have a number of options, and based on your requirements and your budget, you can probably find one—or a combination of several—to meet your specific needs.

- **Full-time employees.** This is just what it sounds like: you put individuals on payroll to get them to devote between 30 and 40 hours (or more) of their time each week to your business.

  Full-time workers can be salaried employees—usually management—who are given a weekly or monthly salary to cover their services that remains the same even if the exact number of hours they work varies from week to week or even day to day. Full-time workers can also be paid hourly.

Do as I do

Your employees will only be as honest and ethical as you are. They will be watching your every move and listening to every word you speak to determine what your ethical standards are and what you expect of them. No matter how idealistic your formal employee code of conduct might be, what really matters is your behavior.

- **Part-time employees.** When you don't need a full-time worker to fulfill a certain function—say you need a shipping clerk just one day a week—it doesn't make sense to hire a full-time employee for the task. Part-timers can work from just a few hours a week to as much as 25 or 30 hours a week. (There are laws that vary from state to state defining what constitutes part-time employees and what constitutes full-time ones.) Generally, part-time workers are paid on an hourly basis.

- **Interns.** Interns are usually students or other individuals just starting out in a profession who are eager to learn the ropes and are willing to work for minimum wage (or even for free) to gain much-needed experience. Working with interns is a great way to get inexpensive help in your business while also infusing energy and enthusiasm into the culture.

- **Outsourced or independent contractors.** A common way for small businesses to staff up is by hiring individuals to perform specific jobs without putting them on payroll. Such professionals can be paid either by the hour or on a project or retainer basis. This allows you to bring them on rapidly or cut back on their services when they are no longer needed without worrying about labor and employment regulations.

Igigi:
Success on a Large Scale

Back in 1997, Yuliya Zeltser opened a clothing studio in San Francisco to design custom couture clothing for upscale customers. Business was good, but it wasn't until two years later that Zeltser found her niche.

After fruitlessly shopping for a fashionable outfit that fit her full-figured mother, Zeltser saw a business opportunity. She decided to design a line of clothing sized 14 to 32 for the mass market. A friend loaned her $2,000, gave her a sewing machine, and let Zeltser use her garage to start Igigi.

At first it was just Zeltser and her sister. But then in 2002, Zeltser met her future husband, Alex Brodsky. Coming from the high-tech world, Brodsky was used to both managing companies and thinking big. "I slowly got sucked into the company," he says. After signing on as the CEO of Igigi in 2003, Brodsky launched an ambitious growth plan for the firm. By 2005, Igigi and its then-five employees were able to move out of the garage; by 2006, it had tripled its revenues and grown into a real office in downtown San Francisco. It had also opened its first retail storefront.

By 2007, Igigi had 22 employees and had grossed more than $3 million the preceding year. "We could have made even more, but we were constrained by production issues," says Brodsky, who says that the garment industry in the San Francisco Bay Area is struggling due to a lack of skilled contract labor. "We're still one of the smaller companies and can't afford to pay the prices they're charging," says Brodsky. After doing extensive research, he outsourced manufacturing of Igigi clothing to Turkey, but products that were supposed to have arrived in August weren't completed until December. "This affected our revenues, but we still grew 30 percent and were still profitable," says Brodsky.

A major coup for the firm is that the star of the hit movie *Hairspray*, Nikki Blonksy, has become an Igigi fan. She wore an Igigi creation to the movie's premiere and again to the Screen Actor's Guild Awards.

Early on, Zeltser financed her business using credit cards. After Brodsky joined the company, the two set out to raise money from friends and family. "The banks wouldn't give us anything, so we turned to people who believed in us," says Brodsky. It took 3-1/2 years, but Zeltser and Brodsky finally raised $900,000. "We wanted to raise more but couldn't," he says. The company is now on track for explosive growth, snagging media attention through the appearance of Igigi customers on "American Idol," the BET Music Awards, and the "Today Show."

Brodsky's advice for young entrepreneurs: "Have a vision but think it through, especially when it comes to estimating how much money you need," he says. "It's very hard to grow, even when you're cash positive—as we are—when you're strapped for funds."

worksheet: Employee Needs

Use this worksheet to identify the tasks you need to accomplish to run your business and then calculate how much time each will take. Next, make a note of what skills, education, and experience you're looking for. Finally, consider how much you'll pay for this work. Use the information you've gathered on this worksheet to help you write an ad and/or identify the right person to hire.

Tasks to Accomplish	Hours per Week	Skills, Education, and Experience Required	Pay Rate

Overtime and the Law

Regardless of whether an employee is full time or part time, salaried or paid hourly, it's important that you know—and follow—the overtime laws in your state or province. The law spells out when you must pay employees time-and-a-half or double time, or provide compensatory time. Labor laws also spell out how much time you must give employees for breaks, lunch, and the like.

Finding the Best Employees

The future of your company depends on the quality of your employees. Yet it's a challenge to find and retain outstanding workers, since competition is always stiff for the best employees. To pull ahead, you must:

- **Give yourself time.** You won't always know in advance that you have an opening, but when possible, start the candidate-hunting process as early as possible. The more time you have, the less pressured you'll feel to hire an unqualified candidate just to fill the position. It's better to leave a job open than to hire the wrong person.

- **Create an ongoing recruitment campaign.** Just as you need an ongoing marketing campaign to attract customers, you need an ongoing employment campaign to attract workers (especially if you have a lot of employees) and to compensate for natural turnover. In a small business, that doesn't mean constantly running ads; it means developing a network of referral sources, reminding everyone in your company to be on the lookout for great employees, and being visible in the community.

- **Be creative in your ads.** When you place a help-wanted ad, create as much attention and interest as possible. For example, if an administrative job entails a wide variety of tasks, you might use the wording "duties from the sublime to the ridiculous" or state, "Some days you'll feel like a rock star; other days you'll feel like a rock star's chauffeur."

- **Be competitive on salary and benefits.** As a small company, you may not be able to pay more than big companies or give as many benefits, but that doesn't mean you don't need to be competitive. You can't be so far apart that any applicant would feel like a fool for accepting your job. Offer creative benefits. Give birthdays as a paid holiday. Offer "well" days when people need to take an occasional day off. Maintain a dog-friendly office, where employees can bring their dogs to work. Little things like that can mean a lot to employees, and make everyone happier—and more productive—all around.

- **Be flexible.** Many applicants want flexible work schedules to avoid rush hour or to be home by 4 p.m. with the kids. You'll have a larger applicant pool if you challenge yourself to think of ways to offer applicants more flexibility.

- **Build a reputation as a great place to work.** Good employees know they're in demand; they're going to be very picky. Sure, all applicants look at tangible rewards such as salary and benefits. But in the long run, what attracts the best employees (and encourages current employees to recruit others) is building a company that's a great place to work.

Hiring Employees

Here are some tips on how to determine whom to pick from what's often a highly qualified pool of applicants:

- **Hire for attitude, train for skills.** Don't get hung up looking for specific skills, such as knowledge of a particular computer program. If you find a smart and willing person, you can send them to a class. There are exceptions, of course—if you need someone to fly a plane, you need an experienced pilot—but most skills can be taught.

- **Hire the unusual.** Increase your applicant pool by expanding your vision of a typical employee. Do you usually hire young people? Try recruiting retirees. Have you considered actively seeking people with disabilities? Sometimes the best employees don't look like the ones you already have.

- **Develop your interviewing skills.** When you're interviewing applicants, don't do all the talking.

The Virtual Team

Do you work alone? If so, you likely juggle a variety of tasks. One minute you're the marketing director, the next you're the computer specialist, and the next you're in charge of accounting. But when you're wearing so many hats, how can you possibly get around to the stuff you actually went into business for—the core functions that make you money?

Just because you have a small business doesn't mean you can't have a "staff" at your beck and call. Find capable professionals, consultants, and assistants, and treat them as your virtual staff. Voila! You're now CEO of a great team!

Here's how to build your virtual team:

1. **Identify the key functions you need addressed.** At the top of this list are accounting and bookkeeping. Next, you probably need help with technology, and you may be smart to find someone to help you with marketing. Of course, it's always advisable to have a good lawyer. If you're very busy, you may need someone to run errands or help with mailings.

2. **Determine whether some "positions" can be filled by companies rather than individuals.** For instance, you can purchase the upgraded tech support service for your most important software, especially for the first few months or even year. That way, the outside company's tech support team becomes your in-house tech team.

3. **Recruit service providers.** Interview a number of potential providers just as you would interview applicants for any job opening—discuss their fees, their services, and your business. Network with other business owners to get recommendations for appropriate and excellent service providers.

4. **Keep your virtual staff on call.** Line up your providers before you need them. If possible, give them a small assignment before you have a big project or big problem.

5. **Recognize this is going to cost you money.** Sure, you're going to have to pay these providers for work you're now doing yourself. But sit down and consider whether your time is better spent finding more clients or doing your own bookkeeping or website building.

Many employers are as nervous as prospective employees when they're in an interview situation and thus tend to talk too much themselves. For the most part, you should let the candidate do the talking. Prepare a few questions in advance; it's not fair to just say, "So, tell me about yourself." Instead, ask what facet of the job appealed to the candidate, what skills they're particularly good at, what it was about their last job that they didn't like, and so on. Also ask questions that give you a sense of the applicant as a person, but be careful not to ask questions that are illegal. It's fine to ask about hobbies, interests, and long-term goals.

■ **Check references.** Even if you have no reason to doubt the honesty of an applicant, you can learn a lot by checking references. Don't look at the reference check merely as a way to confirm employment but also as a way to learn how to work more

What's Legal vs. What's Right

As you'll quickly find out, you'll have to comply with a seemingly endless labyrinth of laws and regulations if you employ workers. There are laws regarding individuals with disabilities; laws dictating that you not discriminate in certain ways when hiring, promoting, and firing employees; and laws involving keeping your workplace safe. Obviously, you must comply with these legal mandates. But there's also a difference between the minimum legal requirements and the right thing to do. You don't want to be mean or abusive to employees. Don't just do the minimum. Do what any ethical and caring individual would do for fellow human beings.

because you have a job to fill. It's better to keep a position open than to be stuck with the wrong person.

Retaining Employees

Once you've hired a great employee, make sure you treat them well. After all, if they're that good, others will want them, too! Here are some tips on getting good employees to stay once you've got them on board:

- **Recognize achievement.** Everyone wants to be appreciated. When employees do a good job, let them know you noticed. Say "thank you" a lot. Find ways to recognize employees who do their jobs well on a day-to-day basis as well as those who accomplish something unusual or significant.

- **Reward hard work.** As important as it is for employees to get verbal recognition for their contributions, it's also great for them to get tangible rewards. This doesn't always have to be a major salary increase or bonus; sometimes just an unexpected treat can go a long way. For instance, when a public relations firm in Houston signed a major new client, the owner rewarded the staff for all their hard work by taking them to a fancy lunch at a nearby mall and giving them each $100 to spend.

- **Give salary increases.** Your employees know what other people in similar jobs earn. They know the salaries you're giving to new employees and what their coworkers make. Don't wait for an employee to become dissatisfied with their pay and ask you for a raise; they may just leave.

effectively with your new employee. Some of the questions you can ask include, "What kind of training, either for skills or for attitude, would you suggest to make the applicant an even better employee?" "What job duties required you to give more direction than others?" "What duties did the candidate particularly enjoy or do well?"

- **Act fast.** Good applicants don't stick around long. If you see someone you really like, be prepared to decide and make an offer. But don't ever hire just

"work for hire"

The work-for-hire relationship is one between a company and an employee in which any work performed belongs to the company, not the individual. This is the reverse of standard copyright law, in which intellectual property belongs to the person who created it. According to the U.S. Copyright Act of 1976:

Works Made for Hire. (1) a work prepared by an employee within the scope of his or her employment; or (2) a work specially ordered or commissioned for use as a contribution to a collective work.

- **Be realistic in your expectations.** It's human nature to focus on what an employee is missing rather than what an employee offers. Let's face it, though, no one is perfect: appreciate employees for what they bring to your organization.

- **Create a "blame-free atmosphere."** Your very best employees want to be able to use their judgment and their brains. They'll thrive in an environment where they know they can make decisions and take chances without getting berated if something goes wrong.

- **Share information and success.** Employees feel a stronger sense of ownership when they understand the company's overall goals and strategy. Share information. Also, look for ways for employees to benefit financially from the company's long-term financial success, whether in the form of bonuses, profit sharing, or an equity interest in the business.

- **Enable employees to grow.** After a while, the best employees get bored doing the same job. If the only way they can grow is by leaving, they will. Instead, invest in your employees. Help them take classes, learn new skills, and take on new responsibilities.

- **Install a "revolving door."** No matter what you do, some employees will want to move on. Be supportive of employees' personal goals. Make them feel welcome to return. Stay in touch with them; invite them to holiday parties. They'll be more likely to return or send other potential employees your way.

Employee Benefits

Good benefits are crucial to making your place of employment more attractive than others. In a day and age when many individuals are choosing contractor relationships with businesses over full-time employment, benefits are one way to lure workers into the fold. There are a number of key benefits that would-be employees are particularly interested in hearing about:

- **Health care.** The quality and quantity of insurance and healthcare benefits offered by employers are rapidly decreasing. Costs for employers are spiraling out of control, and many businesses feel forced to pass some of those costs onto employees, resulting in higher premiums, higher deductibles, and

Good Employees Never Leave?

Many times they do. After all, most people feel the need to change and grow, and they might not be able to do both within a small firm. When this happens, and you can't accommodate their needs, you should encourage your best employees to "follow their bliss"—but you should always welcome them back should new opportunities within your business develop, or if they decide they prefer your organization to others they have experienced.

less coverage. Because of this, companies that offer solid medical and dental benefits look increasingly attractive to jobseekers, especially older and more experienced ones and ones with families. If you can afford it, use these kinds of benefits as a way to attract the best people to your organization.

- **Vacation.** When asked, many people identify "quality of life" and "flexibility" as more important than money when choosing a job. One way to make employees happy in this regard is by being generous with vacation. Start with two weeks paid vacation, not one, and make sure that the time allotted to vacation goes steadily up as job tenure increases.

- **Sick leave/Personal leave.** Rather than going the traditional route of allotting so many sick days and so many personal days, many companies lump them together into one category, where employees get a certain amount of discretionary time off with pay. This simplifies life for your employees who might otherwise be tempted to "call in sick" when in fact they need to wait at home for the plumber to show up, or stay at home because of an ill child.

- **Retirement.** Although pensions are rapidly becoming a thing of the past, having a 401K program where you contribute a generous amount to employees' accounts every year—usually a percent-

worksheet: Creating a Code of Employer Ethics

Use the following worksheet to list the conduct you expect from yourself—as an employer—toward your employees, such as treating everyone with respect, listening to their concerns, acknowledging work well done, paying fair wages, and so on.

I, _____ , pledge:

_____

_____

_____

_____

_____

_____

_____

_____

_____

_____

_____

_____

_____

_____

_____

_____

_____

_____

_____

_____

_____

_____

_____

_____

_____

_____

_____

_____

_____

worksheet: **Creating a Code of Employee Ethics**

Use the following worksheet to list the conduct you expect from your employees, such as being punctual and honest, treating other employees and customers with respect, treating every customer fairly, and so on.

I, _____ , pledge:

_____

_____

_____

_____

_____

_____

_____

_____

_____

_____

_____

_____

_____

_____

_____

_____

_____

_____

_____

_____

_____

_____

_____

_____

_____

_____

_____

_____

_____

Employee Policies

There exist any number of miscellaneous things you might want your employees to do or standards you want them to conform to that don't fall into traditional job descriptions. It's best to document these things and communicate them clearly to all employees. These might include:

- **Dress code.** Perhaps the people in your office can always dress as if they were at the beach. Or perhaps you need them to be in business attire all the time—say you get frequent client visits and you want to give a professional impression. Either way, let your employees know what you expect of them. Be very specific. Don't just specify, "Nice pants," say "No jeans" or "No shorts."

- **Code of ethics.** Many employers want their employees to conform to certain standards of behavior when it comes to conducting business. This can include tenets like "Treat each customer with respect" or "Investigate every claim of product or service defect scrupulously." For this reason, it helps to have a clear code of conduct. However, it won't be your formal policy that matters as much as your own behavior—employees will take their cue from you as to the appropriate way to behave.

- **Training and education.** In addition to providing in-house training to employees, many businesses have tuition reimbursement programs that allow employees to pursue educational opportunities that will directly or indirectly boost their effectiveness and usefulness to your operations. For example, many employers will pay for workers to get college degrees or MBAs—usually by attending classes at night to avoid taking time away from work—so that they can acquire more advanced business skills, which they can then apply to their jobs.

age of salary, or an amount based upon profitability—is much appreciated by employees who are prudent enough to be looking ahead to what happens after age 65.

Laying Off or Firing Employees

Layoffs can be an unfortunate fact of life in the entrepreneurial world. They are generally forced upon businesses when they can no longer afford to have an employee (or employees) on payroll because of financial considerations. But many layoffs at large public companies occur not because the companies can't afford the employees but rather to keep investors and Wall Street happy. This is borderline unethical, and certainly not conducive for acquiring a reputation as a good place to work.

Obviously, you will have to fire employees who are not performing their jobs in ways that meet your performance standards, who engage in illegal or unethical behavior, or who endanger other employees. For legal reasons, you should keep written records that document the performance-related issues you've encountered with problem employees and show that you gave them the opportunity to correct those issues before terminating them. But it's important to do this as humanely and decently as possible, and to give terminated employees severance pay to help them support themselves until they get another job (unless of course they've done something illegal or unethical). Some companies will give employees one-week or two-week notice, but most will ask the terminated employee to leave immediately even if they pay them for that time. It's never a good idea to have a fired, disgruntled employee remain on the job.

One thing that many organizations have found useful is to generate a "code of employee ethics" that lays out precisely the kind of behavior you expect from employees. This can range from the obvious ("I will respect that company property is for business, not personal, use,") to the more esoteric ("I will treat other employees the way I would like to be treated myself).

Managing Finances

Many people are uncomfortable talking about money. Money, after all, is one of the few things left in life that we don't discuss openly with even our closest friends or family members. You may know all of the intimate details of your friends' romantic lives, but they might never reveal how much money they make.

In a business context, this discomfort with money often translates to a reluctance to deal with budgets, bookkeeping, and accounting. Numbers intimidate many people; others simply find it unpleasant to think about cash flow, profit margins, and (especially) debts.

It's time to get over that.

Money and numbers are essential components of business. If you're going to be in business, you have to learn to deal with money and numbers in a matter-of-fact, businesslike fashion. You have to be able to look at your financial reports without thinking of them as report cards on your character, discuss a raise with an employee without feeling you're under attack, and tell clients the price of your services without being embarrassed.

So recognize this: it's OK to talk about money. If a customer's bill is overdue, it's polite to tell them. If you're meeting with a prospective client, it's appropriate to reveal how much you charge. If you're hiring a consultant, it's reasonable to ask not only their hourly fee but how much the whole project will cost and to set limits.

You have no reason to be uncomfortable discussing such matters—they are normal business topics.

This is where financial management comes in: it's a way of staying on top of the money flowing in and out of your business. Financial management is critical because it enables you to come out ahead cash-wise as well as to be profitable—the two related but still very different things that you need to do to stay in business.

Effective financial management will:

- Give you the information you need when you need it

- Ensure that you have sufficient cash to pay your bills

- Safeguard you from being cheated

- Help you manage cash as well as profitability so you can pay rent, pay employees, and manage daily operations

First Steps for Financial Management

Take stock of your current financial situation. When you start a business, you may hope to use other people's money to build your company (see Chapter 15, Finances). Be warned: you're probably going to have to rely on your own money and credit as the primary

Lake Champlain Chocolates: Marshalling Resources Carefully

Back in the late 1970s and early 1980s, Jim Lampman was fond of giving boxes of chocolates to his employees on special occasions. After one such event, Lampman, owner of The Ice House restaurant in Burlington, Vermont, was approached by his pastry chef, who told him that the chocolates he was bestowing on people were not of the best quality. "The chef said he could do a better job," says Alison Stryker, of Lake Champlain Chocolates. "And he did." Before long, Lampman was selling the all-natural chocolates at his restaurant, and they were such a hit that he decided to get into the gourmet chocolate manufacturing business.

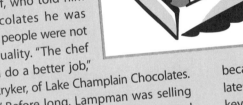

But Lampman wasn't content with being just a local Mom and Pop chocolate store; he wanted to become a national chocolate wholesaler selling into high-end food specialty stores. However, it was tough going at first. "We weren't profitable for the first seven years," says Stryker, "and it was touch-and-go for awhile."

The business slowly grew its channel strategy. Although solely wholesale at first, the firm soon decided it needed to open a retail store for cash flow reasons. Once word began to spread, people started clamoring for the ability to ship the chocolates as gifts. In response, the firm started printing a catalog. Today, it also operates an online store. In 2008, the chocolate company sold 80 percent of its high-quality confections wholesale to markets like Whole Foods and other high-end stores, 12 percent via its own retail operations, and 8 percent through a combination of mail order and Web sales.

The market strategy? "We've always known that if we can just get the chocolates into people's mouths, we can make the sale," says Stryker. So the firm makes a point of giving away lots of chocolates—at trade shows, where influential wholesale buyers might taste them, to the media, and at community events. "We've gotten a lot of great free coverage in newspapers and magazines because someone happened to taste our chocolates," says Stryker. The firm also buys search engine keywords and pays for online banner advertisements on food websites.

Key to the success of Lake Champlain: planned growth. "We're very disciplined," says Stryker. "We have a budget and do sales forecasting as well as estimate our expenses in a way that gives us a financial roadmap for the entire year. It's not that there are never any surprises, but we're usually very well prepared." One challenge is that chocolate is a seasonal business, says Stryker. "Our big sales are driven by the holidays and are usually wrapped up by Easter. Summer is difficult because chocolate melts in the heat." As a result, the company generally runs two production shifts from July through February, and then drops down considerably after that. To leverage the limited workforce of the local population, Lake Champlain works with other local companies to "exchange" employees so that workers get full employment year round, and the businesses minimize their labor costs.

sources of funding—at least until you start making sales!

Thus, as you begin to deal with your new company's finances, take stock of your personal financial situation and monetary assets. You are doing this to determine how much you can afford to put into your business. This will help you plan your expenditures and prepare you to meet with an accountant.

Right from the start, keep track of the money you invest in your new company. There are a few reasons for this. First, you want to be certain you can take every tax deduction you're entitled to, and without records, that can be a lot more difficult. Second, you want an accurate record of all expenses and sources of income. And finally, you may want to treat some of this money as loans you're making to your business rather than as an investment. Ask your accountant about the implications for handling things this way.

Clean up your personal credit record. According to the U.S. Small Business Administration, personal credit cards are the No. 1 source of financing for small companies. Expect to use your personal credit—or give personal guarantees—for many business-related purchases or credit needs. Because of this, you need to make certain you clean up your personal credit record so that you can convince banks, credit card companies, and other sources of credit to give you as high a level of available cash as possible.

This doesn't mean it's impossible to start a business if you have bad credit. But the better your credit record looks, the easier time you'll have getting financing from suppliers, landlords, and lending sources such as banks. You'll also pay lower interest rates. Even investors may check your credit reports. There are a number of critical things to do to be sure that your personal credit record is as attractive as possible:

- Get a credit report

- Learn your credit score

- Make sure everything on the report is accurate

- Pay your bills on time

- Don't increase your debt

- Increase your credit limits

Cash Is the Lifeblood of Business

You can be immensely profitable on paper yet still unable to keep your doors open. How can this be? Well, selling a lot of products or having a lot of clients demanding your services doesn't necessarily translate into immediate cash—and cash is what makes your business stay in business. Think of it this way: it costs you so much to manufacture a product (or purchase one for resale). Or it takes all of your working hours to complete a big assignment for a client—hours that you're not spending on other clients. But what if the customers you sell your products to, or your big client, doesn't pay on time? You can easily run out of cash to pay your rent, utilities, credit card bills, and employees. This has happened to countless entrepreneurs. Learn from their mistakes and pay special attention not just to sales but also to billing and collection. They can mean the difference between life and death for your business.

- Reduce your interest rates

- Make a list of your credit cards, credit limits, and current balances

Set up your books. It's unclear when the term *books* first came to be used for a company's accounts, but that's the basis of the term "bookkeeping." Perhaps it's because the record of a company's financial transactions were written down in a journal or book. In fact, many small businesses still keep their books in an actual book—simple notebooks or lined ledgers that track income as received, billings sent, and expenses.

However, in these days of inexpensive computers and easy-to-use software, this is hardly the most efficient way to track finances. Simple and inexpensive programs enable you to keep track of your company's accounts quickly and give you a lot more power in analyzing your expenses, following up on customers, and preparing your taxes.

worksheet: Financial Resources and Assets

List all of your financial resources here. Obviously, you won't be able to put all of them into your business. In the "available" column, indicate how much you can afford to squeeze from your personal needs to fund your business.

	Specifics (amount, type, etc.)	How Much Available?
Financial Assets		
Savings		
Income from other sources		
Spouse's income		
Credit lines/credit cards		
Stocks and other liquid assets		
Home equity		
Retirement funds		
Other		
Tangible Assets		
Equipment		
Furniture		
Space/Location		
Other		
Total		

worksheet: **Your Credit Cards**

Every business relies on credit cards—but some do so more than others. You may be using credit cards to help finance some of your start-up costs, such as equipment purchases. Or you may be using them to help pay personal bills while your business gets off the ground. You may need to manage your credit card debt before and after you start your business to make sure you have a clean credit report. Use this space to track credit card offers, credit cards you already have, credit card debt you need to pay off, and other information about your credit cards to gain a clearer picture of your credit situation.

Name of Card Issuer	Card Number	Credit Limit	Interest Rate	Other Fees	Current Balance

Check Your Credit

In the United States, you're entitled to one free credit report per year from each of the major credit reporting agencies. Check your credit free at www.annualcreditreport.com—this is the legitimate free website for this information.

Keeping your accounts in bookkeeping/accounting software gives you much more power and information—especially as your business grows. You can more easily see which customers have outstanding balances and which product lines are most profitable, prepare financial reports, and track how your business is growing. Most accounting programs—and certainly QuickBooks, the leading accounting program for small businesses—easily integrate with credit card processing, shipping, and customer management programs. They also make billing and invoicing quick and easy. You'll soon find you can't live without such a program.

Open a bank account. A good relationship with a bank can be a big help to a growing company. Many people just select the bank located close to them or the one with the lowest fees. But that doesn't mean it's the right bank for you, especially as you grow your business. Ideally, you want a bank that will work with you and your company as you grow, and that will provide some understanding of your situation and allow some flexibility in dealing with you. Other services that the bank can provide include loans and lines of credit, direct deposit, automatic bill payments, and other ways to streamline the necessary but time-intensive chores of running a business.

"Interview" a number of banks and meet their business account representatives. Develop a relationship with a good business bank while your business is still small. But expect that relationship to pay off—in terms of credit—as you get larger.

Consider accepting credit cards. You like using credit cards; you can bet your customers do, too. But getting approved to accept credit cards—to be a "credit card merchant"—isn't necessarily easy, especially for a new business. There are lots of "merchant card" processors. Check online to compare rates and policies. Also, check with your bank to see if it can help you become a credit card merchant. Your bank may be a bit more expensive than other credit card processors, but you may also have an easier time being approved by your own bank.

Accepting credit cards benefits you as well as your customers because:

- You receive payment right away.

- The credit card company, instead of you, generally assumes the risk of non-paying customers.

- You have less paperwork, since you don't have to send invoices or statements.

- It increases the number of customers who do business with you.

Line of Credit

The typical form of bank financing available for small businesses is a line of credit, rather than a fixed term loan. With a loan, you get a certain sum of money and then have a period of time to pay it back (typically many years). A line of credit is designed to help businesses manage short-term cash flow needs, such as the time that elapses between when you buy inventory and get paid by a customer. You typically have to pay a credit line down to zero at least once a year.

Hire an Accountant

As you get your business underway, you'll need the assistance of a good small-business accountant to help you manage your money. An accountant who understands small-business issues can help you set up your accounting procedures and books, better understand any financial or tax issues you'll face, and plan for taxes. You'll avoid a lot of problems by getting things set up the right way initially. And you'll almost certainly lower your taxes, too! In virtually all respects, a good accountant will save you more than you pay them.

Some accounting firms can also provide you with bookkeeping or bill-paying services or recommend a reputable outside bookkeeper. If your business will require lots of invoices, bills, or bookkeeping, you may want to ask about these options, especially if you don't have the funds to hire an in-house bookkeeper.

The following are some key financial questions you should ask your accountant:

- [ ] What kind of taxes will I have to pay? What are my tax deadlines?

- [ ] How can I reduce my taxes? Which expenses are deductible, non-deductible, or have to be depreciated?

- [ ] What kind of bookkeeping system should I set up? How can I set up systems to reduce the possibility of theft or embezzlement?

- [ ] How should I pay myself—salary or draw—and what are the tax implications?

- [ ] Should I use the cash or accrual form of bookkeeping?

- [ ] Do I need to keep track of inventory? If so, what method do I use?

- [ ] How do I handle payroll taxes?

- [ ] Do I have to collect sales tax? If so, when and from whom?

- [ ] What are the implications of doing business in more than one state?

- [ ] What kind of retirement program can I set up, and how much can I contribute each year?

- [ ] What other accounting and tax considerations are there for my type of business?

worksheet: Comparing Banks

Use this worksheet to help you compare banks and banking services. Fill it in as you shop for a bank for your business.

	Bank 1	Bank 2	Bank 3
Bank name			
Location/Phone number			
Name of bank rep handling accounts			
Accounts offered and fees charged			
Loan or credit lines available			
Special business services offered			
Your overall impression of this bank and its services			
Other notes			

These benefits come at a cost, however. Some of the fees involved include the following:

- **Discount fee.** The credit card *issuer* (typically a bank offering a Visa, MasterCard, or American Express card, or another card issuer) takes a small percentage (2 percent to 4 percent) of every charge. This is the basic cost of administering the credit and assuming the risk, as well as of marketing.

- **Transaction charges.** These are the charges your credit card *processor* takes. This is usually a small percentage of each transaction plus a set amount (25 cents to 50 cents) on each transaction regardless of amount.

- **Monthly minimums you must meet.** Credit card processors often require you do a certain amount of business each month, or they charge you the difference.

- **Set-up fees**

- **Equipment purchase or leasing.** This includes the cost of the machines you swipe the cards through to process credit transactions (if any).

- **Charge-backs.** This is the amount the issuer will charge any time a customer refuses payment on a charge of yours stating dissatisfaction with the product or service.

Prepare simple financial forecasts. If yours is a very small business, you may only need to prepare a simple budget: a forecast of your estimated sales and a list of how much you plan to spend on the various components of your business. Most other businesses will benefit from preparing at least some financial forms—especially cash flow projections to help determine or

adjust spending (see page 112). And if you're seeking outside financing, you'll need a range of financial documents to give to potential lenders or investors—particularly an income statement (also called a P&L for *profit & loss)* and balance sheet.

Besides helping you figure out your spending, there's another reason to draw up financial forecasts: it helps you set goals. Writing down specific numbers for your anticipated sales gives you a target to work toward.

One key to good financial planning is to create your financial projections at the same time you build your business. If you choose to expand your business in a new town, there are associated costs. If you exhibit at a trade show, that will cost you money, too. Every time you make a change to your business plan, make sure you update your financial forecast.

Learn about taxes. Nobody likes paying taxes, but if you're in business, you're going to have to pay them. In fact, the more successful you are, the more taxes you'll probably pay.

Understanding key tax concerns is critical for most businesses. You will make some decisions—or alter them—based on tax implications. Tax codes are complicated and always changing. Certain tax laws apply to incorporated businesses and not unincorporated ones, or vice versa, and business tax laws differ from regulations for individuals. And of course, each U.S. state has its own tax laws as well.

Chances are good that you won't want to—or won't be able to—deal with all of this yourself. Plan on hiring a good accountant to advise you, prepare the proper forms, and help you comply with the ever-more-complex tax scenario that all companies must face as a part of doing business.

business
BUZZ
words

"net 30"

This simply means that the bill is due within 30 days of its date. You can also have Net 60, Net 90, or any other terms you prefer. Keep in mind, however, that many large corporations have their own policies for when they pay their bills and will frequently ignore the terms you request so be aware of those when negotiating contracts.

Money Management Tips

■ **Review your books regularly.** When you're running your business, you may not take the time to sit down and look at your financials. But you can't manage your money without having the facts. At least once a month, preferably once a week, look at your figures: accounts payable and receivable, expenses, cash flow, and so on.

■ **Bill at regular and timely intervals.** You'd be surprised by how many businesspeople, especially consultants and professional service providers, delay sending out their invoices. You may feel uncomfortable asking someone for money, afraid of being challenged on how much you've billed, or just too busy working. But the longer you wait to send out your invoices, the greater the chance you won't get paid.

■ **Watch your inventory.** If you produce goods, you'll always be tempted to produce more because you get savings based on volume. But inventory can go bad—become outdated, unsellable, and time- or weather-worn. And inventory doesn't just apply to finished goods for resale. You may have "inventory" in the form of marketing materials. Keep an eye on your actual use and make your purchases not only on the basis of price but on whether you can get small quantities only when you actually need them.

■ **Manage your growth.** You want your business to get bigger, but if you grow too fast you may not be able to sustain it. Growth costs money—you incur many expenses before you see additional income. Plan your growth so you have the financial resources to pay for it.

■ **Save.** Every business has income fluctuations. The best way to make sure you have cash when you need it is to put some away when you've got it.

Billing Payment Terms

After you deliver your goods or perform your service, you'll want to get paid. But most of your customers won't just hand over the money they owe you. They'll wait to be "asked." This takes the form of you presenting them with a bill. You have a number of billing options:

■ **Standard billing.** This is the most traditional method of billing clients. Within a certain amount of time after a product has been delivered or a service rendered, you create a bill that itemizes the product or service purchased and lists the amount and the "terms" of billing, specifically, when the bill is due. Generally this is within 30 days of the bill's date, but it can also be 60 or 90 days or even longer if you're running a special promotion to attract customers.

■ **Credit cards.** This is a very attractive option for a number of reasons—most notably convenience for the customer and immediate payment for you.

■ **Upfront deposits.** Sometimes you will ask customers to pay some or all of the fees associated with purchasing a product or service upfront, even before the product or service is delivered. You generally would want to do this with items or services that require you to make a substantial investment in materials or time that you wouldn't be able to use for a different client. For instance, it's typical in any construction work to get upfront deposits for the purchase of materials. This reduces the risk that you will perform a lot of work, or accrue a lot of material expense, and then not get paid due to a change of mind on the part of the customer.

■ **Cash on delivery.** Finally, you may well want to collect your price or fee the moment the product changes hands or the service is performed. This has the obvious advantage of improving your cash flow, making your financial situation more predictable, and reducing the risk that customers won't pay on time, or at all. The downside is that many customers—especially businesses—tend not to operate this way, and it may deter them from doing business with you.

Billing and Collections

All too many small or new businesses ignore a very important aspect of being profitable: billing customers, and then collecting on those bills. Here are some tips on how to do this effectively:

■ Bill promptly. The longer you wait to send out your invoices, the greater the chances that you won't be paid.

■ Make the terms of your billing clear—for example, that you expect payment immediately, within 30 days, or within 60 days.

■ Keep in mind that some businesses are on a payment schedule and will not adjust to meet your demands.

■ Also note that some businesses will pay smaller suppliers (like you) last, especially if they're in a cash crunch.

■ Send out regular, courteous, but increasingly strongly worded letters reminding clients that payment is overdue.

PayPal

One way to accept credit cards right away is through PayPal—an online service originally set up to enable people selling stuff in online auctions (such as eBay) to get paid easily and securely. PayPal may not necessarily be the best long-term solution—or the lowest priced—but it can help you can get going fast.

Learn the Lingo

Once you're in business, you're going to encounter certain money-related terms repeatedly. Don't be afraid to ask what they mean. Here's a list of some frequently used money buzzwords. Learn these, and you'll sound like you've been discussing money for decades.

"Money Talk"

TERM	DEFINITION
Red ink	On accounting ledgers, negative numbers used to be written in red ink. Thus, the expressions "red ink" or "in the red" refer to showing a loss.
In the black	Positive numbers, on the other hand, were written in black ink. So if your accounts finish "in the black," you've come out with a profit.
The bottom line	At the top of your financial statements, you list your income. You then deduct your expenses. The number you're left with on the last line of your profit-and-loss statement is how much money you've made—or lost. That's your company's "bottom line."
Overhead, fixed expenses, or "nut"	These terms refer to the expenses you have each month, even if you don't make a sale. Fixed expenses include items such as rent, utilities, insurance, phone service, and administrative salaries. Your "nut" is the total amount of these fixed expenses.
Burn rate	This is how much money you're going through each month. This can be different than your fixed expenses, depending on what you spend on variable expenses such as marketing, temporary help, buying new equipment, and so on.
Variable expenses	These are the costs that change depending on how many sales you make. In other words, if you run a sporting goods store, your rent is fixed no matter how many golf clubs you sell, but the amount you spend on marketing may change.
Cost of goods sold	This refers to what it costs you to purchase inventory to sell to others or to purchase materials to manufacture your products.
General and administrative expenses	The amount you spend to operate your business other than the cost of goods sold or sales costs. This includes all overhead expenses (such as rent and utilities), salaries, marketing, and so on.
Revenue	Total amount of money received from sales.
Income	The amount of money received from any source. You can, for example, have money coming into your business from loans or as a result of investments.
Profit	Money you have left after deducting your costs from your income.
Gross profit	The amount of money left after deducting the cost of goods sold but before deducting general and administrative expenses.
Net profit	The amount of money you're in the black after deducting the cost of goods sold, sales costs, and general and administrative expenses.
Net loss	The amount of money you're in the red if, after deducting all expenses from all revenue, you have lost money instead of having made money.

sample: **Collections Letter**

May 30, 2009

PAST DUE NOTICE

Dear Aaron:

On March 31, I submitted an invoice to you for final payment for my work writing Web pages for the relaunch of the Telescope Financial Services website, showing a balance of $4,000. Your payment was due no later than April 30, 2009.

I want to remind you that the balance was due upon receipt. According to our agreement, payments received more than 30 days late are subject to a 1.5 percent-per-month late charge, and the attached statement now reflects those late fees.

Please give this outstanding balance your immediate attention and send payment in full without delay. If you've already sent a payment, disregard this notice.

If you have any questions, please feel free to give me a call. Otherwise, I'll expect to receive your payment soon.

Sincerely,

Chris Wong

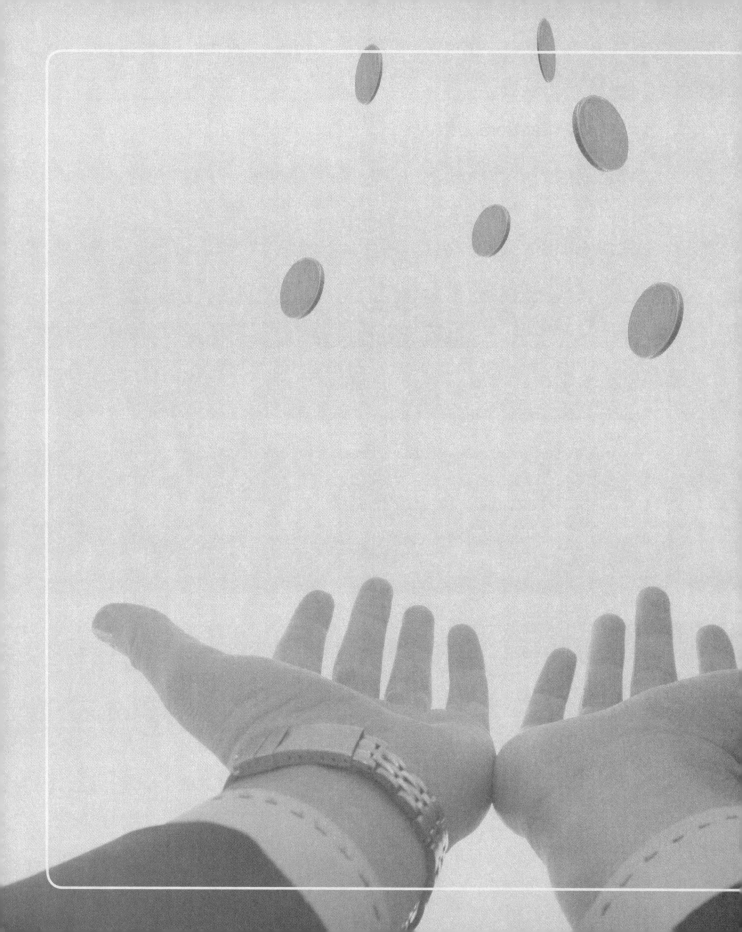

Special Section:
Independent Consultants/ Solo Practitioners

Although this book has covered a lot of ground discussing different types of entrepreneurial ventures, there's one that needs special consideration, because it's by far the No. 1 category of business: *one-person businesses*, especially consultants. In the United States, for instance, of the approximately 26 million businesses that existed in 2006, 21 million or them were solo shops, with receipts totaling nearly a trillion dollars!

Who are these one-person businesses? They can be in construction or catering, real estate sales or property management, engineers, architects, lawyers, hairdressers, or dressmakers. They can be truck or taxi drivers, musicians or artists, book designers or bookkeepers, farmers and fishermen, janitors and house cleaners. They can sell their goods or services to businesses or consumers, on the Web, in stores, and at farmers' or crafts markets. They are butchers, bakers, and candlestick makers.

"Consultants" make up one of the largest categories of one-person businesses. These are individuals who work independently—typically from their own homes or places of business—and provide services to customers or clients. Consultants often provide professional or technical services—in such fields as health care, software, engineering, accounting, law, design, and management consulting. Sometimes they provide only information, expertise, and advice; other times, they actually perform work (such as design, legal services, accounting, engineering, and writing/editing). Consultants can provide these services either to businesses or to individuals.

One of the key distinctions between consultants and those who perform such services as employees is that they are engaged on a "per sale," or contractual, basis for a specific task or period of time rather than participating in an ongoing employer-employee relationship with those they work for. They typically receive no employee benefits (such as health insurance or pension plans), and they must mange and pay their own taxes (rather than have an employer withhold income tax or pay taxes such as Social Security/FICA).

Independent contractors/consultants can be viewed as one of three major types of solo practitioners: consultants, contract workers, or creative talent.

- **Consultants.** These are the independent practitioners who come in for a specified—usually limited—period of time to advise or manage a well-defined project. In other words, there's a definitive beginning and end to the engagement (as opposed to it being an open-ended activity). Consultants may be hired again by the same client for similar engagements, but each time, the consultation or project is limited in time and scope. Consultants are hired for their very specific expertise and generally command higher fees—on a per-hour basis—as a result.

- **Contract workers.** These are workers who act as "outsourcing" resources for a business. They generally are used as less expensive alternatives to regular employees and are hired for more open-ended engagements that can span many months or even years. However, companies that hire such contractors have to be very careful to be on the right side of state and federal tax regulations. The IRS as well as state and local tax franchise boards are very strict about companies that say they have hired contractors, but in all respects other than pay and benefits, these workers are treated like employees. The IRS has some very specific rules as to what determines an independent contractor versus an employee. The overarching premise, however, is that the hiring company only has the right to specify the result of the work being done, not the means and methods of accomplishing that result. The issue comes down to one of control. The more control an employer exerts over workers, the more they are likely to be classified as employees by taxing authorities.

- **Creatives.** Hired for their creative talent, these individuals either perform a service or create a "product" for their employers to use. Creatives can include musicians hired to perform at a wedding, an artist hired to paint a mural for a restaurant wall, a designer employed to develop a logo, a writer contracted to create marketing copy for a brochure, an architect hired to design a new business, and more. Many creatives choose to work with an agent (see "Working with an Agent," page 210).

It's easy to see why being a solo practitioner is such a popular route for entrepreneurs. For the most part, it's a relatively easy and inexpensive way to launch a new enterprise. Start-up costs are, for the most part, minimal. With the exception of certain types of professional or personal services businesses (such as medical or accounting practices or therapists) that require special education, training, certification, or equipment, it's possible to begin with just business cards and a space on the dining room table.

But if you want to make a real living as an independent consultant or a solo practitioner, you'll have to do more than just print up business cards. The most successful solo practitioners make it look easy, but don't be misled when you see them leisurely drinking coffee at Starbucks at 11 a.m on Tuesday morning. They've likely been up all night finishing a project for an impossible-to-please client, or they may have already attended a 7 a.m. networking group trying to drum up new business.

The most successful solo practitioners approach their business as a *business*. They might be their company's only employee, but that company still requires the same commitment, planning, financial management, and marketing as any other type of venture—that is, if they hope to succeed.

As a solo practitioner, what you're selling is your expertise, talent, and hard work. You get paid to help your clients fill a need in their personal or professional lives. That means, of course, that you actually need some kind of expertise or talent to sell, or be willing to learn quickly and work hard.

A solo practitioner usually works for more than one client, either simultaneously or sequentially. They are usually brought in on a project or limited-time basis. They typically set most of their own working conditions (hours, location), provide their own equipment, and work without supervision. They are sought out because of their expertise or special skills. And by contracting with them, their clients get more flexibility than they would by hiring permanent employees.

Advantages and Disadvantages of Being a Solo Practitioner

ADVANTAGES	DISADVANTAGES
You get the flexibility to set your own hours, and determine how much or how hard you want to work.	You have to work hard—often many more hours than you can legitimately bill for.
You get to choose the clients you want to work with.	You may have to work with clients or on projects you don't like to bring in the income you need.
You make more money per hour than you would as an employee.	Uneven income stream can lead to a great deal of financial stress.
You work with a variety of clients, which keeps things interesting.	Your professional life can feel fragmented and scattered because you have to divide your attention among multiple clients.
You can grow in the direction you want to grow and continuously learn new skills.	Your best ideas or work can be discarded or unimplemented.

Working with an Agent

An agent is someone who acts on behalf of a creative professional to market or sell products or services. Writers, artists, actors, and musicians all routinely employ agents. There are both pros and cons to employing an agent:

- **Pros.** You're free to do your work rather than spend you time acting as a marketing or sales person. In addition, an agent is a specialist who should know the market and the major players in that market, and thus sell your work more effectively. They should be able to perform a range of business-related duties (such as billings and collections) much more efficiently and effectively than you could on your own. Although you have to pay an agent a percentage of what you earn on a project or gig—typically 15 or 20 percent— you are likely to make more, because you will probably get more business than you would on your own.

- **Cons.** You give up a percentage of everything you sell, and if you don't have a good agent, you could end up with less money than if you were on your own. Because the agent "owns" the client relationship, you often don't get to personally know your customers—the publisher, gallery owner, or arts patron. An agent may also push you to influence your artistic direction, such as produce more commercially acceptable paintings or music or writing.

Learn to Sell Yourself

One of the hardest parts of being a solo practitioner is learning how to sell yourself. This is something that makes many people uncomfortable, and indeed it's an art to talk positively about yourself without seeming like a braggart. You have to learn how to "toot your own horn" in a way that doesn't make you feel awkward—and which doesn't put people off.

Some tips on how to do this:

- Bring up other successes, especially for clients that are well known in your particular field. Talk about what you've done for others, and you'll very effectively communicate what you can do for prospective clients.

- Get testimonials from previous clients and put them in your marketing collateral and on your website.

- Compile a list of three to five benefits that you offer clients and practice saying them matter-of-factly, without awkwardness. Note that benefits are different from the actual products or services that you provide. For example, rather than just saying, "I design book covers," you could say, "I create compelling book designs that end up selling more copies than you otherwise would, at a price that's half of what you'd pay if you did it in house."

- Bring friends with you when you go to a networking event, and prompt them to brag about you to others.

- Above all, don't put down competitors! Instead, pass on what your clients have said about you.

The Contract

An important thing for solo practitioners to do, no matter what category they fall into, is to get a good contract. A good contract does the following:

- Spells out the nature of the work

- Details exactly how much you'll be paid and who will pay for expenses

- Defines the "deliverables," or what the end results will be

- Specifies how much the solo practitioner will get paid, and at what time that will occur. (Up-front deposit? On the completion of the work? Periodically over the course of the engagement?)

- Lays out what will happen should the scope of the work change in some way

- Describes the terms under which the contract can be ended

- Is very explicit about who owns the work in question

Watch Out for the Legalities

The IRS has a list of things its looks for to determine whether you qualify as an independent contractor or should be treated as an employee. Make sure that you meet the IRS requirements of an "independent contractor." Otherwise, you won't be able to take deductions for your equipment, overhead, and so on, and your client (and possibly you) may be liable for fees or substantial penalties. You may want to become a limited liability company (LLC) or to incorporate yourself to provide additional protection for you and your clients.

The Money

Professional services providers can make very good money; they can also go many months without any income whatsoever. Depending on the type of work you do—and how hard you're willing to market your services—you have to be prepared to ride the income roller coaster.

Early in your career, you can expect to be underpaid. Not only are you learning what the market will bear and how long it takes you to complete a job or assignment, or prepare for a gig, but you may not have the experience to command top dollar. On the other hand, if you charge too little, prospective clients won't think that you're good enough. You therefore need to do your homework as to what the market will bear and price your services accordingly based on your degree of experience and skill.

A big part of being a successful solo practitioner is being comfortable talking frankly about money. You will have to do this a lot—not only when naming your price or putting together a proposal for clients, but in scoping out what the market will bear by asking others what they charge.

Many types of professional services solo practitioners will also need to develop a standard letter of agreement or contract that can be used with all clients just by changing the specific details of the work you're doing for them. You may want to have an attorney review your standard contract. In any case, be sure to spell out payment terms, which expenses are covered and which are not, and what will happen if the scope of work changes.

Don't Get Taken Advantage of

Always keep track of the time you put into a project, even if you're being paid of a project basis rather than for your time. This way, you can begin to see how much time it takes to do a job—and how much time a specific client requires of you. Designing a brochure for one executive might take twice as long as your typical clients, and you need to be able to charge accordingly in such cases.

Whenever possible, try and get money upfront. This commits the client to the project and makes it harder for them to pull out mid-project. Insist on regular payments throughout the course of a project rather than wait for the project to be completely finished before submitting your invoice. Establish milestones for "deliverables" and ask to be paid after each milestone has been reached. And at the slightest hint of unethical behavior on the part of a clients, be on your guard and be prepared to take action—such as demanding immediate payment or even, in some cases, terminating the contract—before you invest more of your valuable time in a job.

Partnerships and Outsourcing

Just because you're on your own doesn't mean you have to do it all without help. Most consultants make it work by partnering with other professional services providers, or by outsourcing key operations. Depending on how busy you are, and how much money your business is bringing in, you may be overwhelmed by all the things it takes to run a successful business. You must determine your "core competency"—that is, the main service you provide to your clients—and sometimes pay other people to do the rest.

Many successful solo practitioners outsource administrative duties, such as bookkeeping, payroll, and tax preparation. In addition to many firms and independent professionals who provide these kinds of services, there are an ever-increasing numbers of online services that will do all of this for you remotely—all you do is submit your invoices, bills, employee timecards, or other documentation online, and the online service will take care of the rest.

Some of the things that solo practitioners typically outsource include:

- Bookkeeping and accounting services
- Technology support, Web design, and hosting
- Marketing and public relations, graphic design
- Legal services
- Management consultants, business coaches
- Agents

The best way to choose an outsource service provider in any of these areas is by asking for referrals from other consultants you know, then thoroughly interviewing multiple prospects. Ask for and check a minimum of three recent references, and use your gut to determine the best fit. Keep in mind that you need to hire professionals you feel comfortable working with—if someone appears very competent, but you worry about a personality clash, follow your instincts.

Setting Up an Office

You will need a space to work—that's a given. The question is, where? You have three basic options: Rent your own space, share an office with other professional services firms, or work out of your home.

Rent your own space. Many solo practitioners choose to lease a space on their own because they either like the independence or they feel it looks better for their professional image if they have their own center of business operations. This is especially true for solo practitioners whose clients frequently need to come into the office, such as accountants, doctors, or dentists. The drawback of going this route, of course, is that it is the most expensive option.

Share an office. To save money, many solo practitioners share office space with other people providing professional services. You see this frequently with medical and legal professionals: often buildings are equipped and dedicated to a certain kind of business, such as doctors' or dentists' offices, or psychologists' suites. There are many office suites that provide shared services like a receptionist, phone system, and janitorial services for one monthly fee. This can dramatically simplify your life.

The Home Office

A home office can take many forms. It might simply be one end of your dining room table, or it could be the guest room (as long as no guests come to visit). You might claim a section of your garage, and build in walls and install a window, shelves, heating, and air conditioning. Wherever you situate your home office, you need to:

- **Install dedicated phone and fax lines.** It's a good idea to have your own business cell phone line or to install a separate business landline if you're working from home even part of the time. When your toddler answers a call from an important client, you'll understand the necessity of this! In addition, if you want to be listed in the Yellow Pages or "business" section of the phone book, many local phone companies require you to have a "business" land phone line. An extra phone line for business also enables you to have a business message on that line and a family message on the other line.

Find a "Business Buddy"

Anyone who works alone needs a business buddy to use as a confidante, trusted advisor, and friend to call up for independent advice, opinions, and "reality checks." This isn't someone you pay—although you may well also hire a consultant occasionally to provide you with insight into a particular issue you're facing in your business—but a personal and reciprocal relationship in which you help each other out when needed pro bono. No money or equity changes hands.

There are two things that are important to building a good business buddy relationship. First of all, you have to keep in mind that relationships go two ways—that is, you have to give as much as you receive. Secondly, as with any relationship, you have to work to keep it viable. Have lunch or coffee with your business buddy as least once a month and put some energy into it. You'll constantly reap the benefits.

- **Install a high-speed Internet connection.** If you're going to be working from your home, get a high-speed Internet connection. You get high-speed connections via DSL (typically from your phone company) or through a cable modem (typically from your cable television provider). If neither service is available in your area, a third option is a satellite system, though this can be a bit more costly and less reliable.

- **Plan how to meet with customers.** If you work out of your home, one of your biggest challenges will be figuring out where and when to meet with customers. If you only meet customers at their place of business, trade shows, or over the Internet, no problem. But if customers are going to come to you, how will you arrange your space so that you look professional? Ideally, you will want to set up your workspace separately from your family surroundings. If possible, have a separate entrance or at least a path to your office that doesn't go through a messy playroom or kitchen. If you're meeting clients infrequently or on a regular schedule, you may be able to use your own living or dining room as a meeting place. Just make sure the rest of the family knows to stay away.

What if you don't want customers in your home but need to meet them somewhere other than their offices? Look for neutral locations such as coffee shops and restaurants. If you have an ongoing need for meeting space, find another company that will allow you to rent an office or conference room on an hourly basis. Executive suite services—short-term office rentals—often offer hourly rentals as well.

■ **Decide if you need a separate business address.** When you work from home, you face a dilemma: what address should you give out? If you use your home address, will you be comfortable putting it on business cards and marketing materials that you hand to strangers or put on a website where the world can see it? If you don't put any address on these marketing materials, you might seem less than professional.

Dealing with Isolation

The isolation that comes with being a solo practitioner is not to be taken lightly. Even the most gregarious people can find themselves feeling alone and separated from the world when they work on their own all day. You need to make sure you get out—in a business as well as personal context. In addition to finding your business buddy, you can join industry associations, get on committees, and be a part of your local business community. You might even consider teaching a class in your area of expertise—anything to get you out of the house and into the company of others at frequent intervals.

One solution is to get a post office box from the U.S. Postal Service. The problem, however, is that then your business address is only a post office box—or "P.O. Box"—number. That may make your business seem somewhat insubstantial. Moreover, the U.S. Post Office usually refuses to accept deliveries from private delivery services such as FedEx or UPS. Another, often better, alternative is to rent a mailbox from one of the many private mailbox providers (such as The UPS Store) also called a "commercial mail-receiving agency." A private mailbox gives you a secure place to receive mail, and there is someone there who can sign for and receive packages for you. They generally will accept deliveries from private services as well as the U.S. Postal Service. Moreover, they often offer other services such as mail forwarding, calling you if you receive a special delivery, packing and shipping items, and allowing you to call in and check your mail if you're on the road. As an added bonus, the address provided by these services often includes a street name and number, instead of a P.O. Box, making your business look more solid.

■ **Understand home-based deductions.** When you work from home, one accounting area you'll need to deal with is understanding which business expenses are deductible and which aren't. If you buy a new worktable that you use for both your office and for the kids' homework projects, is that deductible? If you add a space heater to your office in the garage, can you deduct the extra utility expenses? What if you let your kids use your office supplies?

Tax deduction rules for home offices can be daunting and confusing. If you're setting up a home office, you should add your questions about this to the list when you meet with an accountant. Most normal business expenses that you'd have whether or not you were working from home—postage, office supplies, advertising, wages—are treated the same way as they would be in any other business. You can deduct those expenses as part of your regular deductions for the cost of doing business.

You may also be able to deduct a portion of your rent or mortgage based on the amount of space you use for business. However, there are many considerations before you take the home office deduction. You have to meet the IRS's qualifications for a home-based-business and this is one deduction that frequently leads to an audit. Also, there are tax implications if you later sell your home. So you certainly want to discuss the home office deduction—and whether you should take it or skip it—with your accountant or tax advisor. (See "The IRS Hotline," page 216).

- **Plan ways to separate work life from home life.** One of the most difficult tasks for people who work from home is establishing a clear distinction between work and family life. If you're not disciplined, you may find yourself distracted by non-business matters. One woman said her house was never cleaner than when she worked from home, since she did housework to avoid taking care of business. On the other hand, many people who work from home find they never leave "work." They end up working day and night, much to the annoyance of family and friends.

  Separating your work life from home life can be especially difficult when you live with others: a spouse, children, or guests who come to visit. Friends and relatives often view home-based entrepreneurs as people who are always available. They don't understand why, in the middle of a workday, you can't run an errand, go to a movie, or pick up the kids from school. The best way to deal with working at home is to be as professional as possible during the time you set aside for business, but allow yourself some of the flexibility you want from working out of your home.

- **Deal with kids and pets.** Many parents find the greatest appeal of a home office is being at home for their children. However, many former work-from-home parents have found, after a year or so of working with crying or demanding children in the background, an office away from home becomes a necessary expense. You need to be realistic about the demands that children place on you. It's not realistic to expect to get work done with kids coming in and out, wanting to be driven places, needing a snack, or demanding that you settle an argument. Realistically, depending on your children's' ages and the nature of your work, you may need to

Questions to Ask on Home Office Deductions

- [ ] What percentage of my rent or mortgage can I deduct?

- [ ] Can I deduct costs of remodeling? Rewiring?

- [ ] Can I deduct these expenses the first year, or do I have to capitalize them over a number of years?

- [ ] Is it wise for me to take the home office deduction?

- [ ] What are the tax implications if I later sell my home?

- [ ] What percentage of my phone or Internet connection costs can I deduct?

- [ ] What furniture and equipment expenses are deductible? Office supplies?

- [ ] What transportation expenses can I deduct for getting from my office to my customers, if any?

- [ ] Can I deduct expenses for artwork, décor, stereos, or other amenities in my home office?

- [ ] What other business expenses can I deduct?

make child care arrangements during your working hours. Some businesses are more flexible in terms of deadlines, hours, or phone calls. Others are truly difficult to run when you have a needy 2-year-old or teenager.

You also have to factor pets into the equation. If you work at home, a pet is a great companion. A dog or cat makes working at home less lonely. But just as you can't have a screaming child in the background of your business calls, you can't have a barking dog, a screeching parrot, or any other animal that makes persistent and loud noises.

The IRS Hotline

The IRS answers questions about the tax implications of running your business from your home. For online help, go to www.irs.gov/taxtopics/tc509.html.

Putting It All Together

As a provider of professional services, perhaps you always intended to go into business for yourself one day. The business world is used to working with independent consultants and contractors—in fact, many businesses prefer it. You'll find that many companies want to work with you on a contract basis again and again—forging business relationships that last for years and make your income more secure. Technology makes it even easier to run your business efficiently—even on your own—and to present a polished, professional image. It's a great time to be an independent entrepreneur. Enjoy the ride!

Index

a

Accountant, 98, 101, 107, 195, 201
    key financial questions for, 199
Advertising, 38, 42, 56, 109, 130
    Internet, 133, 194
    message, repeating, 133, 134, 152
    traditional, 133–39
        billboard, 137
        print, 134–36
            newsletters, 136
        media contact information, 140
        media kits, 134
        radio, 136–37
        TV, 138–39
    timing of, 138
    word of mouth, 141–42
See also Branding; Marketing; Public relations
Agent, 81, 83
    of solo practitioner, 210
Agreement
    with client, 168
    letter of (sample form), 95
    non-compete (with employees), 93
    non-disclosure (with potential investors), 93, 126
    partnership, 89
    service-level (SLA), 179
See also Payment: terms of
Associations
    entrepreneur, 144
    industry, 27, 144, 155
    trade, 101
Attorney. *See* Lawyer
Avocation, 4, 16

b

Balance sheet, 109, 115
Balanced business, 14–15
Banking, 198, 200
Barriers
    to entry, 49
    to switching (for customers), 41
Benefits, employee, 9, 51, 186
Big business, 48, 49

Billing, 108, 195, 198, 202, 203. *See also* Cash
        flow; Collections; Payment
Body care services, 88
Bookkeeping, 195, 202
    software, 198
Bottom line, 204
    triple, 51
Branding, 56, 68, 130. *See also* Advertising;
        Marketing; Public relations
Business
    concept, 31–39
    growth, 15
        managing, 202
    selling, 15, 22
    starting, 10
    values, 17, 125
    viability, 22
Business to business (B2B) sales, 36. *See also*
        Customer
Business to consumer (B2C) sales, 36. *See also*
        Customer
Business model, 35–36, 109
Business name, 57–58
Business plan, 123–27
    components, 125–27
    social responsibility, 53
    writing, 124, 126
See also Marketing: plan

c

"C" corporation, 87
Career
    advancement, 8
    changes, 7
Cash flow
    burn rate, 204
    management, 109, 124, 193, 105
    projection, 105
See also Billing; Costs; Collections; Expenses;
        Payment
Cash flow statement, 114
Catering service, 149. *See also* Food business
Change, responding to, 9, 124–25

case studies

worksheets

Acknowledgments

Rhonda Abrams would like to thank:

Entrepreneurship professors and instructors, who responded to the surveys and interviews we conducted to identify the issues and concerns they had when teaching cross-campus entrepreneurship students and courses. Their insights helped shape this book from the outset.

Alice LaPlante, whose research and writing skills helped make this book possible. Alice is a consummate professional and a delight to work with. She is one of the best writers I know, and her grasp of small business issues is outstanding. Alice has helped make this book come alive.

Jill Simonsen, Editorial Project Manager, who took over this project mid-stream and saw it to its successful conclusion. Without Jill, and her organizational skills, editorial excellence, and years of professional publishing experience, this book might still be sitting on my computer. Aloha, Jill!

Rosa Whitten, Office Manager and all-around go-to woman of The Planning Shop's team. Rosa makes sure that everything in The Planning Shop actually works and that the bills get paid. She is an organizational champion and is invaluable—in terms of both her skills and her positive outlook. We are fortunate, indeed, to have her.

Diana Van Winkle, who now oversees the design of all books in The Planning Shop line and brought her graphic expertise to the design of this book. She is talented, responsive, and a delight to work with. Diana's skills ensure that The Planning Shop's books continue to be easy and pleasurable for readers to use.

Maggie Canon, Managing Editor. Maggie shepherded this book from conception. Maggie's professionalism was an invaluable addition to The Planning Shop. She was founding editor of *InfoWorld* and numerous other technology magazines and was also managing editor of the bestselling *America 24/7* series.

Mireille Majoor, Editorial Project Manager, who oversaw the bulk of the editorial process of this book. Mireille is a consummate professional and both The Planning Shop's books and readers have benefited from Mireille's commitment to excellence.

Kathryn Dean, who developerd a thorough Index, making it easy for readers to find exactly what they need quickly.

Arthur Wait, who originally designed the overall look and feel of The Planning Shop's line of books and products and developed our first website and electronic products. We are always amazed (though no longer surprised) by the range of Arthur's talents.

Every successful business starts with a plan.

If you're starting a business, you need to make sure you've accurately assessed your market potential, costs, revenue, competition, legal issues, employee needs, and exit strategy *before* you start investing your (or someone else's) money.

Fortunately, *The Successful Business Plan: Secrets & Strategies* by Rhonda Abrams will show you how to develop a well-crafted, clear, meaningful business plan—step-by-step—that will help ensure you don't end up facing any costly surprises down the road!

Named by *Inc.* and *Forbes* magazines as one of the top ten essential books for small business, *The Successful Business Plan* is the best-selling business plan guide on the market, used in the nation's top business schools and by hundreds of thousands of successful entrepreneurs.

Whether you're seeking funds from outside investors or bankrolling your start-up on your own, *The Successful Business Plan* will be your guide to planning your business in a sound, profitable manner.

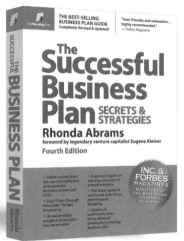

Book features:

• 99 worksheets to help you get started quickly, taking you through every critical section of a successful business plan

• Sample business plan offering guidance on length, style, formatting and language

• The Abrams Method of Flow-Through Financials, which makes easy work of number crunching—even if you're a numbers novice

• Special chapters addressing issues of concern for service, manufacturing, retail, and Internet companies, plus advice on starting a business in a challenging economy

• Nearly 200 real-life insider secrets from top venture capitalists and successful CEOs

"User-friendly and exhaustive...highly recommended."
Forbes Magazine

"There are plenty of decent business plan guides out there, but Abrams' is a cut above the others..."
Inc. Magazine

Available from your bookseller or at www.PlanningShop.com

thePlanning**shop**

You're ready to launch your business: Now what?

You're ready to follow your passions and get going on your entrepreneurial dreams. Now you're ready to get your business started!

Six-Week Start-Up is carefully designed to show you, step-by-step, how to get your business up and running—*quickly* and *successfully*.

From licenses to bookkeeping to marketing to hiring employees to setting up shop, this book guides you through every critical step, ensuring that you understand how to take care of even the smallest details. Nothing is left to chance—you'll be given all the information you need, as you need it.

The book is divided into six main chapters—one for each week—allowing you to pace yourself and take care of each task in its proper sequence. The book's unique

format significantly streamlines the startup process, allowing you to start making money faster.

Book features:

• **Week-by-week checklists:** See exactly what you need to do on a weekly basis, along with detailed information on how to complete each item.

• **"Red Tape Alerts":** Stay out of trouble in areas related to taxes, laws, employment regulations, and more.

• **"Questions to Ask":** Before you meet with accountants, lawyers, investors, or other professionals, review these lists of important questions to ask.

It's all here! Get your business up and running fast! Order your copy of *Six-Week Start-Up* today.

Available from your bookseller
or at www.PlanningShop.com

the**Planning**shop